上海市人民政府 | 面向未来30年的
发展研究中心系列报告 | 上海发展战略研究

上海2050
崛起中的全球城市

联合国首届世界城市日
全球城市论坛实录

The Record of Global City Forum
on the First UN World Cities Day

肖 林 主编　Chief Editor Xiao Lin

格致出版社　上海人民出版社

PREFACE

序

　　城市是人类文明的产物。当今人类一半以上都居住在城市。随着工业化和城市化的发展，城市在使人们享受美好生活的同时，也带来了交通拥堵、环境污染、资源紧缺、文化冲突等诸多挑战。2010 年，以"城市，让生活更美好"为主题的世界博览会在中国上海成功举办，世界各国充分展示城市文明成果、传播先进城市发展理念，给人类留下了丰富的精神遗产，对实现城市可持续发展产生了深远影响。

　　为弘扬上海世博会理念，激励人类为城市美好未来而不懈努力，2014年 10 月 31 日，联合国首届"世界城市日"活动在上海隆重举办。作为首届世界城市日系列论坛之一，由上海市人民政府发展研究中心和世界银行主办、上海师范大学承办的全球城市论坛也于同一时期在美丽的黄浦江畔举行。本次论坛以"上海 2050：崛起中的全球城市"为主题，吸引了来自联合国、世界银行和国内外城市研究领域的一流专家参与，与会嘉宾从城市创新、全球化、城市治理等不同角度出发，对全球城市发展趋势和 2050年上海发展战略等问题展开深入研讨，贡献了众多富于智慧的真知灼见，堪称一场思想的盛宴，令人获益匪浅。

　　呈现在各位读者面前的《上海2050：崛起中的全球城市——联合国首届世界城市日全球城市论坛实录》，就是这场思想盛宴的精彩再现。这本实录以充分反映与会嘉宾的思想观点为宗旨，生动再现了论坛现场的交流盛况，详实记录了与会嘉宾的真知灼见，详细总结了全球城市建设的先进经验，为研究者留下了宝贵的历史资料，希望能够对关注全球城市发展的人们有所裨益，并启发我们以前瞻性的眼光，在更广阔的视野探索全球城市发展和上海的未来。

　　世界城市日带给我们无限的希望和憧憬。展望未来，上海将在实现中华民族伟大复兴中国梦、打造中国经济升级版中承担更大的责任和使命。上海将立足全局、把握大势，因势而谋、顺势而为，谋划和实施面向未来30 年的发展战略。让我们齐心协力，以更加前瞻的视角、更加开放的胸怀、更富智慧的行动，共同打造世界的上海、中国的上海、我们的上海，迎接上海充满活力与梦想的明天。

是为序。

上海市人民政府发展研究中心主任、党组书记

2015 年 8 月

A city is the product of human civilization. Today, more than half of the world's population lives in cities. With the development of industrialization and urbanization, the cities are able to provide a better life for people. However, cities are also confronting us with quite a number of challenges, including traffic congestion, environmental pollution, resource shortages and cultural conflicts. In 2010, a splendid World Expo, with the theme of "Better City, Better Life", was held in Shanghai, China. Countries from all over the world fully displayed their achievement in urban civilization and spread their advanced ideas and theories of urban development, and it left us an abundant spiritual heritage with a profound impact on achieving sustainable urban development.

Aiming to promote the theme of the Expo 2010 and inspire mankind to make unremitting efforts for a better city and a better life, on October 31, 2014, the first "World Cities Day" of the United Nations was solemnly held in Shanghai. As one of a series of the First World Cities Day Forums, the Global City Forum had a spectacular opening on the bank of the beautiful Huangpu River, which was hosted by the Development and Research Center of Shanghai Municipal People's Government as well as the World Bank, and was organized by Shanghai Normal University. With the theme "Shanghai 2050: A Rising

Global City", Shanghai Global City Forum gathered leading experts and professionals both at home and abroad, including those from United Nations and the World Bank. Guests held a further discussion on global city development trend and "Shanghai 2050" development strategy from different perspectives, such as city innovation, globalization and urban governance. Numerous profound insights full of wisdom and intelligence were contributed to the forum, which can be rated as an evocative and beneficial brain storming thought feast.

Shanghai 2050: A Rising Global City—The Record of Global City Forum on the First UN World Cities Day is the original presentation of this thought feast. Based on the principle of recording the authentic viewpoints of the speakers, this book vividly shows the heated discussions of the event, the detailed insights of speakers and the advanced experience of global city construction, which offers precious materials for the researchers. We hope that this book will be of benefit to people who are concerned about global city development and will inspire us to shape the future of global city and Shanghai in a broader horizon with foresightedness.

World Cities Day brings us more hope than ever before. Looking into the future, Shanghai will take greater responsibilities in realizing the "Chinese Dream" of the rejuvenation of the Chinese nation and boosting China's economy. Shanghai will consider the overall situation, fulfill its potential, seek opportunities and plan and implement its strategic development in the next three decades. Let's make concerted efforts in a more foresighted, opener and wiser way to build Shanghai into a megacity nationwide, a megacity worldwide and to embrace a Shanghai full of vitality and dreams in the future.

Director General of the Development Research Center

of Shanghai Municipal People's Government

Xiao Lin

August, 2015

上海市务副市长屠光绍会见参加全球城市论坛的联合国和世界银行官员专家

Tu Guangshao, Executive Vice Mayor of Shanghai, meets with officials and experts from United Nations and the World Bank

上海市常务副市长屠光绍和与会嘉宾亲切交谈

Tu Guangshao, Executive Vice Mayor of Shanghai, is having a cordial talk with the guests

全球城市论坛现场盛况

The spectacular of Global City Forum

与会人员认真聆听嘉宾发言

Participants are listening to the speeches carefully

CONTENTS

目 录

闭幕演讲

闭幕致辞

附录

318　后记

OPENING ADDRESSES

KEYNOTE SPEECHES

SPECIAL SPEECH

PARALLEL FORUMS

Forum I   Global City Strategy for Shanghai under Multiple Angles

Forum II   Innovation and Competitiveness Enhancement of Global Cities

CLOSING SPEECH

CLOSING ADDRESS

APPENDIX

OPENING ADDRESSES

开幕致辞

上海市人民政府发展研究中心主任、党组书记肖林
在全球城市论坛开幕式上致辞

Xiao Lin, Director General of the Development Research
Center of Shanghai Municipal People's Government,
addresses at the Opening Ceremony of the Global City Forum

致辞—

肖 林
上海市人民政府发展研究中心主任、党组书记

本届全球城市论坛的主题是"上海2050：崛起中的全球城市"，这一主题反映了我们的共同思考和期盼。当今全球化和信息化加快发展，各国日益成为利益交融的命运共同体，同时也面临着更加纷繁复杂的全球性挑战。如何定位城市战略，促进城市可持续发展，是世界各国城市共同面临的紧迫课题。上海在城市发展过程中，既遇到世界其他城市遇到的共同问题，也面临着一些独特的挑战。再过几年到2020年，上海就将实现基本建成国际经济、金融、贸易、航运中心和社会主义现代化国际大都市的战略目标，站上新的历史起点。在新的历史阶段上海何去何从，亟待通过战略研究来探索方向、统一思想和明确思路。本届全球城市论坛就是在这样的背景下召开的。

未来30年，全球化将继续深化，区域合作将更加迫切，经济增长的重心将逐渐东移，人民币将成为国际货币中的一个重要分支。上海要努力把握全球开放合作的巨大机遇，通过市场化的方式来提升全球资源配置能力。未来30年也是实现"两个一百年"中国梦的重要时期，上海要把自身发展置于中国未来发展的大局大势中，以实现"两个一百年"中国梦、尤其是新中国成立100年的发展目标为引领，把未来30年发展放到更长的时间跨度、更大的空间范畴中来研判，进一步明确未来发展的战略目标，凸显上海在"两个一百年"中国梦中的地位和作用。

今天，在美丽的黄浦江畔，我们汇聚了全球城市领域的著名学者和上海最高层次的专家进行研讨，为未来30年上海城市发展战略和核心竞争力的提升出谋划策。我们希望通过这样的开放式、互动式研讨，交流观点，凝聚共识，明确方向，把此次论坛打造为推进未来30年上海发展战略研究的标志性活动。

促进城市发展是一项需要坚持不懈的事业。我们将积极搭建国际交流平台，与国内外专家学者共同探讨，集各方智慧，为全球城市可持续发展作出新的贡献。

上海师范大学校务委员会主任陆建非
在全球城市论坛开幕式上致辞

Lu Jianfei, Chairman of the Council of
Shanghai Normal University, addresses at the
Opening Ceremony of the Global City Forum

致辞二

陆建非
上海师范大学校务委员会主任

"世界城市日"是联合国认可的国际日，它来源于 2010 年中国上海世博会的精神遗产，以"城市，让生活更美好"为主题。"世界城市日"具有鲜明的时代特色，对人类社会的可持续发展具有重大意义。

上海师范大学是一所多学科的综合性院校，以教师教育为其最鲜明的特色。自成立时开始，上海师范大学不仅见证着上海的发展，也为这座城市的发展作出独特的贡献。作为坐落在上海的一所颇具影响力的大学，我们选择了将上海和其他国际大都市的开放性研究作为我们的研究主题之一。2013 年，我们建立了城市发展研究院，这是我们学科结构战略性调整的一个里程碑，也是教育体系的一次变革。它的教育和科研活动涵盖了多种不同学科，包括地理、人文、经济、商业和旅游业等。在未来发展中，我们将会持续关注城市研究，努力将上海师范大学建成一个培养城市发展人才的基地，提供政府咨询参考的基地。

上海师范大学城市发展研究院是一个向全球范围内大学和研究机构开放的研究平台。2006 年，上海师范大学和鹿特丹伊拉斯谟大学共同成立了中欧城市比较研究中心，这也是上海师范大学在城市研究方面的首个国际性合作研究平台。在这之后我们也开始与其他研究机构合作，与澳大利亚、日本的研究人员进行沟通和合作，我们希望这类合作能够进展顺利，带来更多的有益成果。

2014 年，我们参与了上海市政府"面向未来 30 年的上海"系列研究，负责其中一个课题"上海提升全球城市品牌形象与增强城市吸引力研究"。对上海来说，未来竞争力的提升不仅依赖于经济发展水平，也和城市软实力紧密相关。文化因素和城市品牌对于增强城市软实力具有重要意义。我们期待通过这项研究，能够对上海建设全球城市发挥积极的促进作用。

"上海2050：崛起中的全球城市"这一全球城市论坛是由联合国发起的2014年"世界城市日"系列活动之一。我们非常荣幸有机会邀请到许多城市研究方面的著名专家和研究人员，一起讨论关于上海转变为全球城市的这一重要战略议题。这些讨论对于上海未来建设全球城市非常重要。在迈向全球城市过程中，上海将广泛学习国际上的先进经验，取长补短，相互借鉴。世界城市日带给我们无限的希望和憧憬，让我们共同铭记这一天。

Address I

Xiao Lin

Director General of the Development Research
Center of Shanghai Municipal People's Government

The theme of this Global City Forum is "Shanghai 2050: A Rising Global City", which reflects our common thinking and expectation. Globalization and informatization are developing rapidly, and all the countries are becoming a unity where they are closely interdependent and intertwined. At the same time, they are also confronted with more intricate global challenges. How to position cities' strategy and promote the sustainable development of cities is an urgent issue that all the cities in the world are faced with. Shanghai, in the development process, encounters common problems which other cities in the world have met, but of course it is also faced with many particular challenges. In 5 years, Shanghai will basically accomplish the strategic object of being the center of international economy, finance, trade and maritime as well as the international metropolitan with socialist modernization characteristics. That will make a historical starting point for Shanghai. At the fresh historical stage, what path Shanghai should follow requests Chinese strategy research to explore the direction, to unify and clarify our thinking. This is the background for the holding of Global City Forum.

In the future 30 years, globalization will develop further in depth. The need for regional cooperation will get more urgent. RMB will become one of the important branches of international currency, and the economic center will move eastward. Shanghai has to seize the great opportunity of the further open cooperation between countries and regions, and promote its international resources allocation capability by integrating market. Next 30 years is a significant stage for the realization of Two Centenary Goals. The development of Shanghai will follow the overall trend of the future development of China, with the two Chinese Dreams as its guide, especially the 100 years' development objective since the People's Repubic of China was founded. We should see the development of Shanghai in the next 30 years in a longer time span and larger space category, so as to clarify the strategic objectives of Shanghai's development, and establish the important status and role of Shanghai in the realization of two Centurial Chinese Dreams.

Today, near the bank of the Huangpu River, we are honored to invite many famous international scholars in many fields of urban studies and the top-level specialists of Shanghai to discuss suggestions on the development strategy and the enhancement of core competitiveness of Shanghai in the next 30 years. We hope that we can exchange our opinions, build consensus and clarify the developing orientation of Shanghai through this open and interactive discussion. And we also hope this forum can be regarded as a milestone activity which signifies a full swing of the studies of development strategy for Shanghai in next 30 years.

Promotion of city's development needs our persistent endeavor. We will make great effort to build platforms for international communication so as to discuss relevant issues with domestic and international scholars and specialists to make new contributions for the sustainable development of cities around the world.

Address II

Lu Jianfei

Chairman of the Council of Shanghai Normal University

World Cities Day is derived from the spiritual heritage of Expo 2010, Shanghai, China, and takes "Better City, Better Life", the theme of Shanghai World Expo, as its general theme. So World Cities Day bears distinct features of the times and plays a very important role in the sustainable development of human society.

As you know, Shanghai Normal University is a comprehensive, multidisciplinary university with teachers' education as its most distinctive feature. Since its founding, we have not only witnessed but also promoted the development of Shanghai. As an important and influential university located in Shanghai, we have chosen open studies of Shanghai and other global metropolis as one of our major research themes. In 2013, the Institute of Urban Studies (IUS) was established. The founding of the IUS is a milestone of our strategic adjustment of scientific disciplines and a reform of our education system. The education and research activities of the institute cover many different disciplines including geography, humanity, economics, business, tourism, etc.. We will continue focusing on the research of urban studies, making Shanghai Normal University a base for educating city talents, and a think tank of government on our urban development.

IUS is a research platform open to the universities and researchers from all over the world. In 2006, Shanghai Normal University and Erasmus University at Rotterdam jointly formed Sino-European Comparative Urban Research Center, which is the first international cooperation research platform of Shanghai Normal University in urban studies. After that we entered into cooperation with institutes and researchers from Australia and Japan. I expect this cooperation will continue to be successful and produce more valuable results.

In 2014 we are requested by Shanghai government to conduct a research project of "Facing the Future, the Development Strategy of Shanghai in the Next 30 Years". We are in charge of one of the research topics, that is, city brand building and attractiveness of Shanghai as a global city in 2050. For Shanghai, city competitiveness in the future is not merely based on city's GDP and economical growth development level. More importantly, I think, attractiveness relies on multiple factors that are closely related to the city's soft capacity, among which are cultural factor and city brand. We expect that this research project can promote the process of building Shanghai into a global city.

"The Global City Forum—Shanghai 2050: A Rising Global City" is one of the series activities of World Cities Day initiated by the UN in 2014. We have the honor to invite many famous domestic and international scholars, experts and researchers in urban studies to discuss about this very important strategic topic of Shanghai when it turns into a global city. These exchanges are beneficial for further clarifying the 2050 vision of Shanghai and are useful for the real practice. Shanghai will be able to learn from international experiences, on the way to be a global city with international competence and attractiveness. So I should say remember the day, World Cities Day, which brings us more hopes than ever before.

KEYNOTE
SPEECHES

主旨演讲

联合国副秘书长吴红波
在全球城市论坛上作主旨演讲

Wu Hongbo, Under-Secretary-
General, United Nations，delivers
a speech at the Global City Forum

可持续发展的城市与上海

吴红波

联合国副秘书长

城市的可持续发展，对中国未来的繁荣乃至全球可持续发展都具有不可估量的重要性。当今世界城市化进程不断加快，一半以上的人口都居住在城市。因此，如果策略得当，城市将为可持续的繁荣发展提供重要机遇。一直以来，城市都是经济发展、创新与就业的中心，也是教育、文化和科技创新的中心，带动了人类文明的不断进步。但是，随着城市不断发展，管理城市也变得愈加复杂。在许多国家，城市的过快发展和规模膨胀都带来了巨大的挑战。关注这一领域的专家已经达成共识，城市未来可持续发展是一场复杂的战役，胜负难以预料。四年前 2010 年上海世博会的主题正反映了这一关切，那就是"城市，让生活更美好"。

实现可持续发展并不容易。城市是一个复杂、多维、相互联结的系统，推动着文明的演化和发展。它既是经济发展的引擎，也是经济高度发展的结果。城市中经济活动的集聚，对一个国家乃至全球的经济发展都具有十分重要的作用。我们来看一组数据，有些可能大家都很熟悉。城市贡献了全球 GDP 总量的 80%，其中 60% 来自约 600 座城市。在发展中地区情况也大致如此。比如，非洲 60% 的 GDP 来自城市；在中国，地级市和其他中心城市贡献了全国 GDP 的 61%。

我们要用动态的视角看待这一现象。大家都知道，城市的扩张起源于 19 世纪 60 年代开始的工业化进程。此后，城市逐渐成为世界经济增长的引擎和催生新科技、新发明的创新中心。未来 30 年我们面临的重大挑战在于，如何充分发挥城市化的潜在成效，同时将其负面影响降到最低，从而实现包容性发展。亚洲和非洲在未来城市化中将面临严峻的挑战。随着人口持续增长和城市化的加速，到 2050 年全球城市人口将增加 15 亿，而其中 90% 来自亚洲和非洲。并且大部分人口增长并非来自大城市，而是来自相对较小的二线城市或市镇，这些地方贫困率相对较高，基本公共服务远不能满足需求。那么，亚洲和非洲的城市能否容纳这些新增的人口，这些城市的管理者将面临诸多难题。比如，外来人口越来越多，这些城市能否创造足够的就业机会？学校、医院、交通基础设施和住房等能否满足新增人口的需求？在城市快速发展的同时如何保护环境？而这些仅仅是政府需要解决的问题的一部分而已。

不仅发展中国家面临着城市化进程中诸多问题的挑战，工业化国家也同样如此，有些问题与其类似，有些问题则有不同的特点。首先是人口结构的变化。比如，和很多发达国家城市一样，上海面临着一系列的人口问题，诸如低出生率和人口老龄化。其次是基础设施老旧和经济停滞。在欧洲和北美，很多城市的基础设施都已有百年之久，需要修补或替换。在经济发展缓慢、停滞甚至下滑的环境下，它们面临着很大的财政压力。第三，在经济增长缺乏包容性的情况下，很多城市面临极大的贫富差距和社会鸿沟。一些社区居住环境差，教育质量低，社会两极分化严重，空间隔离严重，让低收入和边缘化群体很难找到价格合理又体面的住房。第四，收入提高还伴随着私家车保有量上升和住房的拥挤，使生态环境面临更大压力。以上这些都说明，管理好城市的发展已经成为 21 世纪最大的挑战之一。

气候变化也给城市提出了减灾防灾的要求。联合国国际减灾署的数据显示，自 1975 年起，全球城市面临的自然灾害频率上升了 4 倍。城市在极端天气和气候事件面前变得日益脆弱，比如热浪、严重干旱和洪水，这些都可能影响城市供水、居民健康、基础设施以及生态环境。对于沿海城市来说还存在海平面上升和飓风等风险。我在纽约就见证了"桑迪"飓风的灾害，造成了几亿美元的损失。面对日益频繁剧烈的自然灾害，城市做好应对准备了吗？如何保护城市基础设施？在城市规划与发展中如何提升抗灾能力？无论是上百年历史的城市，还是发展中国家的新兴城市，在灾害预防和灾后重建中都面临着同样的挑战。

国际社会越来越关注城市可持续发展。在联合国可持续发展大会（又称"里约 +20"峰会）上，各国一致认为，如果城市能够进行良好的规划和管理，将从经济、社会、环境等方面极大地促进可持续发展。大会呼吁，为有效应对未来几十年的人口增长，应当有更多大都市、城市和市镇对可持续发展进行规划。联合国正在开展的 2015 年后发展议程，就是从气候变化、工业化、基础设施建设、经济发展、健康、教育以及环境保护等多个方面，对可持续发展进行规划，其核心是坚持以人为本，建设可持续的城市。

作为世界级的大城市，上海如何应对可持续发展的挑战，不仅对中国的发展十分重要，对国际上其他城市也同样具有借鉴意义。上海是中国最大的城市，人口密度高，经济活动高度集聚，要保持良好的环境难度更大。这方面上海取得的成就是令人瞩目的。上海在加快发展的同时，在环境保护上进行了大量投入，在经济发展和环境保护之间保持了良好的平衡。上海在交通基础设施建设上也进行了大量投资，建立了以轨道交通、公交、出租车为基础的发达的公共交通体系。上海的快速轨道交通体系，包括地铁与轻轨在内，覆盖了中心城及周边地区的每个角落。

然而，上海接下来还有许多工作要做。经济持续发展将对环境产生很大的压力，上海应对这些压力的举措将给世界上其他快速发展的城市很大启发。如何在不断改善环境质量的同时，保持上海经济持续增长？如何充分运用科学和工程手段解决上海的环境问题？如何推进城市可持续发展？在此我想抛砖引玉，基于此前所做的工作，作个简要回答。

第一，从长远和系统视角出发规划城市可持续发展。城市不仅是实体的基础设施，还是思想、商业、文化、教育和社会发展的中心，因此我们必须有一个综合的战略。

第二，积极推进农村地区发展。城市没有边界，从长远看，只有让周边农村地区分享发展成果，城市才能真正繁荣发展。

第三，让利益相关方共同参与。正如我前面所说，城市是一个非常复杂、交叉性很强的系统，没有任何部门或个人可以单独规划或管理，因此在城市规划过程中，各个方面的利益相关方必须充分参与进来。

第四，发展先进的公共交通体系，并降低对私家车的依赖。在这方面，上海已经做了大量卓有成效的工作，相信还会取得更大的进展。

第五，大力发展服务业。与中国其他大城市相比，上海服务业遥遥领先，2013 年上海 60% 以上的 GDP 都来自服务业。下一步，还将继续大力发展金融服务业、航运业和文化产业。

第六，推行完备的垃圾处理方法，包括循环处理和废物利用。垃圾处理是全球性的难题。随着城市化的推进，预计到 2025 年固体废弃物将是现在的两倍，这将给城市环境和公共健康管理带来很大压力，上海也不例外。

第七，提高灾后重建能力，减少灾害易发地区的建筑物数量。我之前也讲过这个问题，我认为这将是上海市政府长期面临的挑战。

第八，为农民工提供良好的就业机会，并将其纳入城市规划之中。这对世界上很多城市都是艰巨的挑战，上海在创造就业方面采取了前瞻性的策略，重点关注服务业和创新型经济增长。我相信上海会解决好这个问题。

最后我想用一句话来概括我的观点：城市可持续发展事关我们每一个人。这不仅是政府的责任，也是我们每个人的义务，我们都应当为此作出贡献。我们应该更多使用公共交通，节约利用水、能源和其他资源，减少废物排放，促进循环利用，积极参与到社区活动当中。让我们牢记，城市在未来可持续发展中发挥着关键作用。城市，让生活更美好！让我们共同努力，充分发掘城市的潜力，拥有我们想要的未来。

世界银行中国局局长郝福满
在全球城市论坛上作主旨演讲

Bert Hofman, World Bank's Country
Director for China, delivers a speech at
the Global City Forum

从世界和中国的趋势
看上海的未来

郝福满

世界银行中国局局长

30 年是一个很大的时间跨度。30 年前，谁能想到纽约能够成为世界顶级城市？谁能想到美国制造业的中心底特律会濒临破产？谁能想到伦敦能够成为世界金融中心之一？在那时几乎没有网络的情况下，又有谁能够想到，阿里巴巴今后会成长为中国最大的公司？情景规划是一个复杂的科学问题，但我认为它对中国和上海来说十分必要。世界银行在全球不少城市和农村发展问题上都有丰富经验，我们很乐意为上海提供帮助。

20 年前，浦东陆家嘴地区只有一条隧道连接浦西地区，而如今浦东和浦西之间有众多的隧道和桥梁，两岸的面貌都发生了巨大的变化。中国改革开放后，创造了举世瞩目的经济奇迹，而上海一直走在中国的前列。中国能成为世界经济供应链中最重要的一环，作为长江三角洲制造业中心的上海功不可没。上海已经是世界最大的港口，其规模超越了鹿特丹和新加坡。目前上海的 GDP 规模相当于葡萄牙，可能超过了比利时。而上世纪90 年代，整个国家的 GDP 才勉强与比利时相当。由此可见，这些年发生了多么巨大的变化。未来上海经济应该向服务业和创新型产业转型，关键是如何实现这一进程。

城镇化是一个重要的趋势。中国的城镇化时间不长，且伴随着经济的高速发展和经济社会转型。然而，拉动经济增长的出口导向型工业发展模式的压力日显。同时，剧烈的社会变迁、收入不平等加剧和人口老龄化也构成新的挑战。空气污染、能源使用和温室气体排放造成的环境破坏，对国内和全球都带来危害。

亚洲再度崛起，成为全球 GDP 的重要贡献力量。到 2050 年，预计将占到世界经济总量的 30% 至 35%（按不变价计算）。再投资发展现有产业已不能为中国带来相同的效益，中国的工业生产率仅为经合组织国家的

50% 左右。中国的制造业成本虽然仍很低廉，但也在快速上升。印度凭借其人口优势，最有可能填补中国的劳动力人数空缺，成为下一个制造业基地。因此，中国需要提升发展服务业所需的创造力和创新力，也迫切需要更好地利用资本和人才创造经济价值。中国的航运业仍有巨大潜力，并已拥有多个世界最大港口。上海港是世界最大的货运港口，上海有望在区域层面继续发挥在全球制造业和供应链中的作用。

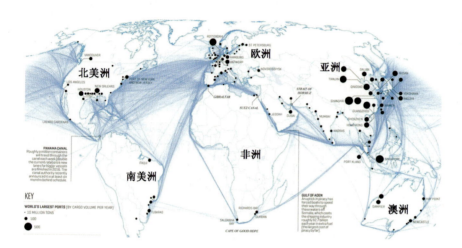

图 1
世界港口分布情况

　　随着中产阶层的人数不断增加，中国将成为重要的消费市场，从生产型社会逐渐转变到消费型社会。虽然中等收入陷阱没有得到充分证实，但有证据表明，当一个国家的人均收入达到 1 万—1.5 万美元时，经济增长速度往往会放慢。好消息是，很多走出中等收入陷阱的国家都在东亚地区。如今，欧洲仍是世界最大的消费中心，但到 2030 年亚洲特别是中国和印度将成为主要的消费中心。

　　与此同时，中国及亚洲各国的收入不平等现象日益增加，但全世界的不平等现象却在下降。随着中国的经济增长速度放缓，高度的收入不平等可能催生经济和社会问题。亚洲城镇化和老龄化日益加剧，对传统社会造成压力，对社会和公共服务的需求不断增加，因此如何管理就成了严峻的挑战。世界各国的经验表明，社会凝聚力对于构建具有可持续性和韧性的经济十分重要，对于像上海这样一个城市的繁荣发展也是一个重要因素。

　　人口问题也需要关注。各个国家情况有所不同。到 2050 年，尼日利亚经济会明显好转，人口将呈爆炸式增长，出现人口红利。而印度将面临老龄化等城市化进程带来的问题。日本的老龄化问题已经非常严重，在 2050 年前必须找到解决问题的方法。对于中国我们预计到 2050 年，劳动

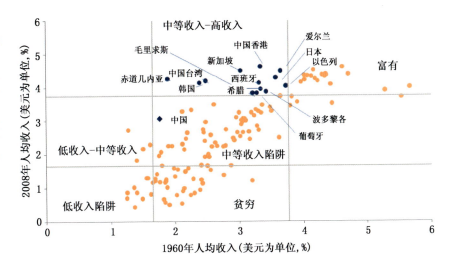

图2

1960 年和 2008 年
人均收入

资料来源：世界银
行、国务院发展研
究中心研究报告，
《2030 年的中国：建
设现代、和谐、有
创造力的高收入社
会》，2012 年 3 月。

人口总数会减少，而老龄人口总数将迅速上升。

　　未来几十年世界将会如何发展？事实上很难预测。主要有两大驱动因素，一是人口状况和创新能力，二是社会凝聚力。综合起来可能有四种情况。

　　（1）如果增长速度快、社会凝聚力强，所有的社会问题都能得到解决，那么城市会有无限发展机遇，人们可以生活得很好。

　　（2）如果经济增长速度很快，而社会凝聚力不强，世界将严重分化，任何改革都无法推行。

　　（3）如果经济增长速度慢，社会又动荡，就出现大家普遍不满的"严冬"。英国在 70 年代后期就是如此，国民对此普遍不满。

　　（4）如果经济增长速度慢，但社会凝聚力很强，它仍是一个宜居、和谐的国家，但人们对未来的期望也很低。日本过去 20 年就是这样。

　　未来出现哪种情况很难预知。无论如何，上海都应当奋发努力，努力实现繁荣发展。对中国而言，上海在未来发展中扮演着十分重要的角色。在亚洲和世界经济体系中，上海都有着广阔的发展前景。

国务院发展研究中心发展战略与区域经济部部长侯永志
在全球城市论坛上作主旨演讲

Hou Yongzhi, Department Director of Development Strategy and
Regional Economy, Development Research Center of the State
Council, delivers a speech at the Global City Forum

不确定的世界，谋划
一个确定的未来

侯永志

国务院发展研究中心发展战略与区域经济部部长

要研究 2050 年的上海，有很多的不确定性。但是谋划一个确定的未来还是可能的，这个未来是确定的，也即我们要有一个美好的上海，一个令人向往的上海。

1. 谋划 2050 年的上海具有重要意义

我们知道世界是充满不确定性的，在一个不确定的世界谋划一个确定的未来确实不是一件容易的事情。回顾 30 年前，当人们把手表、缝纫机、自行车作为三大件的时候，当人们把上海生产的真丝手绢作为城乡青年的定情之物的时候，当广大农村的孩子把上海生产的大白兔奶糖作为梦寐以求的奢侈品的时候，谁能想象到今天，我们的飞机满天飞，轿车遍地跑，互联网也兴起了，渗透到社会生活的每一个角落里。大山里的青年来到了上海，有从事蓝领工作的，也有从事白领工作的。世界各国的人士纷纷来到上海，有来到上海洽谈生意的，也有旅游逛大街的。想想这 30 多年的变化是巨大的，这在那个时候是很难想象的。但是，有一点是可以肯定的，即技术的进步引起了生产力的发展，而生产力的发展又会导致生产经济结构、社会结构和文化结构的变化。同时，应该看到技术进步也会导致经济空间结构的变化。

纵观世界近代史，可以清晰地看到技术进步对于生产方式的影响。18世纪 70 年代以来，在技术革命的推动之下，世界经济进入了一个完整的以 50 年为周期的波浪。每一波长都有各自清晰的地理特征：K1 时期，技术领先的国家是英国、法国和比利时；K2 时期，德国和美国成为技术领先国家的新成员；K3 时期，德国和美国成为技术最先进的国家；K4 时期，日本、瑞典和其他工业化国家跻身于技术领先国家行列；K5时期，美国、日本、韩国等是技术领先国家。

展望未来，我们还会看到技术进步，这里有麦肯锡预测的十几种颠覆性技术。第一个是移动互联网。第二个是智能型工业自动化，将来我们的自动化不仅仅是解放人的手，还解放人的脑，我们的脑力劳动也要被机械所替代。第三个是物联网技术。第四个是云计算。还有先进的机器人技术、新一代的基因技术。自动化的交通工具会减少二氧化碳排放，能量的储存技术会帮助太阳能的输送和使用。还有3D打印，最近看到还有4D打印这个说法，就是我们打出来的东西还会变形。还有先进的材料、石油勘探技术等。这是对未来10年技术进步的估计。

未来30年的情况又是怎么样的？这确实需要我们思考。对于技术进步的影响也有不同的估计。我最近看了两本书，一本是《零边际成本社会》，这本书谈了11个城市，将来随着互联网技术的发展，可能每个人都会成为创新者，都会在网上进行创新，成果会让大家共享。所以将来知识产权这个概念可能就不存在了，只剩笼统的社会。另外一本书就是《互联网的误读》，它认为互联网也没有那么神奇，也就是一般的技术而已，也不会有那么颠覆性的影响。以上是两种不同的观点。

除了技术进步之外，我想还有一个观点基本可以肯定，即中国将成为世界第一大经济体。回看过去中国经济增长，如果按7%的标准，实际上中国的经济已经快速增长了50年，未来中国的经济增速会有所下降，但是，在相当长的时间内仍然可以保持6%—7%的增长。不管怎么样，总的来说如果说没有意外的话，如果说不会掉到中等收入陷阱里，中国成为第一大经济体应该是有可能的。

另外，会有越来越多的国家将被卷入工业化和城镇化的浪潮当中。这些变化无疑将改变世界的格局，但世界经济格局将发生哪些具体的变化呢？实际上是很难说得清楚的。

但是不管怎么样，我们总是希望上海有一个美好的未来，我觉得我们建设一个令人神往的上海应该是确定无疑的目标，所以说要在一个不确定的世界谋划一个确定的未来，这个确定的未来就是上海要成为一个令人神往的地方。

最关键的是什么？就是要做一个规划。我们的规划不一定能完全实现，但是我们做规划总比不做要好，早做规划总比晚做要好，这是肯定的。中国古代有一句话：处天下之事不可以不因其事。我们如何做到因其事，就是首先要认清大势，做好规划。

有一本书，《解除束缚的普罗米修斯》，这本书解释为什么工业革命会发生在西方，还有长期的财富积累等问题。还说到政府所提供的某些最基本的社会稳定，例如首先是安全问题，如果没有安全，会引起社会的动荡，也就是 riot of society，政府就是无效的管理。另外，做规划其实也相当于提供了公共安全，政府在发展过程中不是可有可无的，必须起到应有的作用。

总的结论就是，上海在中国经济和世界经济都处于重大转型的关头谋划未来 30 年的发展是必要的，也是可行的。

2. 如何思考上海的定位

我们应该怎么来思考上海的定位？谋划发展定位，首先要对发展有全面和深刻的理解。我们对于发展的理解，有一个从狭义到广义的变化。最初，我们认为发展等于增长，有了经济增长之后，一切发展的问题就解决了。后来，我们发现仅仅有增长是不行的，必须考虑到如果增长不能带来其他方面的变化，不能带来社会结构的改善，也是不行的。所以，后来发展是多方面的，包括经济、文化、社会等方面的结构变化。新中国成立的时候，发展生产主要是满足人民群众的基本生活需求。那时候，能想象楼上楼下都有电视电话吗？可是现在这些都有了。现在有不少老人还用上手机，这些在当时能想象得出来吗？所以我们对于发展的内涵也是在不断地变化。

《人文地理学》这本书里有这么一句话，发展是一个变形重版的概念，它是根深蒂固的，并且是无处不在的，因为它隐含着一个最美好的意愿。我认为这讲到了发展的本质。

对于发展问题，社会各方面、学者、各国政府以及联合国都在考虑，中国共产党也一直在思考什么是正确的发展。在中共第十八次全国代表大会上，中国共产党在总结中国发展的历史和世界各国发展经验的基础上，明确地提出了中国要建设社会主义市场经济、社会主义民主政治、社会主义先进文化、社会主义和谐社会、社会主义生态文明。我理解可以把发展概括为五个方面，也就是经济发展、政治发展、文化发展、社会发展和生态发展。我认为这五个方面，可以作为我们思考上海 2050 年发展的逻辑和起点。

中国古代著名的思想家和诗人屈原有九问，我想上海2050年的发展定位也有这样九个问题：

一是2050年的时候上海在中外公众中的整体形象是什么？上海作为一个全球城市，这是一个概念。随着中国经济地位的上升，上海在全球公众中形象究竟是什么？

二是2050年的上海应该有什么样的经济结构？服务业、制造业到底相对的地位是怎么样的？有的人认为上海不要搞制造业了，也有的人认为制造业很重要，究竟如何考虑？

三是2050年的上海对中国和对全球生产要素的配置能起到什么样的作用？接下来的问题就是上海能不能起到当今的纽约在全球资源配置中所起到的重要作用。因为现在美国是全球经济的老大，所以纽约在全球的地位是比较高的。那么，当中国成为第一大经济体的时候，上海能不能起到像纽约一样的作用？

四是上海在即将到来的人类社会大转型中能否起到一个垂范作用？最近《文化纵横》杂志有篇文章，认为不仅仅是中国处在一个发展转型期，整个人类社会、世界都要转型，这是面向21世纪的思考。

五是面对资源环境问题、社会问题，同样具有挑战性。上海将来在资源环境问题、社会问题上能不能探索一条道路，怎样才能又和谐又繁荣？

六是在东西方文化相互交流和碰撞中，上海在促进文化交融方面可以发挥什么样的独特作用？

七是在全球气候变暖等生态问题日益突出的背景下，上海在改变人类生态足迹方面可以发挥什么样的作用？能不能创造一个新的人类生活方式，减少二氧化碳排放？

八是在互联网触及社会的每一个角落，城市质地日益复杂的背景下，上海是否可以探索一条新的道路？

九是在发展的五个方面——经济、社会、政治、文化、生态，在上海这块大平台上形成什么样的逻辑关系，才能有助于上海自身的发展定位？这也是值得一问的。这是因为经济是基础，但不是发展的全部内容。只有经济与其他领域形成良性的互动关系，经济才能够发展，其他领域才能发展。《难以抉择：发展中国家的政治参与》这本书讲到国民生产总值的增长不会自动带来更公平的收入分配，不会自动增加下层群众的教育和就业机会，也不会自动地产生一个平衡和健康的都市长远发展模式，或者是去实现其他一些现代化的目标。

3. 构建一个高质量的经济体系

经济活动分为两种，一种是高质量的经济活动，一种是低质量的经济活动。高质量的经济活动，体现在产出的增长速度、技术进步水平、竞争状况、工资水平、职工素质和工作积极性等方面。为什么要追求高质量的经济活动？因为物质生产是人类社会存在和发展的基础。正如一位著名的思想家所言，历史过程中的决定性因素归根到底是现实生活的生产和再生产。

实现上海的发展定位，最核心的是要建立一个高质量的经济体系。上海未来的发展肯定会面临不少的挑战，必须突破自然环境对增长的制约，减轻发展对环境的压力。只有建立高质量的经济体系，才能应对挑战，才能在资源、环境因素制约日益增强的情况下，实现物质的较快增长，才能在物质财富增长的同时使生态环境保持良好的状态。

上海虽已完成城市化进程，但未来还会有外地人口源源不断地来到上海，给上海的社会治理带来严峻挑战。《落脚城市——最后人类大迁移和我们的未来》一书认为人类涌向城市以及过渡性都市飞速的发展对许多人造成直接的影响，而城市化走错了方向所造成的灾难，包括各种苦难，很大程度上往往是由于这种盲目现象所导致的直接后果。我们的思考未能虑及这些大量人口融入的问题，结果新进人口因此陷入困境，遭到排斥，心怀愤恨，这个时代的历史有很大一部分是由失根造成的。他们因公民权遭到了剥夺，于是采取了很极端和暴力的手段，以求在都市体制中取得一席之地。将来我们的城市化仍会有外来人口涌入的情况，城市化还有新人进来。我们只有建立高质量的经济体系，才能为人们提供相对稳定的就业和高水平的收入。

4. 实现上海战略定位的关键

实现上海战略定位的关键在于娴熟驾驭四个变量。《国际市场中的城市》一书认为，决定城市发展的有四种力量：一是市场条件，二是政府支持，三是公共控制，四是地方文化。市场条件和政府支持为驱动变量，公共控制和地方文化为转向变量。市场条件实际上是为城市提供发展资源，为投资提供更多的机会，即市场是不是能够为人们在这里投资和工作提供机会。政府支持提供发展所需要的基本要素，比如公共服务和基础设施。公共控制引导公众注意力的方向，比如创造工作机会、加强环境保护、正确处理经济发展增长与保护环境的关系。地方文化决定着城市的凝聚力和城市的形象。实现上海战略，关键是怎样驾驭这四种力量。驾驭这四种力量有三种方式：一是社会属性，强调政府起更大的作用；二是以市场为中心的，强调市场起更大的作用：三是混合式的。

关于上海的选择，一是要让上海的市场发挥重要的决定性作用。但是，对市场要有一个全面的认识，怎么样起到一个正确的决定性作用？很多产能过剩实际上就是市场在起盲目性作用的时候出现的。二是要让政府发挥更好的作用。这是两个驱动变量。三是要让公众参与，要有更多的建设性意见。四是要让文化更有包容性和开放性，要接纳不同的文化，不仅是西方的文化，乡土文化也可以接受，包括上海当地传统文化。

上海市人民政府发展研究中心主任、党组书记肖林
在全球城市论坛上作主旨演讲

Xiao Lin, Director General of the Development Research
Center of Shanghai Municipal People's Government,
delivers a speech at the Global City Forum

我们的上海，中国的上海，世界的上海

肖 林

上海市人民政府发展研究中心主任、党组书记

　　城市是现代文明的标志，是经济、政治、科技、文化、教育的中心，也是人类的共同家园。2008年，全球城市居民人数首次在历史上超过农村居民，我们的星球已经进入城市时代。中国的城市化与工业化同步，目前已形成具有中国特色的城市化模式。上海作为中国城市化水平最高和经济最发达的城市，从21世纪初就已经进入后工业化时代。上海在城市发展过程中既遇到了其他城市遇到的共同问题，也面临一些独特的问题和挑战。城市功能的发展在中国、在发展中国家都具有典型意义。中国改革开放以来，上海城市的发展方向和功能定位已经发生数轮转变，其对城市经济社会发展发挥了重大而深远的牵引作用。

　　目前，上海正在同时开展三个面向未来战略规划的重大研究。第一个是到2020年，上海"十三五"经济社会发展规划研究，主要是解决今后五年上海的发展问题。第二个是到2040年，上海城市总体规划修编研究，主要是解决上海未来的城市定位、城市功能以及空间战略问题。第三个是到2050年，面向未来30年的上海发展战略研究，对未来的发展目标、发展趋势、战略路径做出预判。

　　这三大战略研究之间有着非常紧密的关系。首先，"十三五"规划要与中国共产党建党100周年时全面建成小康社会，以及新中国成立100周年时建成富强、民主、文明、和谐的社会主义现代化国家这两个百年目标来衔接，要更加注重以解决长远问题的办法，来应对我们面临的挑战。其次，2040年城市总体规划的城市发展愿景和城市定位，要以面向未来30年发展的上海战略研究为依托。因此，开展面向未来30年的上海发展战略研究意义非常重大，上海各方面的专家、社会力量都在积极参与这一重大研究。目前，有上海社会科学院、上海财经大学、华东师范大学、复旦

大学、同济大学、中共上海市委党校、上海市发展改革研究院等30多所高校、研究机构的80多个研究团队，汇集了上海以及国内的一些顶级专家和学者来开展综合研究和专题研究。国务院发展研究中心和世界银行也分别从国家战略和全球视野角度对上海未来30年的发展开展研究。

展望未来，世界与中国的变化可能比过去30年更快、更大，上海也将在打造中国经济升级版图、实现中华民族伟大复兴中国梦中承担更大的责任和使命，上海将胸怀大局、把握大势，因势而谋、因势而动、顺势而为，谋划面向上海未来30年的发展战略。

1. 上海城市功能的历史变迁

中国改革开放以来，上海城市功能发生了根本性的演变。上海宋代成镇、元代设县、明代筑城，在中国古代璀若明星的众多城市中并不是特别耀眼，上海的崛起从近代开始，随着条约口岸的开放，形成了新的生产力和生产方式，因港设县，以商兴市。在20世纪30年代，上海就已经成为远东地区的国际经贸中心、商业中心、金融中心、交通枢纽和文化重镇。新中国成立以后，由于西方国家的战略遏制和经济封锁，加上国家以农业为基础、工业为主导的发展方针，上海必然地承担起了工业重地的历史任务，由消费型城市转变为生产型城市。

上海曾开展过多次发展战略研究，这些研究中确定的愿景目标和功能定位对上海选择发展方向、制定发展目标、统领发展思路发挥了重要作用。其中最重要的是20世纪80年代和90年代的上海经济发展战略、浦东开发开放战略，以及迈向21世纪的上海战略研究。通过战略研究，上海明确了城市发展的方向和功能定位，实现了从原来的以工业为主的单功能经济结构向综合型多功能经济中心城市转变，从计划经济向市场经济转变，实现了跨越式的发展，逐步成为国际经济、金融、贸易、航运中心和社会主义现代化国际大都市。

纵观历史，上海发展战略研究有一条主线和脉络基本没有变过，这就是城市的功能定位。20世纪80年代上海的发展战略明确了要发展对外开放和多功能的中心城市作用，努力建设成为开放性多功能、产业结构合理、经济繁荣、文化昌盛和科技发达的社会主义现代化国际经济中心城市。90年代，浦东开发开放成为国家战略，通过开发浦东，加快城市功能的转变。20世纪末，上海提出迈向21世纪的上海发展战略，提出要积极成为国际经济中心城市，建成国际经济、贸易、金融中心。进入21世纪以后，又逐步发展成为建设国际经济、金融、贸易、航运四个中心，明确到2020年基本建成"四个中心"和社会主义现代化国际大都市的基本目标。2014年5月，习近平总书记在上海考察期间，又对上海提出了向具有全球影响力的科技创新中心进军的新的战略定位，全球科技创新中心与产业经济中心协同共进，使上海国际化大都市的未来更加丰富和充实。

上海城市的发展具有独特的因素和规律，城市是具有生命的个体，拥有城市的共性因素，但是每个城市又是不同的。历史上上海的城市功能调整，无不显示其具备无法被其他城市替代的特殊因素，所以上海从来没有被复制为世界上另一个城市。上海独特的城市因素对城市功能的演进具有重要的影响。首先，自然禀赋和地理位置决定了城市发展方向和城市形态，决定了城市发展的产业结构和城市功能。上海地处长江入海口、中国沿海经济带的地理中心，由此，上海得以成为远东的商贸节点和要素集散中心，引导国际经济中心城市框架的形成。其次，人口自然构成、人口地域构成和人口社会构成决定了城市活力的显性特征。上海作为现代开放性的国际城市，是典型的移民城市，拥有东西方文化融合的海派文化，海派文化是600多年来中国江南文化与西方优秀文化碰撞所遗留下来的文化精髓，具有多元开放、兼容并蓄的特征，是中国优秀文化传统的组成部分，是中华伟大文明的体现。第三，上海城市的发展战略始终密切联系着国家战略。无论是计划经济时代还是市场经济时代，上海作为全国中心城市的定位始终没变。新中国成立至改革开放前夕，上海作为当时全国工业技术最好、设备最优的城市，成为全国最大的工业基地和传统工商业城市；改革开放以后，突破体制束缚的上海通过一系列的不懈努力，持续开放，改革创新，把握全球化和信息化两大机遇，由传统的全国经济中心和国际大都市向全球城市嬗变。

2. 上海城市转型的战略背景

未来30年，上海将进入功能转型的战略机遇期。

第一，全球的产业结构加速调整，世界经济重心逐步东移，上海提升全球资源配置能力将迎来重大机遇。全球金融危机以后，以中国、印度为代表的新型经济体逐渐崛起，世界经济重心向亚太地区转移，这为上海吸引国际人才和金融资源的流入、提升在全球产业价值链中的地位提供了重要的机遇。

第二，以物联网、云计算和下一代通信网络为代表的新一轮信息技术革命为上海城市功能转型带来了重大机遇。随着新技术、新业态的快速发展，信息技术与传统产业的不断融合，催生出新的商业模式和服务业态，将推动上海产业结构调整和加快升级。

第三，"一带一路"和长江经济带国家战略为上海打造全球城市和中心节点带来了历史性机遇。上海地处丝绸之路经济带、海上丝绸之路和长江经济带的交汇节点，"一带一路"和长江经济带国家战略将进一步释放上海的发展潜能，发挥上海的中心辐射作用，提升上海的城市能级。

第四，中国崛起和经济发展方式转变，调结构、扩内需，经济加快转型给上海带来先行先试的机遇。上海城市功能的转型离不开整个中国整体的发展战略，进入 21 世纪以来，中国转变发展方式的要求更加紧迫，而作为中国经济中心城市，上海需要在全国发挥示范引领和改革开放的带动作用。

第五，长三角地区发展成为国家战略。区域同城化进程加快，上海城市功能转型拥有长三角作为重要依托。上海是长三角城市群的首位和中心城市，上海发展要放在长三角城市群的战略空间中加以考量。长三角城市群协同能力的不断提升，会对上海的产业结构升级、技术创新、城市管理、环境保护和资源的要素激活产生巨大的促进作用，从而促进长三角区域协调发展和共同发展。

第六，中国全面深化改革和对外开放战略的深入，为上海提供转型的动力。中国（上海）自由贸易试验区和浦东新区的深化改革、扩大开放，不仅极大地激发了上海城市发展的巨大潜力和活力，也将引领中国新一轮的改革开放，成为中国改革开放和创新转型的试验田。

同时，上海发展也面临着一些挑战，这在一定程度上也倒逼城市功能的转型。

第一，城市功能的转型、结构调整与稳定增长的挑战。在城市转型过程中，上海不能出现大规模的经济衰退和大量的失业。2014 年，上海加大城市转型的力度，但是仍然保持了一定的经济增长速度，这在世界上是一个奇迹。未来上海不能以牺牲稳定增长来换取城市转型，在转型过程中，必须通过劳动生产率的持续提高来实现城市经济社会的稳定和发展。

第二，资源环境的挑战。目前，能源、土地、水资源等自然资源已经成为制约上海发展的关键因素，尤其是土地资源，上海建设用地占总面积比重超过 40%，远高于北京、天津等国内大城市，也超过国际化大都市的平均水平。污染物排放和环境吸收容量也已接近饱和。

第三，人口问题的挑战。上海城市人口存在着结构、规模双重压力，一方面人口规模过大、增长过快，加重了城市的负荷；另一方面，新增人口主要是外来人口，平均受教育水平不高。人口老龄化等社会结构性的矛盾日益凸显，上海户籍人口的老龄化水平已经达到 24.5%。

第四，空间结构的挑战。目前上海的城市空间、城市形态和城市功能存在着一定程度的不匹配，基于中心外围结构的网络型大都市区尚未完成。上海常住人口空间分布已经呈现郊区化趋势，但经济活动仍过于集中在中心城区，从而产生了庞大的潮汐式通勤人口。

在城市转型中，我们既要把握这些重大机遇，也要直面这些矛盾挑战，在不确定的未来中把握确定的目标。

3. 未来的上海将建成什么样的全球城市

科学制定城市发展战略是引领城市未来发展方向的路标。2050 年，中国将实现中华民族伟大复兴的中国梦；再过 5 年，上海就要实现 2020 年基本建成国际经济、金融、贸易、航运中心的宏伟目标，上海将站上新的历史起点。在新的历史阶段，上海将何去何从？我们期待通过战略研究来探索方向、统一思想、明晰思路。未来上海城市功能的转型要顺应内外环境变化的潮流，要追寻城市功能演变的客观规律，要依据上海城市禀赋的独特因素，树立系统的观点、智慧的观点、可持续的观点和开放引领的观点，依托长三角区域建设经济、文化、生态、环境共生的世界性全球城市，用系统的观点来看上海未来全球城市的发展转型。

从城市发展愿景看，上海应当成为体现文明特质的综合型、世界性全球城市，全球城市网络中最重要的节点城市，世界版图中最重要的门户，成为基于长三角全球城市区域网络的核心城市。基于这样的发展愿景，应从多个层面的城市功能共同形成面向未来 30 年的上海城市功能体系。

从资源层面看，上海应当成为全球资源配置管理协调功能的控制节点，高端资本、商品、信息和人流的交换枢纽；集聚具有全球影响力的科学原创中心、研发总部、制造高地。

从现代文明层面看，上海是一个东方大国的东方城市，如果不具备文化软实力，上海城市的影响力和竞争力就是无根之萍。因此，上海应当成为东西方文化交流共建的中心、全球创新思想的汇聚高地、现代社会治理的全球典范。

从生态层面看，信息技术、大数据、云计算等科技创新日新月异，将催生出新的商业模式和服务业态，也必将改变城市居民的生活方式，新一轮的技术革命必将着力于人与人的协调发展、人与城市的协调发展、人与自然的协调发展。未来上海要建设的城市必然是智慧的、自然的全球城市。

可持续发展是每一个国家、每一个组织、每一个人的共同责任，应当用可持续的观点看上海未来全球城市功能的转变。2012年6月，联合国可持续发展大会通过了成果文件《我们憧憬的未来》，表达了全人类对可持续发展的期盼。城市是可持续发展的主要阵地，城市可持续发展是一种全新的城市发展观，其核心是在保证城市经济效率和生活质量的前提下，使能源和其他自然资源的消费、消耗及污染最小化，重新思考未来全球城市可持续发展的内涵是一个全新的命题。

上海必须坚持以人为本，走城市可持续发展之路。未来上海要建成的全球城市，必然是可持续发展的全球城市，成为人居之城，绿色、低碳、生态之城。要用开放引领的观点来看上海未来全球城市功能的转型。上海是中国长三角城市群、长江经济带以及丝绸之路经济带、21世纪海上丝绸之路的龙头，引领着长三角城市群、长江经济带与"一带一路"的发展。

面向未来30年，建设全球城市是上海市民追求幸福生活的共同梦想。在追梦、圆梦的奋斗过程中，上海将与世界各国城市一道，共同为城市的发展、进步和文明创造美好的未来。

Shanghai and
Sustainable Cities

Wu Hongbo

Under-Secretary-General, United Nations

The importance of sustainable cities for China's future prosperity and for the future of global sustainable development is inestimable. In today's increasingly urbanizing world, more than half of the world's population now lives in cities. Consequently, if well managed, cities can offer important opportunities for sustainable development. Cities have always been the focal points for economic growth, innovation, and employment, as well as major sites for education, culture, and scientific and technological innovations, thus enriching our social and cultural fabrics. Nevertheless, as cities grow, managing them becomes increasingly complex. In many countries, the speed and the scale of the urban transformation present formidable challenges. Therefore, experts working on a broad range of sustainable development issues have come to this conclusion that the future battle of sustainable development will be won or lost in cities. Four years ago, this message was vividly captured in the theme of the World Expo 2010 Shanghai, "Better City, Better Life".

Achieving sustainable city development is no easy task. Cities are complex, multi-dimensional and interlocking systems, which epitomize the advancement of our civilization. They are both an engine and a consequence of the fruits of our economic growth. The concentration of economic activities in cities contributes significantly to national and global outcome. Let me share with you some statistics, some of which may be familiar to you. Worldwide, cities generate 80 percent of the global GDP, 60 percent of which comes from just 600 cities. This is also more or less the case in developing regions. For example, in Africa, 60 percent of the region's GDP is created in cities. In China, prefecture-level cities and other large urban centers generate 61 percent of China's GDP.

This phenomenon should be viewed dynamically. We are aware that cities began to expand after the start of the industrialization in the 1860s. Since then, cities have been the reliable engines of the world economy and centers of technologies and innovations. The critical challenge for the next 30 years will be to take full advantage of the potential benefits of urbanization while lessening the negative impacts in an inclusive way. Asia and Africa will face enormous challenges in their future urbanization processes. Continuing population growth and urbanization are projected to add 1.5 billion people to the world's urban population by 2050, 90 percent of which will come from Asia and Africa. Most of this population growth will not occur in the largest cities or towns but in smaller secondary cities and towns where poverty rates are higher and where the existing coverage of basic public services is far from comprehensive. Will cities in Asia or Africa be able to absorb more than 2 billion new urban residents? Local authorities or mayors will have to address a series of problems as follows. Will the cities create enough jobs for an ever increasing number of migrants? Will there be enough schools, hospitals, transport infrastructure or housing to meet the growing needs? And how can we protect the environment as our cities are growing? These are some of the questions local governments will have to contend. However, the problems associated with cities are not just the preserve of the developing world. Across the industrialized world, cities are also home to a growing set of challenges, some shared with cities in developing countries, others unique to cities in industrialized countries. First, demographic change. Shanghai, like many other cities in the developed world, is facing a series of demographic challenges, such as low birth rates and the aging population. Second, aging infrastructure and economic stagnation. Many cities in Europe and North America are grappling with century-old infrastructure which needs repair or replacement, which is an enormous fiscal challenge in a climate of slow economic growth, together with the threat of economic stagnation or decline. Third, without an inclusive growth, many cities continue to face large and persistent income disparities and a great economic segregation. Some neighborhoods are characterized by poor housing, low-quality education, social polarization and spatial segregation, making it increasingly difficult for low-income or marginalized groups to find decent and affordable housing. Fourth, higher income is associated with a rise in private vehicles and smaller house size, which threatens local ecosystems. All of these factors underscore that managing urban growth has become one of the biggest challenges of the 21st Century.

The climate change also raises the issue of disaster risk reduction for cities. According to UN Office for Disaster Risk Reduction, worldwide cities have witnessed a four-fold increase in frequency of urban natural disasters since 1975. Cities have become more exposed and vulnerable to extreme weather and climate events, such as heat waves, intense droughts, and floods, all of which can compromise water supplies, human health, infrastructure and eco-systems in cities. For coastal cities, impacts can include sea level rise and storm surges. I personally witnessed Hurricane Sandy in New York City, which cost hundreds of millions of dollars. Are cities prepared for more frequent and intense natural disasters? How can cities protect their infrastructure? How can cities build disaster resilience into urban planning and city development? Cities with century-old infrastructure as well as new and emerging ones in developing countries face the same challenge in disaster preparedness and resilience.

The international community has accorded increasing attention to sustainable city development. During the United Nations Conference on Sustainable Development— also known as Rio+20, Member States stated that cities can promote economically, socially and environmentally sustainable societies if they are well planned and well developed. They further emphasized that there should be more metropolitan regions, cities and towns that plan for sustainable development in order to respond effectively to the expected growth of urban population in the coming decades. The ongoing United Nations post-2015 development agenda plans for the sustainable development across a number of focus points and areas, including climate change, industrialization, infrastructure, economic growth, health, education and the protection of the environment. At the center of this interlocking agenda is the perspective of human-centered approach to sustainable urbanization and sustainable cities.

How well Shanghai, as one of the world's largest cities, is able to respond to the challenges of sustainable development not only will be important for China, but will offer important lessons for the rest of the world to follow. Shanghai is the largest city in China, and its population density and concentration of economic and industrial activities are among the highest in the country. It is thus a great challenge for a city like Shanghai to maintain its environmental quality. The achievements of Shanghai with respect to environmental management are significant. Its rapid development has been matched by large investments in environmental protection. Shanghai has shown how it is possible to balance environmental protection and rapid economic growth. The city has also invested heavily in transportation infrastructure and has built an extensive public transport system based on metros, buses and taxis. Shanghai's rapid transit system, the Shanghai Metro, incorporates both subway and light railway lines and extends to every corner of urban district as well as neighboring suburban districts.

Yet, much work still remains to be done. Continued economic development will exert even greater pressure on the environment. How Shanghai responds to these challenges can inform other cities around the world that are undergoing similar rapid transformations. How economic growth can be achieved while improving the local environment? How can Shanghai solve its environmental problems with scientific and engineering expertise? How can Shanghai achieve a sustainable development? Let me venture a short answer, based on the previous work of my Department.

First, by applying a holistic approach to sustainable city development with a long-term vision and integrated planning perspectives. Cities are more than mere physical infrastructure; they are also hubs for ideas, commerce, culture, science, education and social development. So we need an integrated approach.

Second, by promoting rural development. Today's cities have no city walls. Over the long run, cities will prosper only when the rural areas around them share the same prosperity.

Third, by engaging all stakeholders. As I said earlier, cities are complex and interlocking systems. No single department or individual can plan and manage such complex systems alone. So stakeholder participation is an absolute imperative.

Fourth, by developing strong public transport systems and reducing reliance on private vehicles. In this regard, Shanghai has already done a remarkable job and I'm sure the city will see more achievements in the future.

Fifth, by fostering the service sector. Compared to other large cities in China, Shanghai is well ahead in the sector. In 2013, more than 60 percent of Shanghai's GDP came from service industries. Shanghai is also taking action to further develop its financial services, logistics and cultural industries.

Sixth, by encouraging sound waste management practices, including recycling and recovery. This is a worldwide challenge. Growing urbanization is estimated to double the volume of municipal solid waste annually by 2025, challenging environmental and public health management in the world's cities. Shanghai will not be immune from this challenge.

Seventh, by developing resilience to natural disasters, and reducing settlements in risk-prone areas. I spoke about this earlier and I am sure this will remain a major task for the Shanghai Municipal Government.

Eighth, by providing decent job opportunities for rural and migrant workers and integrating them in the urban planning. This is a daunting task for many municipal governments across the world. Shanghai has taken a forward-looking strategy to job creation by focusing on service sector and innovation-driven growth. I am confident the city will overcome this challenge.

I would like to conclude my remarks with one appeal. Sustainable city development is everybody's business. It is not just the responsibility of the government; it is also everyone's duty and we should all contribute. We should use more public transport, reduce unnecessary water, energy and other resource consumption, reduce waste, do more recycling, and participate more in activities of local communities. Let us not forget, the future of sustainable development will be won or lost in cities. Better City, Better Life. Let us work together to make sure that we take full advantage of the benefits of cities so that we can achieve the future we all want.

On Shanghai's Future through Current Trends of China and the World

Bert Hofman

World Bank's Country Director for China

30 years is a long time. 30 years ago, who would have thought that New York could be a top city in the world? Who would have thought that Detroit, which used to be the manufacturing center of the United States, would be on the verge of bankruptcy? Who would have thought London would have become a financial center of the world? And who would have thought that Alibaba, when the Internet did not objectively exist, was actually going to be the largest company in China? Scenario planning is a complex scientific problem, but I still think it will be very useful for China and for Shanghai. The World Bank is very humble to help Shanghai Municipality with experience from its global practice in urban and rural social development.

20 years ago, at Lujiazui there was only one tunnel connecting Pudong and Puxi, but now there are numerous tunnels and bridges between the two areas. Things on both sides have changed greatly. Since the Reform and Opening-up, Shanghai has been the vanguard of China's tremendously impressive economic miracle. And as China became the basic role in the supply chain, Shanghai gives a strong hand with its manufactures in the Yangtze River Delta. Besides, Shanghai is already the world's largest port and has taken over Rotterdam and Singapore. Also, Shanghai has a GDP as the size of Portugal and might be larger than Belgium. Yet, in the 1990s, the whole country's GDP was barely larger than Belgium. You can think what tremendous developments have occurred since then. In the future, Shanghai should shift its economy to the service and innovation industry, but the question is what will be needed to make that happen.

Urbanization is a critical trend. China is a late comer with a very dramatic growth rate and economic transformations. However, China's export-driven industries, its growth engine, are faced with increasing pressure. At the same time, China is also being challenged by dramatic social changes, the growing income inequality and an aging population. Besides, both China and the rest of the world are being jeopardized by environmental problems from air pollution, energy use and greenhouse gas emission.

Asia is on the rise and has become a prime contributor to the world's GDP. By 2050, Asia is projected to account for 30%-35% of the world economy (at constant prices). China's investments on current industries cannot generate similar benefits as before, and its productivity is only about 50% of OECD countries. The cost of manufacturing is currently desirable, but is still on the rise. And India, with its demographic advantages, is most likely to take China's place as a new manufacturing base. So China should improve its creativity and innovation ability for the service sector, and it will be massively important for China to use its capital and people more efficiently. China also has huge potential in the shipping industry and is home to many world's largest ports. As the world's largest freight port, Shanghai is expected to continue its role in the global manufacturing and supply chain.

As the middle class is expanding, China will become an important consumption market and will shift from a producing society to a consuming society. Though the proof for the Middle Income Trap is not yet sufficient, there is evidence that the economy growth of a country slows down when the income per capita reaches 10-15 thousand dollars. Fortunately, many East Asian countries have walked out of the trap. For now, Europe is still the biggest consumption center in the world. By 2030, Asian countries, particularly China and India, will be the largest consumption centers of the world.

At the same time, the income inequality is growing in China and other Asian countries, while this is the opposite for the rest of the world. As China's economy growth slows, high income inequality can turn into economic and social problems. Asia is increasingly urbanized and aging, and the traditional society will be challenged and there will be continuing demand for social and public services, so the management becomes paramount. Also, as other countries have shown, social cohesion is a critical factor for building a sustainable and durable economy, which is also the case for the prosperity of Shanghai.

Another challenge is the population, which varies in different countries. By 2050, Nigeria will become a much better economy where the population will explode, and it will enjoy the demographic dividend. India is going through the aging problem as well as other troubles from urbanization. In Japan, the aging problem is already serious and it has to find a solution by 2050. As for China, as we have projected, it will have less laboring population and more aging population by 2050.

So it is very hard to predict how the world is going to develop in the next decades. There are basically two main drives: demographics and its innovation, and social cohesion. And there are four futures to think about.

(1) With high growth and social cohesion, all social problems will be solved, and cities have more opportunities than ever and all people will enjoy a quality life.

(2) With high economic growth and low social cohesion, the world will be heavily divided where no reform can be carried out.

(3) With low economic growth and low social cohesion, it is going to be "winter", as was the case for United Kingdom in late 1970s, when nobody was satisfied with the status quo.

(4) With low economic growth and high social cohesion, it is still going to be a livable and harmonious world where people have low expectations for the future, as has been the case for Japan for the past 20 years.

So it's difficult to foresee. In whichever scenario, Shanghai should try its best towards prosperity, because for China, Shanghai is an important part of its future. And Shanghai also means great expectation for Asia as well as for the whole world.

Planning a Certain Future in an Uncertain World

Hou Yongzhi

Department Director of Development Strategy and

Regional Economy, Development Research

Center of the State Council

Although there would surely be many uncertainties when we try to study Shanghai in 2050, it is still possible for us to plan a certain future. The future is already certain, that is, we want a beautiful, desirable Shanghai.

1. Significance of Shanghai 2050

We all know that the world is full of uncertainties. It won't be easy to plan a certain future in an uncertain world. Thirty years ago, people took the watch, sewing machine and bicycle as three major pieces for a marriage; they took the silk handkerchief produced in Shanghai as a token of love; and a large number of children in rural China took the White Rabbit candy produced in Shanghai as their dream luxury. Who at that time could possibly imagine today our planes fly around the globe, cars take us here and there, and the Internet has risen and penetrated into every corner of our society. Children from the mountainous areas have come to Shanghai as workers, as white collars and blue collars. People from all over the world have come to Shanghai for business, shopping and visiting. Admittedly, so many changes have taken place in the last 30 years, which we could hardly imagine back at that time. However, there is one thing we can be certain about, that is, technological progress advances the development of productive forces, which then bring about changes in the economic, social and cultural structure of the production. In the meantime, it can be seen that technological progress itself also brings about changes in the economic spatial structure.

Looking through the modern world history, we see clearly the impact that technological progress has on the production mode. Since the 1770s, driven by the technological revolution, the world economy has entered a wave with a period of 50 years. Each wave length has its own clear geographical characteristics. In the first period (K1), countries with leading technologies were UK, France and Belgium. In K2, Germany and the US became new members of the leading countries. In K3, Germany and the US were the countries with the most advanced technology. In K4, Japan, Sweden and other industrialized countries ranked among the leading countries. K5 is the US, Japan, South Korea.

Looking into the future, we will see more progress of the technology. Here is a list of a dozen of so-called subversive technologies that McKinsey has predicted. The first is the mobile Internet. The second is intelligent industrial automation, that is, in the future the automation will liberate not only our hands but also our minds—our mental labor is to be replaced by the machines. The third is the Internet of Things technology. The fourth is the cloud computing. Also there are advanced robot technology and the new generation of gene technology. The automation of vehicles will reduce carbon dioxide emissions. The energy storage technology will benefit the transmission and use of solar energy. Moreover, there is the 3-D printing technology. Recently we have even heard about the 4-D printing, which prints something that can be transformed. Still there are the advanced materials and the oil exploration technology. This is an estimate of the technological progress for the next decade.

What will happen in the next 30 years? This is indeed a question worth thinking about. There have been different estimates of the technological progress. Recently I have read two books. One is *The Zero Marginal Cost Society*. This book, covering 11 cities, proposes that with the development of Internet technology, in the future maybe everyone will become an innovator, innovating on the Internet and letting everybody else share their products. Then the concept of intellectual property rights might cease to exist in the future, leaving a generalized society behind. The other book is *Misunderstanding the Internet*. It holds the opinion that the Internet is not as magical as we have thought. It is nothing but a common technology, which won't have that subversive effect. That is to say, there are two different viewpoints regarding the impact produced by the Internet.

Besides the technological progress, I think there is one more thing we can be certain about, that is, China will become the world's largest economy. Over the past years, China's economy, according to the standard of 7% growth rate, has maintained a rapid growth for 50 years. Admittedly China's economic growth rate will decline, but it will still keep at 6%-7% for a long time. Generally speaking, if China encounters no unexpected and unwanted circumstances and does not fall into the middle-income trap, it is highly possible to become the largest economy in the world.

In addition, there will be more and more countries involved in the wave of industrialization and urbanization. There is no doubt that these changes will reshape the structure of the world. But what specific changes might happen to the world economic structure? This is in fact something hard to say.

But anyway, we will always hope that Shanghai has a bright future. I think the goal is certain that we should build a fascinating Shanghai. This is why we talk about planning a certain future in an uncertain world. The certain future means that Shanghai should become a fascinating place.

To achieve this goal, the key is to make a plan. Although our planning may not be fully realized, it is still better to make plans than not, and better to plan earlier than late. This is something certain enough. A saying in ancient China goes that matters in the world should be handled by their own rules. How do we comply with their own rules? The answer is to fully recognize the trends and make plans accordingly.

A book *The Unbound Prometheus* explains such questions as why the industrial revolution would occur in the west, as well as the long-term accumulation of wealth. Also it discusses some of the most basic social stability functions that the government can provide, among which safety is the top priority—the absence of safety would cause social unrest, namely the riot of society, and then the government would suffer ineffective management. As a matter of fact, planning is also providing public safety. The government in the process of development should not be dispensable, that is, it must play its part.

To conclude, it is both imperative and feasible for Shanghai to plan its next

30 years of development when the economy of China and the world are both at a critical moment of major transformation.

2. How to Consider Shanghai's Orientation

How should we consider Shanghai's orientation? When we plan its development orientation, we should first of all have a comprehensive and profound understanding of development itself. Actually our understanding of development has gone through a changing process from its narrow sense to the broad one. Initially we believed that development equaled growth, and that with economic growth all the problems of development could be solved. Later we found that only growth is not enough, given the fact that if the growth could not bring changes in other aspects, could not bring the improvement of the social structure, then it is far from enough. Thus development involves multiple aspects, including structural changes in the economy, culture, society, and so on. When the People's Republic of China was founded, the development of production mainly aims to meet the need of people's basic life necessities. Could people at that time possibly imagine living upstairs and downstairs, using televisions and telephones? But we do have these now, and many senior citizens are using mobile phones now. How could they imagine it at that time? Therefore our connotation for development is also in constant change.

There is one sentence from the book *Human Geography*: development is a concept about transformation and rebuilding, deep-rooted and omnipresent because it contains a most wonderful aspiration. I think this reveals the nature of development.

Development has been considered by all social aspects, scholars, governments and the United Nations. The Communist Party of China has also been considering what the right development is. At18th CPC National Congress, the Communist Party of China, learning from the development history of China and the development experience of the other countries, put forward that China is to establish a socialist market economy, a socialist democracy, an advanced socialist culture, a harmonious socialist society and a socialist ecological civilization. That is, according to my understanding, to summarize development from five aspects—economic development, political development, cultural development, social development and ecological development. I think these five aspects can be used as our logic and starting point when we consider Shanghai's development in 2050.

About Shanghai's development orientation, I have got nine questions. In ancient China there was a famous thinker and poet Qu Yuan who once had nine questions. I just think that we can also put forward such nine questions for Shanghai's development orientation in 2050.

First of all, in 2050, what would be Shanghai's overall image in the eyes of both the Chinese and the foreign public? Now we speak of the overall image—Shanghai is a global city. This is a concept. With the rise of China's economy, what would be Shanghai's public image around the globe?

The second question: What kind of economic structure will Shanghai have in 2050? That is to say, what should be the relative status between the service and manufacturing industries? Some people think that Shanghai could do without the service and manufacturing industries, while there are also others who regard manufacturing as highly significant. How should we consider it?

The third question: What role will Shanghai in 2050 play in the global allocation of production factors? The next question is whether or not Shanghai could play as important a role as New York plays today in the global allocation of resources. Since the United States now is the largest economy in the world, New York enjoys a relatively high status. Then when China becomes the first economy, will Shanghai play its part just as New York has?

The fourth question: Will Shanghai play an exemplary role in the forthcoming major transformation of human society? Recently there is an article from the magazine *Wenhua Zongheng* (*Cultural Crossing*), saying that the whole human society more than merely China is in a transition period of development and that the whole human society, the whole world is about to transform. This is the thinking for the 21st century.

The fifth question: There are also arduous resources and environment problems as well as social problems, which are as challenging as the others. Could Shanghai in the future discover a way to solve such problems? How could we achieve both harmony and prosperity?

The sixth question: In the cultural exchange and collision between the East and the West, what unique role could Shanghai play in promoting cultural integration?

The seventh question: In a context that ecological problems such as global warming become increasingly prominent, what role could Shanghai play in changing the human ecological footprint? Could Shanghai create a new lifestyle for the mankind so as to reduce carbon dioxide emissions?

The eighth question: Could Shanghai discover a new path in a context that the Internet reaches every corner of the society and the city texture becomes increasingly complex?

The ninth question: In the five aspects of the development—economy, society, politics, culture and ecology, what logical relations should they form so as to benefit Shanghai's development orientation for itself? This is also worth considering. Because although the economy is the basis of development, it is not the whole story. Only when the economy fosters a good relationship of interaction with the other fields can the economy as well as the other fields be developed. In the book *No Easy Choice: Political Participation in Developing Countries*, it is already said that the growth of GDP will not automatically bring a more equitable income distribution, it will not automatically increase the chances of education and employment for the lower class, and it will not automatically produce a balanced and healthy urban development pattern, let alone accomplish other goals of modernization.

3. Establishing a High-quality Economic System

The economic activities can be classified into two kinds—one is the high-quality economic activity and the other is the low-quality one. The high quality of economic activities are reflected in the output growth, technological progress level, competition conditions, wages, workers' quality and their work enthusiasm, etc. Why do we pursue high-quality activities? Because material production is the basis for the existence and development of human society. As is said by some famous thinker, in the process of history, the decisive factor is after all the production and reproduction in real life.

To realize the development orientation of Shanghai, the core is to establish a high-quality economic system. Shanghai's future development is bound to encounter many challenges. It is a must to break through the restrictions of the natural environment on growth and in the meantime ease the pressure that development imposes on the environment. Only by establishing a high-quality economic system can we stand up to the challenges, achieve rapid material growth in a period of increasing resource and environment restrictions, and endeavor to keep the ecological environment in a good state at the same time of material wealth growth.

Although Shanghai has completed the urbanization process, the future will still see outsiders coming continuously to Shanghai, which will bring severe challenges to Shanghai's urban governance. In the book *Arrival City—the Last Human Migration and Our Future*, it says that the migration of mankind to the cities and the rapid development of transitional cities have a direct impact on many people. The disasters caused by the urbanization going astray, including all kinds of sufferings, are to a large extent usually the direct consequences of this phenomenon of blindness. Our thinking has not covered the integration of the large population, consequently this group of new-comers are easily trapped in a predicament, being ostracized and thus becoming resentful. A large part of the history in this era is caused by the problem of dislocation. Their civil rights deprived, these people are inclined to adopt extreme and violent means in their attempt to survive in the urban system. In the future we will see more outsiders coming in. There will be new-comers in the process of urbanization. Only by establishing a high-quality economical system can we provide our people with relatively stable employment and high-level incomes.

4. Key to Realizing Shanghai's Strategic Positioning

To control the strategy of Shanghai and realize its strategic positioning, the key lies in mastering four variables. According to the book *Cities in the International Marketplace*, four forces determine the urban development: firstly the market conditions, secondly the government support, thirdly the public control and lastly the local culture. Among these, the former two serve as the driving variables and the latter two serve as the steering variables. The market conditions are meant to provide resources for urban development and more opportunities for investment, that is, in terms of development whether or not the market can provide opportunities for people willing to invest and work there. The government support provides the basic elements needed for development, such as pubic services and infrastructures. The public control guides the direction of public attention, such as creating jobs, strengthening environment protection, and correctly handling the relationship between economic growth and environment protection. The local culture determines a city's cohesion and image. To realize Shanghai's strategy, the key is to control these four forces. To control these four forces, there are three means: one is the social attribute, emphasizing that the government should play a bigger part; one takes the market as the center, emphasizing that the market should play a bigger part; also there is a third one which is a hybrid.

As for the choice of Shanghai, the first thing is to allow its market to play a decisive role. But first of all we should have a comprehensive understanding of the market and know well what we could do to ensure this decisive role. As a matter of fact, much of our excess production capacity takes place when the market plays a role of blindness. The second is to let the government play a better role. These are the first two driving factors. The third one is to involve the public and welcome more constructive ideas. The last one is to make the culture more inclusive and open. It should be able to embrace different cultures, not only the western culture, but also our indigenous rural cultures including Shanghai local culture.

Shanghai—A Megacity Nationwide, a Megacity Worldwide

Xiao Lin

Director General of the Development Research

Center of Shanghai Municipal People's Government

City, the mark of modern civilization, is the center of economy, politics, technology, culture and education, and is also the home for humankind. In the year of 2008, the number of urban residents for the first time in our history surpassed that of the rural residents—our planet entered the era of cities. As for China, urbanization has synchronized with industrialization and by now it has developed an urbanization mode with Chinese characteristics. Shanghai, as the most urbanized and economically developed city in China, entered the age of post-industrialization at the beginning of the 21st century. In the process of its urban development, Shanghai has encountered not only common problems faced also by other cities but some unique problems and challenges. The evolution of urban function is of typical significance to both China and other developing countries. Ever since China's reform and opening up, Shanghai has experienced several major transformations in its development direction and function positioning, which have produced significant and profound impact on its economic and social development.

At present, Shanghai is conducting simultaneously three major researches on its future strategic planning. The first, lasting to the year 2020, is Shanghai's "Thirteenth-Five-Year Plan" for economic and social development, mainly to solve Shanghai's development problems in the next five years. The second, lasting to 2040, is a research on the revision of Shanghai's urban planning, targeted at the issues of Shanghai's future orientation, city functions and space strategies. The third, lasting to 2050, is a research on Shanghai's development strategy for the next three decades, aiming to make predictions about the future development goals, trends and the strategic paths.

These three researches have very close relations. First of all, the "Thirteenth-Five-Year Plan" will combine with the goals of the 100th anniversary of the foundation of CPC and that of PRC, with the former to establish an overall well-off society and the latter to realize the great rejuvenation of the Chinese nation, focusing on coping with the challenges to be faced through long-term solutions. Besides, the goal of urban planning and city orientation of 2040 will be based on the strategic researches targeted at Shanghai's future development in the next three decades. Therefore, it is of great significance to conduct strategic research on Shanghai's future development in the next three decades. Various social forces including scholars from different fields are working on this research already. Currently, comprehensive and monographic researches have been done by over 80 research teams initiated by 30 educational institutes, including major universities such as Shanghai Academy of Social Sciences, Shanghai University of Economy and Finance, East China Normal University, Fudan University, Tongji University, and organizations like Shanghai Party Institute of CCP, Shanghai Academy of Development and Reform. In addition, Development Research Center of the State Council and the World Bank are also conducting researches on Shanghai's city development in the next 30 years from national strategic and international perspectives.

Looking into the future, the world and Shanghai are changing more rapidly and broadly compared with the past three decades. Under this circumstances, Shanghai will take greater responsibilities in boosting China's economy and realizing the "Chinese Dream" of the rejuvenation of the Chinese nation. Shanghai will aim higher, seizing the overall situation, utilizing its potential, seeking opportunities and making thoughtful plans for its strategic development in the next three decades.

1. The Historical Changes of Shanghai's Urban Function

Since China's reform and opening up, the urban function of Shanghai has experienced fundamental evolution. Once a town in Song dynasty, Shanghai gradually developed into a county during Yuan dynasty, and in Ming dynasty its fortification was built. Unlike other marvelous ancient cities in China, Shanghai remained insignificant until the approaching of modern times when it became an open port under the colonial treaties. The opening of treaty port brought new productivity and production modes to Shanghai. Counties came into being from the port and the city flourished because of business. In the 1930s, Shanghai has already become a center for international economy and trade, business, finance, transportation and culture in the Far East. After the foundation of People's Republic of China, under the strategic suppression and economic restriction by the western powers, coupled with China's development guideline with agriculture as the base and industry as the leading factor, Shanghai undertook the historical responsibility of an industrial stronghold, and transformed itself from a consumption-oriented city to a production-oriented one.

Many researches have been done on Shanghai's strategic development. The visions and urban functions of Shanghai defined in those researches played a significant role in determining development directions, formulating development goals and leading development thoughts for Shanghai. Among these researches, Strategy for Shanghai's Economic Development in the 1980s, Strategy for the Development of Pudong in the 1990s, and Strategy for Shanghai's 21st Century were considered the most valuable. Also it was through those researches that Shanghai determined its development direction and function positioning, completed successful transition from an industrial-oriented single function economic structure to a comprehensive and multi-functional economy, from a planned economic system to a free market oriented one, realized leap-forward development, and became an international socialist metropolis and a center for global economy, finance, trade as well as shipping.

Through the history, one main line has remained basically unchanged in the research on Shanghai's development strategy, which is the city's function orientation. Shanghai's development strategy in the early 1980s has clearly defined the goal to play its part as an open and multi-functional central city, and to endeavor to build a socialist modern international economic center city with much openness, multi-functions, reasonable industrial structure, prosperous economy and culture, and advanced technology. In 1990s, the development of Pudong became a national strategy, through which the transformation of

Shanghai's city functions was accelerated. At the end of last century, Shanghai proposed the development strategy, namely strategy for Shanghai's 21st Century, which aims to develop Shanghai into an international economic center, as well as an international economic, financial and trade center. With the arrival of the 21st century, Shanghai is further developing into four centers—the international center for economy, finance, trade, and shipping. This along with the building of a socialist modern international metropolis will be accomplished by the year of 2020. In May, 2014, President Xi Jinping, during his visit to Shanghai, proposed a new strategic positioning for Shanghai that it should march towards a science and technology innovation center with global influence, and that the building of a global science and technology center should keep pace with that of the industrial economy center, thus enriching the future of a metropolitan Shanghai.

There are unique factors and laws for Shanghai's urban development. Cities are individuals with vitality. Though sharing the common factors for a city, they remain quite different from each other. Among Shanghai's urban function adjustments in the history, each of them showed some special factors that made Shanghai irreplaceable for other cities. That's why Shanghai has never been replicated into another city in the world. The unique urban factors of Shanghai have a large part to play in the evolution of its urban functions. First of all, the preferential natural conditions and geographical location of Shanghai have determined its urban development direction, urban morphology, its functions as well as industrial structure. Its special location at the geographical center of the Yangtze River estuary and China's coastal economic belt has enabled it to become a commercial node and a hub for the elements distribution, thus guiding the formation of the framework of an international economic center city. Secondly, the natural, regional and social composition of population determines the dominant characteristics of the urban vitality. As a modern and open international city, Shanghai is a typical immigrant city, embodying a culture of the eastern and western cultural fusion. Shanghai culture is the cultural essence left by the 600 years of collision of the Chinese Jiangnan culture with the western culture. With the diversified, open and inclusive characteristics, Shanghai culture is an important part of the Chinese excellent cultural tradition and a reflection of the great Chinese civilization. Thirdly, Shanghai's urban development strategy is closely linked to national strategies. Whether in the era of a planned or a market economy, Shanghai's positioning as a national center city has remained unchanged. From 1949 to the eve of the reform and opening up, Shanghai, with the best industrial technologies and equipment then found across the country, became the largest industrial base and traditional industrial and commercial city of China; ever since the reform and opening up, Shanghai, after breaking through the restrictions of system, grasped the two major opportunities of globalization and informationization, and transformed itself from a traditional national economic center and an international metropolis to a global city through a series of endeavor and continuous opening up, reform and innovation.

2. Strategic Background of Shanghai's Urban Transformation

In the next 30 years to come, Shanghai will enter the strategic opportunity period of function transformation.

First, the acceleration of global industrial restructuring and the gradual eastward of world's economical center have provided a great opportunity for Shanghai to enhance its ability of international resource allocation. After the global financial crisis, new economic entities represented by China and India have risen rapidly and the world's economic center is transferring to the Asian-pacific area, which have brought an important opportunity for Shanghai to attract international talents and financial resources and to enhance its position in the global industry value chain.

Second, a new round of information technological revolution represented by Internet of Things, Cloud Computing and Next Generation Network has provided great opportunities for Shanghai's urban function transformation. With the rapid development of new technology and new business, the constant integration of information technology with the traditional industry has created new business models and services, which will promote the optimization and upgrade of Shanghai's industrial restructuring.

Third, the national strategies of the Yangtze River Economic Zone and "One Belt and One Road" have brought historical opportunities for Shanghai to become a global city and a central node. Located at the intersection of the Yangtze River Economic Belt, the Silk Road Economic Belt and the Maritime Silk Road, Shanghai will further release its potential by taking advantage of the national strategy of the Yangtze River Economic Zone and "One Belt and One Road", playing its part as the center and upgrading its city level.

Fourth, with the rise of China and its transformation of economic development mode, there has been structural adjustment and domestic demand expanding. The accelerated economic transformation has brought great opportunities for Shanghai to take a lead. Shanghai's urban function transformation largely depends on China's overall development strategy. Since the new century, it has become more urgent for China to transform its development mode. As China's economic center, Shanghai should play an exemplary role across the country and take a lead in the reform and opening up.

Fifth, the Yangtze River Delta has developed into a national strategic area. During the acceleration of urban areas integration, Shanghai's urban function transformation has greatly depended on the Yangtze River Delta. As the most important city in the Yangtze River Delta, Shanghai's development should take the strategic space of Yangtze River Delta into consideration. The constant progress of the cooperative capability in the city cluster of Yangtze River Delta will contribute immensely to Shanghai's industrial structure upgrading, technological innovation, city management, environmental protection and resources activation, thus facilitating coordinated and common development of Yangtze River Delta.

Sixth, the comprehensive deepening of China's reform as well as the deepening of the opening-up strategy has provided impetus for Shanghai's transformation. The deepening of reform and the expanding of opening-up in China (Shanghai) Free Trade Zone and Pudong New District will not only greatly stimulate the huge potential and vitality for Shanghai's urban development, but also lead a new session of reform and opening-up, enabling them to become an experimental field for China's further reform, opening-up and innovation transformation.

At the same time, Shanghai is also faced with some challenges, which to some extent forces the urban function transformation.

First is the challenge from the urban function transformation, structural adjustment and stable growth. In the process of urban transformation, Shanghai will not see large-scale recession and unemployment. In 2014, Shanghai increased its intensity of urban transformation, but it still maintained a certain economic growth rate—this is a miracle in the world. In the future, Shanghai should not accomplish transformation at the expense of stable growth. Instead, during the process of transformation, the urban economic and social stability and development must be achieved through constant improvement of labor productivity.

Second is the challenge from the resources and environment. Currently, the energy, land, water and other resources have become key factors that restrict Shanghai's development, especially the land resources. The land for construction in Shanghai has taken up for over 40% of the total urban areas, which is far higher than that of such large domestic cities as Beijing and Tianjin, and higher than the average level of the international metropolises. What's more, its capacity of pollutants discharge and environmental absorption is already close to saturation.

Third is the challenge from the population. There are pressures on both the scale and structure of Shanghai's urban population. On one hand, the huge population scale as well as its rapid growth has aggravated the load for the city; on the other hand, the newly added population is mainly outsiders, who shared lower level of education. Social structural problems such as the aging of population have become increasingly prominent. Among the census register population, Shanghai's aging population has reached 24.5%.

Fourth is the challenge from the space structure. There exists some mismatching between its urban space, morphology and its urban function. The construction of a network metropolis based on the "center-peripheral" structure has not yet been achieved. Although the spatial distribution of permanent resident population has shown the trend of sub-urbanization, the economic activities are still concentrated in the central urban area, consequently leading to a huge commuting population.

During the urban transformation, we should not only seize the great opportunities but also face the challenges, grasping the certain goals in an uncertain future.

3. What Kind of Global City Will Shanghai Build in the Future?

Mapping out scientifically the urban development strategy is the landmark that guides a city's future development. In 2050, China will realize the Chinese Dream of the great rejuvenation of the Chinese nation. In five years' time, Shanghai will be at a new starting point of history as this city achieves the goal of building an international economy, finance, trade and shipping center by 2020. Which direction should Shanghai take in a new historical stage? We are hoping to explore the direction, unify thoughts and clarify thinking through the research on strategy. During the future transformation of Shanghai's urban function, it is necessary to comply with the trend of the changing internal and external environment, follow the objective rules of the urban function evolution, and accord with the unique factors endowed on this city. It is necessary to form a systemic, wise, sustainable, open and leading perspective, relying on the Yangtze River Delta to build a cosmopolitan global city in which economy, culture, ecology and environment coexist with each other. Also it is important to view Shanghai's future development of a global city from a systematic perspective.

Seen from the visions for city development, Shanghai ought to become a comprehensive global city that embodies the civilization traits, the most important node city in the global urban network, the most important portal across the world, and a core city in the Yangtze River Delta. Based on such visions, an urban function system oriented for the next 30 years should be developed from multiple levels.

From the aspect of resources, Shanghai should become a controlling node in the global resources management and allocation and a hub for the exchange of high-end capital, goods, information and talents, agglomerating those original science centers, research & development headquarters, and manufacturing industries that are of global influence.

From the aspect of modern civilization, Shanghai is an eastern city in an Oriental country. Without cultural soft power, there will be no city influence and competitiveness for Shanghai. Thus Shanghai should become a center for the exchange and common development of the Eastern and Western cultures, for the convergence of global innovation thoughts, and also a global model for the modern social governance.

From the aspect of ecology, the future transformation of Shanghai's global urban function, and the rapid development of technological innovation such as the Information technology, big data and cloud computing will bring new business and service mode and change the life-styles of urban residents. A new round of technological revolution will certainly focus on the coordinated development between the people, between man and nature, as well as man and the city. The future that Shanghai aims to build will be a wise and natural global city.

Sustainable development is a common responsibility shared by every country, organization and man. The future transformation of Shanghai's global city functions should be viewed from a sustainable perspective. In June, 2012, the document *The Future We Yearn* that was passed on the UN Conference on Sustainable Development expresses the anticipation of the whole mankind for sustainable development. Cities are the main carrier of sustainable development. Sustainable urban development is a new kind of urban development, whose core idea is to minimize the consumption and pollution of energy and other natural resources under the premise of guaranteeing economic efficiency and life quality. It is a new proposition to rethink the connotation of sustainable urban development in the future.

Shanghai must adhere to the people-oriented principle and the path of sustainable urban development. The future global city that Shanghai intends to build will for sure be a sustainable one, a green, low-carbon and ecological city that is suitable for living. We ought to view Shanghai's future transformation to a global city from the perspective of being open and a leader. As a forerunner in China's Reform and Opening up, Shanghai is now leading the development of the Yangtze River Delta city group, the Silk Road Economic Belt, the Yangtze River Economic Belt, and the Maritime Silk Road in the 21st Century.

In the next 30 years, to build a global city will be a common dream shared by the Shanghai citizens in their pursuit of a happy life. During the process of pursuing and realizing this dream, Shanghai will, along with all the other cities in the world, endeavor to build a better future for urban development, progress and civilization.

SPECIAL SPEECH

专题演讲

加拿大多伦多大学教授、城市数据全球委员会
总裁兼首席执行官帕特里夏·麦卡尼
在全球城市论坛上作专题演讲

Patricia McCarney, University of Toronto, Canada,
President & CEO of the World Council on City Data,
delivers a speech at the Global City Forum

全球城市数据标准化与
上海未来发展战略研究

帕特里夏·麦卡尼

加拿大多伦多大学教授

城市数据全球委员会总裁兼首席执行官

世界城市日的设立，无论对上海还是联合国来说都是一件值得纪念的事情。我想简单介绍一下城市数据全球委员会的由来，它对我们研究者来说具有什么样的意义，我们怎样在全球建立起包括 20 个城市在内的合作网络。事实上，上海已经是这个合作网络的核心城市之一。

1. 全球城市数据受到广泛关注

首先我想解答的一个问题是，为什么现在我们都非常关注像全球城市、全球指标这样的话题？为什么我们关心城市数据及其应用？为什么当前全世界都在谈论这些问题？

城市受到如此高的关注，最显而易见的是经济原因。令人难以置信的是，全球 70% 甚至将近 73% 的 GDP 是由城市创造的。人口方面的原因也很明显，目前城市人口占了全球总人口的 53%。因此，综合考虑人口和经济这两个因素，城市在世界舞台上扮演着越来越重要的角色，它是两个因素共同作用的结果。当然还有其他因素，比如能源等。

城市需求规模与基础建设投资大大增加了对城市数据的需求。城市投资和基础设施的规模在未来 10—15 年间将会不断增长，而需求规模由人口数量决定，并受到基础设施缺口的影响。到 2025 年，中国百万人口以上的城市将超过 220 个，而欧洲现在一共才 35 个，由此带来的大规模基础设施投资需求在历史上是从未有过的。这些需求缺口以及更具智能、更富信息的城市建设计划，也就是现在全球范围内提倡的智慧城市发展计划，都影响着投资规模的扩张。如果我们将城市看作一个经贸发展、韧性增长、可持续发展的物流信息平台，我们需要考虑城市基础设施在其中的关键地位和作用。随着城市结构的不断变化，我们感到在研究城市在全球舞台上的作用时有些力不从心，于是就开始思考如何建立全球标准的城市数据来记录全球城市发展历史上的关键时刻。

2. 全球城市数据国际标准不断凝练而成

面对城市数据需求的全球增长，我们开始考虑如何在国际层面上推进城市数据的标准化。国际标准化组织过去没有参与任何有关城市的标准化问题研究。ISO 标准管理系统一般是制定房间的白墙指标标准、电脑零部件标准等，大家的手机内部零件和其他设置大概就有 6 个或 7 个 ISO 标准。然而，针对城市的 ISO 标准还从未有过。因此，从 2008 年开始，我们就与世界银行、联合国人居署和其他的合作伙伴一同研究建立一个城市数据的国际标准。

众所周知，建立城市数据库面临不少关键挑战。首先就是城市边界的问题。城市边界的不同定义使我们无法比较城市间的数据，甚至无法得到城市的确切排名。例如上海某些方面的排名，有时排第二、有时排第三、有时排第五等等，其实这些排名都取决于边界如何划分。东京也是这样，它被认为是世界上最大的城市，但如果和墨尔本、上海—南京走廊地区进行比较，再重新去看它的边界划分，情况就有不同了。因此，我们必须解决城市边界的定义问题，明确衡量的内容和方法。从 2008 年开始，我们对 75 个指标规定了标准化的定义、方法、相关分子和分母。2012 年，我们将这些指标报告给国际标准化组织，该组织也因此建立了技术委员会（TC268），专门致力于城市指标标准的构建。

这个标准化的进程早在 2012 年就开始了。我们有法国同事在研究如何使管理体系标准化，也有日本同事在研究如何使城市度量和基础设施度量标准化。当时我们和法国、日本的同事一同到日内瓦的国际标准组织，我们从加拿大带去了 75 个标准化城市指标。目前在 TC268 委员会，我们有 20 个拥有投票权的国家会员，已举办了六次国际会议，第七次会议将于 2015 年 1 月举办。纵观过去的研究历程，各有关城市对全球城市国际标准（ISO37120）付出了辛勤的劳动。从 2012 年各城市对 ISO 城市指标毫无概念，到 2014 年 ISO 标准的推出，均是由各城市自己来决定。问题是哪些指标应该被纳入这个标准，哪些指标应该作为核心指标。ISO 37120 标准研究小组收到了来自各城市的 300 条建议。经过五次修改，最终指标增加到 100 个。这些指标用来衡量一个城市生活质量的各方面表现，涉及 17 个主题指标。根据 ISO 的统一进程，草案经历了多次的投票表决，在投票过程中，许多城市和国家问到新的城市指标，尤其是城市韧性。韧性指标对城市提出了新要求，需要城市有更好的应急措施、更完备的应急预案、较好的污水处理系统和基础设施建设。因此，我们正在努力创建新的标准（ISO37121），这是针对城市可持续发展与城市韧性的一个新标准。

3. 城市数据全球委员会诞生与数据应用

由于第一个城市国际性标准（ISO37120）发布的需要，城市数据全球委员会就应运而生了。也就是在几个月前，这个委员会在加拿大多伦多市正式成立，旨在更好地推进城市数据的标准化工作。该委员会是 ISO37120 的执行机构。目前，该委员会已经拥有 20 个奠基城市，来测试城市对 ISO37120 的采用情况。这些城市来自全球各地，它们在地理和人口规模上很有代表性。比如，西亚和东非的阿曼、迪拜、麦加，澳大利亚的墨尔本，北美的波士顿和多伦多，南美的波哥大、圣保罗。欧洲也有不少，包括赫尔辛基、鹿特丹、阿姆斯特丹、伦敦、巴塞罗那。从 2008 年起，我们就与这些城市建立了合作关系，对标准进行检验，并不断加以完善。我们很骄傲地告诉大家，上海是第一个加入我们的城市，成为奠基城市之一，也是这方面的领军城市，我很高兴能够在这方面与上海市人民政府发展研究中心合作。

那么，如何应用全球城市数据呢？我们能用这些数据做些什么？我可以举出很多方面，但最重要的是有了标准化的数据，城市之间就能够进行交流，它们就有一个好的平台来进行比较，交流城市建设经验，相互学习。有了标准化的数据，我们就能通过分析数据来管理城市，提出发展目标，制定行动计划。在过去六年里，合作城市的实践告诉我们，要想说服政府进行投资，拥有可靠数据是非常重要的。不管是各方面都堪称良好的城市，还是一些仍有欠缺的城市，在说服政府投入时都需要以数据为依据，这样他们就可以说，与世界上其他城市相比，我们表现如何，并用相关城市数据加以诠释。我们也发现，这些数据能够帮助城市提高安全指数。我们都知道，在亚洲的一些地方自然灾害频发，如飓风桑迪、卡特里娜，各种风暴潮和海啸等，而依靠准确的数据，城市就能及时作出反应，从而保持韧性的适应力，满足居民基本的安全需求。

通过充分运用数据，城市管理者就能准确把握自身所处位置，看看和同一层次的城市相比，自己做得怎么样。过去，他们只能从与本国城市比较的角度来回答这个问题，但现在不同了。就拿我所在的城市多伦多为例，多伦多喜欢拿来比较的城市群并不是加拿大的城市，有几个是美国的，像洛杉矶和芝加哥，但是最喜欢拿来比较的一个城市是澳大利亚的墨尔本。中国情况也是这样，上海的主要比较对象可能不在中国。因此，在国际平台上获得好的、标准化的数据，来和伦敦、东京及其他像上海这样的大城市对话成为时代的需求。很多企业也在积极运用城市数据来协助作出决策。实际上，过去几十年来一直与我们合作的很多企业对于这些问题都有着浓厚的兴趣。

这里我想举几个数据运用的例子。联合国儿童基金会最近利用这些标准化数据，建立了一个儿童友好型城市指数。我们也建立了一个城市人口老龄化指数。老龄化是人类面临的严峻挑战，就拿撒哈拉以南非洲来说，未来 20 年 65 岁及以上的老年人口将会增长 36.6%，这是非常惊人的。诸如城市老龄化指数、健康指数、宜居性指数、竞争力指数、人口流动性指数、全球城市指数等，这些指数都能够为城市间进行比较提供参照。由于很多城市对如何使用数据、如何进行衡量和与其他城市比较等存在疑问，我们正在建立全球通用的数据比较分析模型，配有范例和教程，帮助不同国家的同类城市进行横向比较。

城市数据的另一用途就是可以帮助我们重新定义城市边界。起初我们使用城市的行政边界作为城市边界，但后来我们发现，城市的界限扩张实际上超过了其行政边界。因此我们在蒙特利尔和多伦多等地区开发了一种数据聚合工具，它能够整合大多伦多地区几个行政区的数据，我们想看看数据统计上它的作用怎么样。然后开始测试，仿照美国国家航空航天局的方式进行拍摄，观察夜间照明情况，界限划到差不多是城市里人口最密集的地区，然后将数据累加，将其与芝加哥、洛杉矶海湾地区以及上海—南京走廊地区相比较。这个项目中我们本来想要讨论城市人口流动性或是环境问题，但这 25 个大多伦多地区周边的行政区更加关心城市竞争力。所以，我们根据城市竞争力整合了各项指标。以高等教育指标为例，当我们根据这些地区高等教育的指标数据来综合分析时，发现多伦多城市区域和洛杉矶海湾地区以及硅谷非常相近，而此前我们并不知道会出现这样的结果。通过运用各种工具和应用软件，对大量数据进行分析处理后，就能清晰地划出城市的界限，如多伦多地区、上海—南京走廊、墨尔本等。由此可见，城市数据的应用潜力是无穷的。在 20 个试点城市中，阿根廷的布宜诺斯艾利斯正在运用城市数据衡量城市可持续发展水平，多伦多也在运用这些数据测量城市竞争力。

4. 上海运用城市数据研究 2050 年发展战略的思考

我们先看一些数据。上海 GDP 比挪威、比利时和其他不少国家的 GDP 都高，上海有 2 400 万人口，上海的人口数量和 GDP 都令人吃惊，市长相当于其他国家的总统或首相。通过在联合国世界城市日建立的城市网络，上海能够成为全球网络的一部分并且参与交流。对城市以及城市在国际舞台定位感兴趣的人都认为，这对上海来说，是一个蕴藏巨大潜力的事件，是一个惊人的转折点。

从上海目前面临的挑战看，比如老龄化，我们发现上海这个问题不算严重。其他城市像米兰，65 岁以上老年人口已达 24%—25%，也就是说 4 个米兰市民中就有 1 个年龄超过 65 岁。而在北京和上海，老龄人口比重大约小于 10%，所以老龄化问题目前并不是很紧迫，但是随着下一代成长到工作年龄，这个问题可能会变得非常严峻。此外，与多伦多、纽约或伦敦相比，上海人口的增长速度令人吃惊。

城市排名随城市边界划分不同而不同。在城市群排名中上海位居第三，但在都市区域排名中位居第二，当只考虑城市本身时排在第五、第六位。排名情况的变动取决于边界，在不同领域我们有相应的数据。ISO 标准报告显示，在工商业资产、商业评估和人口控制等方面，上海在首批 20 个奠基城市中表现非常好。

接下来我简单讲一下城市数据对上海 2050 发展战略研究的作用。这个项目非常有趣，它有几个研究领域，由上海市人民政府发展研究中心主持。我相信，ISO37120 能够帮助预测城市需求、制定一个明智的发展战略。

第一个研究领域是战略环境。上海市人民政府发展研究中心一直关注未来世界经济发展趋势、结构调整、技术革命、中国经济增长对上海未来 30 年的影响等，这些问题既是中国的，又是世界的。城市数据全球委员会和 ISO37120 标准有许多指标能够支持趋势分析和研究。我们不断拓展的成员城市网络，能够帮助上海将自己与世界各大城市的发展指标进行比较，从而推进 2050 发展战略研究。现在我们有 100 个基于 ISO 标准的城市指标，其中核心指标 46 个，辅助指标 54 个。

第二个研究领域是战略性资源，涉及资源潜力、人口结构变化、城市空间、教育、健康、文化、交通等等。在这方面，通过运用城市数据可以开展全面、有可比性的全球城市调查，从而帮助预测并得出相应的趋势分析结果。我们可以在不同领域的国际比较中，进一步明确上海的全球定位。

第三个研究领域是战略驱动力，涉及可持续发展、全球化、区域经济规划、长三角区域发展等。关于这一主题，我觉得除了需要支持趋势分析的指标外，还需要补充对其他地区的分析，尤其是可以借助某种工具综合分析长三角区域的数据。我们已研发出这种工具，上海可以通过这个工具，与世界其他区域进行比较研究。

第四个研究领域是关于发展趋势预见与分析，涉及城市的规划蓝图、城市目标以及城市化趋势和全球城市的风险。另外，该课题研究资源优化和发展，这些指标都能够帮助上海在实践中做到最好。这些指标的运用可以帮助城市建立良好的制度，而数据则可以用来预测、解决未来的挑战和困难。

Global Cities Data Standardization and Shanghai Development Strategy in the Future

Patricia McCarney

University of Toronto, Canada

President & CEO of the World Council on City Data

It's such a tribute to Shanghai and a tribute to United Nations since we have a World Cities Day. I'm going to start with a video. I've been asked to speak a little bit about World Council on City Data and our role in building an ISO standard for city indicators. So I'm going to speak a little bit about city data, how we're building this World Council, what it means for all of us as researchers and how we build incredible partnership across 20 cities already, Shanghai being one of the principal cities in this network.

1. Global City Data has Caught Much Attention

So I would like to begin in asking this question like global cities, like global metrics, why are we all concerned these days with these questions, and why are we so concerned with data, and big data and its exercise, why are we talking these questions on the global stage.

One of the clearest reasons of course is the economic. With 70 and even now I believe it's closer to 73 percent depending on which, just if you believe these days, 73 percent of global GDP as generated by the cities. The economic argument is clear, but we also have the demographic argument whereby also 53 percent of the world's population is in the city. So when you put just those two factors, the demographic and economic together, the increasingly important role of cities on the world stage is just the result of these two. Of course others that we would be addressing here in this form have to do with the energy, all the challenges and opportunities for example that cities command.

The need for city data is also driven by the whole scale of demand and the scale of infrastructure investment that are giving rise over next 10-15 years. The scale of demand is not only driven by demographics but also by infrastructure deficit. We know by 2025, more than 220 Chinese cities will cover one million population, while Europe has only 35 at present. So the scale of investment, the sale of demand for infrastructure are unparalleled in our history's to date. The scale of investment is also driven by this deficit and the need for smarter, more informed city project, so called smart city development and initiatives now underway worldwide. So if we started to think about cities as logistics platforms for economic development and trade, for resilience, for all kinds of sustainability, challenges and opportunities, we need to start to think about how infrastructure can be placed into this. So as a result of all the changing dynamics and this growing pressure to consider cities on the world stage, we are starting to think about how to build globally standardized city data to help to inform this very critical moment in our history.

2. ISO Standard for Global Cities Data—the Result of Persistent Endeavor

Facing the increasing demand for global cities data, we start to think about the standardization of cities data at an international level. There's never been an ISO standard for cities. Generally ISO standardizes the white wall in this room and computer parts. The cell phones that you carry probably have 6 or 7 maybe more ISO standards inside and other builds. But there's never been an ISO standard for cities, and there's certainly never been any ISO standards for city indicators. So we have been building with an effort that started in 2008 with the World Bank partners with UN Habitat and other partners to start to think about standardizing city data.

As many of you know, there are key challenges around data. One has to do with the boundaries, how we define our city boundaries and how we govern them. Without a unified definition for city boundary, we can't compare data of different cities, and we can't even get the ranking of cities. If you look at some rankings for Shanghai, they're second, they're third, they're fifth, depending on where the boundary is being drawn. The same with Tokyo, it's considered the largest city. But when you look at how the boundaries are being drawn again, it's not that comparative to cities like Melbourne, Shanghai and Nanjing corridor for example. So we have to fix this. We have to standardize definitions on what to measure and standardize methodology on how to measure. So we have basically rewritten 75 indicators, definitions, methodologies, numerators, denominators standardizing all of that since 2008. And we took that to ISO in 2012. We built something called the TC268 in the ISO which is dedicated to standardized metrics for cities.

This is new. It's just started in 2012 when we went to ISO Geneva from Canada with Japanese colleagues and French colleagues who were also thinking about standardizing metrics and infrastructure metrics from the Japanese colleagues, management systems form the French colleagues. We came from Canada with standardized indicators for cities at set of 75. Over the course of ISO development, 20 countries are now voting members of ISO TC268. We have had 6 international meetings and next one is in January. This ISO standard ISO 37121 went through five drafts for 300 commends, and as a result it grew to 100 indicators. We came out in 2014 with an ISO standard that is called ISO 37120 on sustainable development of communities. So we measure performance in cities, performance and also quality of life. The themes are as usual suspects in what cities are asking to measure. Cities generally measure indicators across all of the 17 themes, so the cities actually were demanding which indicators should be in the standard and which one should be prioritized as the core indicators. As a result of the vote, we kept drafting and redrafting and redrafting again the ISO standard, and it went through a number of ballots whereby many voting cities and various countries kept asking for the new indicators especially resilience. So resilience is a new demand for cities to have better measures on emergency, prepare emergency response, wastewater, infrastructure, etc. So as a result, this process we are now still building ISO 37121 to be a new standard on sustainable development of resilience of cities.

3. The Birth of WCCD and the Application of Cities Data

It was really a critical moment when we publish ISO 37120. It was published on May 15 in Toronto Global City Summit. And once it was proved and published, we then lunched what is known as World Council on City Data. This is a host for the ISO37120. We've now developed foundation set of cities with 20 cities. The cities in our first foundation partners are from all over the world. We have a very nice list of cities with very rigid geographic representation and also demographic size. So for example, in West Asia and East Africa, we have Oman and Dubai and Mecca for example. Melbourne has just recently joined us in this effort. We have cities in North America including Boston and Toronto. We want two to represent that region. In South America we have areas on Bogotá, St. Paul. In Europe, we have a number of important cities joining us around foundations, 20 foundations city partners including Helsinki, Rotterdam, Amsterdam, London and Barcelona. So we have rigid geographic representation test for moving forward with all the partners we've built since 2008. We're very proud to say that Shanghai is the first city to join this effort, so Shanghai is one of our foundation cities in building the World Council on City Data, testing how cities can best conform to the ISO standard. Shanghai is a leader on this, and I'm so pleased to be working with the development research center here in Shanghai.

So how is global city data being used? What are we going to do with the data? I can make a list, but one of the key things is of course, once you have standardized data, cities can start to talk to each other. They can actually start to have a good sound comparative data platform to learn from each other and exchange experiences. Once you have standardized data, you can also start to manage performance decisions through the analytics as we move forward. You can benchmark, you can target, you can get a plan for city planning. What we are finding from a number of cities we've been working with over the last 6 years are also telling us that it's very important to have good data to leverage funding from senior levels government. Whether you are a well performing city or a city that requires some more work on certain indicators, cities are telling us they are using the data to actually start to leverage senior levels of government to say: well, here's how I am doing relative to my peers worldwide, and here's why, with the evidence. We are also finding increasingly that it's beginning to help especially with this new resilience indicators to answer the questions of insurance for cities. As we know hurricane Sandy and Katrina, and the various storm surges and tsunamis, etc. happen horribly in certain parts of Asia. The requirement for cities to be insured is requiring better data as well, so this globally standardized data can help cities react to those disasters timely, keep a resilient adaptability to satisfy the basic insurance of residents.

By making full use of those data, the city managers can get a precise position of their cities, how they are doing relative to their peers. And in the past city managers have only been able to answer that in terms of cities and everything in the same country, but now, Toronto being one example where we are from, the peer groups of cities that Toronto likes best to compare themselves to are not in Canada. There're a few in the United States like LA and Chicago. But one of their favorite comparators is Melbourne, Australia. The same is true for China. The main comparators for Shanghai may not all be in China. So there's a need on global stage to actually have a good standardized data to talk to London and Tokyo and other large cities like Shanghai. So this ability to actually start to measure cities in the informed and accurate way is also being picked up by many of our corporate partners. There's a very strong interest by many of the corporate partners we've been working with over the past decades to actually understand those issues.

Here I want to show you a few example about the application of this data. Recently we helped UNICEF to build a child friendly city index using the standardized data which we've been working on with them for last year and a half. And we are also looking at an additional index on aging in cities, which is a very important challenge where in Sub-Saharan Africa. For example, the aging population over the next 20 years is around 36.6 percent, and 65 and plus category of that age cohorts. So aging index, healthy city index, resilience city index, livability index, competitiveness index, mobility index, global city index, all of the data is coming in for helping cities to actually build its comparative tools in the future. We are also building some of the visualization and comparative analytics because cities are asking us how we use this, how we actually benchmark and compare ourselves. So we've started to build analytics just in general. I think we have examples and educations as well.

Another way that the data can be used is to help us correct the problem of boundary issue. At the beginning we use the administrative boundaries of cities.

It's the only way to get a standard. But then what we were finding is that cities of course are expanding far beyond those boundaries and economic functional area. So we developed tool in Montréal and other Toronto region. We developed tool to actually start to aggregate the data up across a number of municipalities in the greater Toronto region just to see how this worked out statistically and what kinds of uses we could apply. And then we looked at the night lights NASA shots. It's pretty much lined up to densest part of the city. We then started to aggregate the data and compare that to greater Chicago, the San Francisco Bay Area and the Shanghai-Nanjing corridor. We thought they were going to want to talk about mobility or environment, but in fact the cities, the 25 cities around the greater Toronto region want to talk about competitiveness. So we aggregate the indicators of 5th competitiveness, and this is just one example of higher education degree. So it turns out we did not go this. When we aggregate the data in higher education degrees, in fact, the Toronto urban region is rather close to the bay area, to Silicon Valley. We didn't know that before we drew that. So the tools and applications and the endless possibilities of good data when you aggregate comparatively, you create the boundaries comparable in corridor Toronto region or the Shanghai-Nanjing corridor or the corridor Melbourne or corridor Sao Paulo. I mean it's endless how we can use this. Buenos Aires is one of the cities in the 20 and they're already working on monitoring sustainability and benchmark with the tool, with the data. In Toronto, they are benchmarking competitiveness.

4. How to Inform the 2050 Development Strategy of Shanghai through City Data Application

We just put together a little bit of data. So Shanghai's GDP is 516.5 billion USD. That's bigger than Norway's economy, Belgium's economy and other national governments. With 24 million people and GDP larger than most countries, the mayor of Shanghai must be a very busy man. He's like a president or Prime Minister of any other countries, with this staggering number of People and staggering high GDP. These kinds of networks are built around the UN world cities day, the frameworks for Shanghai to exchange and be part of network globally are an amazing potential and incredible turning point for all of us interested in cities and in the positioning on the global stage.

I just put a few other things together about aging population of Shanghai that shows so well with this data, with 81 percent of the working age population. So it's not so much as in Beijing city at this point. Unlike some other cities like Milan, it's 24-25 percent already over 65. So one in four citizens of Milan is over the age of 65, but in Shanghai and Beijing it's still around minor 10 percent. So this aging phenomenon is actually not pressing at this point, but will be in the future as the next age cope work which is incredible working age population matures. In terms of growth rates, when you try to relate to Toronto or New York City or London, you can see the tremendous growth rates of Shanghai.

And I just put the slice here because it really does show the difference of how these rankings and boundaries. This is, as you know, the top title is urban agglomeration. So in this ranking, Shanghai ranks third. But when you look at the metropolitan area, it ranks second, and when we look at the city itself, it's just behind four or five others. So it moves depending on the boundary issues. With the appointment and property, Shanghai is already showing very well in these first 20 cities at the report of ISO standard around on the appointment commercial industrial properties, commercial assessment and population limiting property. Shanghai is doing very well on the global stage relative to other big cities like London.

So how the WCCD can help with the new development strategy over these next coming 30 years? I'm sure many of you have already read about the objectives of the 2050 strategy that I summarized here and the main research subjects which are being developed under the Shanghai Development Center. This new research project is really very interesting in looking at Shanghai for the next 30 years and they divided it into several categories. For the next 30 years, ISO37120 we believe can help to predict what is needed and also to develop a smart strategy to get there—one based on science and data.

So the first research area is about strategic environment. The development research center in Shanghai is talking about the growth trends, economic structure, global government's technology, global systems, influence of China's economic growth in the next 30 years on Shanghai. Those issues are significant both for China and the world. The WCCD and ISO37120 have indicators to support trend analysis, forecast and research. The network of the WCCD cities which has grown beyond twenty as recorded on November 18 when we opened it to all cities globally. This data platform can also help to build this network of Shanghai and the world in comparing the frameworks for moving forward on the 2050 plan. We have one hundred indicators in the ISO Standard, 46 core ones and 54 supporting ones.

The second effort is about strategic resources, which involves resource potential, the major barriers to resource efficiency, changing demographics, urban land, or the spatial aspects of the city, also education, health, cultural resources and transport, etc. That whole strategic resources, strategy, again, we hope that the indicators can help just report the trend analysis that Shanghai is looking for, both to forecast and to carry a very informed and comparative global research, city research. And also this learning in exchange platform that will build the WCCD can help to position Shanghai relative to other cities.

The third topic that Shanghai Development Research Center is looking at is the theme called strategic driving force. There they're looking at sustainable development, globalization, regional economic program, also the Yangtze delta area development, and the triangle global-city region of Shanghai. Here I think the indicators to support the trend analysis can be also supplemented by access to other regions and this analytic tool specially in aggregating data to the Yangtze delta region. Because as this tool has been developed, it's now being built into a website. So when Shanghai records its data into the web portal over the next two years, they can actually engage with this tool of aggregation to the Yangtze regions, start to explore that with other regional aggregations in the world.

Fourth and the second last is development trend envision analysis, which involves the risk and the blueprint of the city. In addition, they are also looking at optimizing resources and the development of thought. I think in this case all of the indicators can help to amount that, and can help Shanghai do best in practices. This application of those indicators can help city to build a great system, and the data can be used to predict risks so as to help solve challenges and difficulties in the future.

PARALLEL FORUMS

平行分论坛

FORUM I

分论坛一

Global City Strategy for Shanghai under Multiple Angles

多元视角下的上海全球城市战略

世界银行首席经济学家索拉尔
在全球城市论坛平行分论坛一上作专题演讲

Somik V. Lall, Lead Urban Economist,
delivers a speech at Parallel Forum Ⅰ
of the Global City Forum

基于全球经验的上海
长远发展战略

索拉尔
世界银行首席经济学家

在 1987 年，上海有 1 265 万人口，人均生产总值为 1 166 美元，从那时起，上海发生了天翻地覆的变化。过去的 30 年间，像上海大众这类公司引领了地区性工业革命，它们在大都市区域内创造了巨大的收入，不仅提高了数十亿工人的工资，还吸引数亿工人从乡下、郊区迁移到城市。2011 年上海大众公司生产汽车 150 万辆。如今，上海已经成为生机勃勃、充满活力的都市经济体。过去 30 年，上海人均收入从 2 000 美元增长到 2 万美元，与经济合作与发展组织其他国家相比不分上下，经济繁荣发展。上海中心大厦约 600 米高，它将会成为中国第一、世界第二高的摩天大楼。上海在过去十年内的经济增长速度为 10%，而人口与 1987 年相比也呈翻倍增长（图 1）。

在以往成功经验的基础上，在座的各位正讨论着另外一种转型，我认

图 1
2014 年十大国际城市的人口增长趋势比较

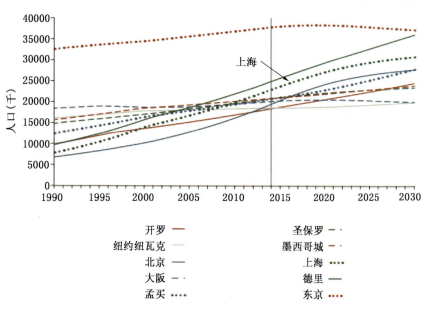

为这种转型是基础型转型。过去 30 年里，上海因其产品而家喻户晓。但是，接下来的 30 年，上海应该走什么样的发展道路呢？在我看来，上海应该因其创造出的产品、理念以及服务而闻名于世。这种从制造到创造的转型能够帮助上海在拥有高收入的同时进一步提升竞争力，让这座城市更适合生活，而不仅仅是一个生存的地方。

那么为实现此转型需要做哪些努力呢？作为一名经济学家，我给大家提供一些基本的框架和建议。

一方面，我想提出一个城市工资溢价的概念。这种溢价来自生产率的提高、创新能力的增强以及对高技能工人的培养等方面，与城市整体经济环境息息相关，经济学家称其为集聚经济。

另一方面是城市成本损失。当出现以下情况，比如城市形态管理欠佳、交通费用不断增长、环境污染迫在眉睫、多数市民无法得到服务保障或买不起住房等，城市就会产生成本。如果处理不当，集聚经济和城市生产力就会削弱。因此，从更广泛意义上说，政府的挑战来自如何在城市工资溢价和城市成本损失之间找到平衡。

放到实践层面，我所表达的意思是什么呢？上海和中国大都市的作用是连接中国经济和全球经济。通过出口生产服务和财政服务，上海已经很好地实现了这种连接作用。但同时上海也遇到了挑战。相比其他全球城市如东京、首尔和香港（图 2），上海在经济、商业和金融服务等方面所占比重相对较小，并且过去十年中服务业比重并未明显提高（图 3）。除了经济潜力之外，更重要的问题是创新和技术改造问题，这方面中国是有优势的。中国在研发方面投入的资金占 GDP 比重比印度等国家高，与同等收入水平时的韩国和马来西亚相比，比重也更大（图 4）。

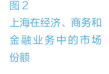

图 2
上海在经济、商务和金融业务中的市场份额

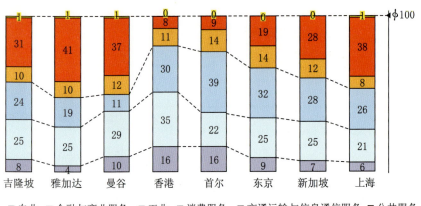

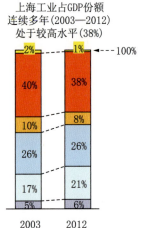

农业　金融与商业服务　工业　消费服务　交通运输与信息通信服务　公共服务

上海工业占GDP份额连续多年（2003—2012）处于较高水平（38%）

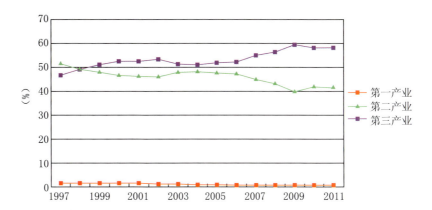

图 3
上海近年来产业结构
变化情况

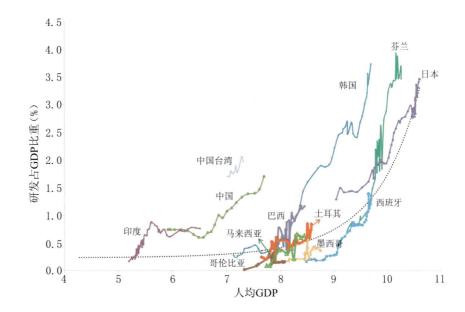

图 4
中国的研发绩效

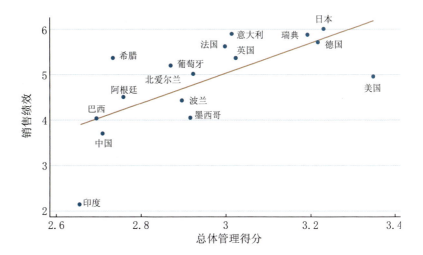

图 5
中国研发的管理情况

然而，上海所面临的挑战是，仅增加研发投资只是解决问题的一个步骤，把科学知识转化成产品优化是关键，这方面中国面临的不利条件较多。世界银行比尔·莫拉尼（Bill Maloney）的研究显示，中国的研发管理水平不足（图5）。提升中国的管理能力是需要解决的主要问题。

可以告诉大家的好消息是，世界上很多例子告诉我们怎么实现管理能力的升级，比如像丰田这种具有良好管理能力的公司。丰田运用5S管理① 来帮助管理者维持生产过程，提高生产力。这一模式已经被美国以及其他行业所运用（图6）。

图6
丰田的 5S 管理方法

怎样提高管理能力？
日本的一个例子：5S管理法

- 20世纪70年代，丰田研发
- 主要目的是帮助管理者简化生产流程，并提高生产率
- 这一框架后来被美国采纳并扩展到其他行业
- 管理能力的积累过程需要时间
- 新加坡和韩国的经验表明强制公司加快速度只会导致资源的浪费

整理：
区分需要的和不需要的

清洁：
"分类"，"整顿"和"清扫"

素养：
维护已指定的程序

整顿：
把需要的产品放在正确的位置

清扫：
保持工作环境的清洁

接下来是城市成本损失。这方面证据不断增加，在上海，拥挤与污染已成为主要问题，它们不断拉低上海的生产率，使得居民家庭的成本更加昂贵。数据显示，2012年交通费用占上海家庭消费支出的8%，而东京和香港仅占4%。这个问题一方面是由于交通管理不当，换言之，未能为居民提供上下班时使用私人或公共交通的选择。更重要的是，没有协调好土地使用和基础设施建设的关系。当土地使用和交通决策制定好以后，这些决策将为市民服务100年甚至更长，与他们的利益息息相关。所以，今天我们所犯的错误，如果等到上海人均收入变成8万美元时再纠正，我们会付出更高的代价。

世界上其他全球城市也面临着同样的挑战，它们都积极采取应对措

① 5S管理是日本企业常见的管理方式，分别是整理Sort、整顿Set In Order、清扫Shine/Clean、清洁Standardize、素养Sustain，可用于物流管理、仓存管理、生产管理、电脑档案、数据库和个人物件分类等。

施。纽约前任市长布隆伯格（Bloomberg）提出了拥挤收费项目。为了这个项目，他借鉴了伦敦、斯德哥尔摩的很多经验，研究了怎么增加城市收入，怎样减少交通堵塞，怎样才能促进健康的生活方式等问题。当他启动这个拥挤收费项目时，地铁生机也得以恢复，公共汽车服务增多，新的交通服务增加。这是一个明智的定价方案，公共交通得到改善。

伦敦曾经是个制造中心，但现在已成为了全球领先的金融中心，这正是上海所向往的方向。上世纪 80 年代伦敦的土地使用规划出现了不少问题。伦敦当局通过改变城区规划、改善交通基础设施等方法，探索了城市再开发的新路。伦敦市内形成了多个复杂的经济活动中心。在这一过程中，低价值的经济活动移出市中心，而高价值的经济活动则进入金融中心。如今，伦敦的竞争不再是基于价格，而是基于创新。

现在上海正处于转折点、转型期，拥有从制造者变成创造者的机会。这不仅需要提高生产率，提升创新能力，而且需要降低生活和工作成本。这种转变过程艰难，但如果转型成功，将会有很大的收益。

上海市经济学会会长周振华
在全球城市论坛平行分论坛一上作专题演讲

Zhou Zhenhua, President of Shanghai
Economics Society, delivers a speech at
Parallel Forum Ⅰ of the Global City Forum

上海全球城市核心竞争力的战略定位和实施路径

周振华

上海市经济学会会长

我想讲的第一个问题是，全球城市是上海未来城市发展的升级版。因为到 2020 年上海要基本建成"四个中心"和现代化国际大都市，在此基础上上海未来 30 年怎么走？它的升级版就是全球城市，但是这不是一个简单的概念转换。升级到全球城市在内容上有非常深刻的现实性，因为国际大都市很早以前就开始被用来描述在世界经济中占主导城市的概念，但是全球城市确实是当今全球化和信息化交互作用下，新型世界体系的一个空间表达，所以它在概念上是完全不一样的。具体来讲，上海要迈向全球城市，必须在四个方面实现根本性转变。

第一，从中心城市转向节点城市。国际大都市源于传统的中心空间分布理论，突出的是中心地的概念，所以是一种贸易场所、港口、金融中心或者工业中心的角色。中心地有明确的地理边界、地点空间，所以强调的是商品与服务的集聚、垂直的通达性、单向流动、交通成本等因素。而全球城市存在于全球城市网络之中，是这一网络中的主要节点城市，其基本特色表现在与其他城市有更广泛和更密集的相互作用上。所以，节点这个概念意味着有强大的非本地关系，城市之间建立顺畅的内部联系并持续相互作用，因此全球城市就不单纯是一个地点空间，更是作为网络节点的流动空间，具有地点空间和流动空间的双重空间结构。

第二，从竞争性的大都市转向合作协同的大都会区。国际大都市作为中心地，是与周边及其腹地形成一种"中心—外围"的主从关系，从而处在垂直的系统当中的顶端城市，或者我们讲的首位城市。由于这种"中心—外围"的关系是一种对空间的零和博弈的完全竞争关系，因而国际大都市就像一个黑洞一样不成比例地聚集资源和财富，并通常在周边地区形成"灯下黑"的现象。而基于全球城市网络的全球城市改变了这种关系，呈现的是一种基于平等的、非零和博弈的合作协同关系。特别是像纽约、伦敦、东京这样的超级全球城市，正通过城市网络全面融入到区域、国家和全球经济的各个层面，其中一个重要方面，就是通过高度的地区交流与合作，包括高度发达的资本信息以及人力资源流动，与毗邻的周边城市形成强大的内在联系并整合在全球经济体系之中，因此全球城市是寓于全球城市区域发展之中的。

第三，从内部结构转向外部连通性功能。国际大都市的概念是运用功能主义和结构主义基本方法体现出来的，即通过城市结构分析来解释其内部特征及其功能，并由此来界定城市的特征和地位，所以通常使用的是关于经济实力、市场规模、竞争力等重要指标来进行静态的衡量。而全球城市则通过网络分析来解释其外部连通性特征及其功能，并由此来界定城市的特质和确定城市的地位。因此一个城市在网络中的重要性，取决于它与其他节点之间的关联程度，取决于它们之间交流什么，而不是它们那里有什么东西。因此，全球城市感兴趣的是其中流进流出的途径，加速与减速的收缩和扩展，它不是依靠所拥有的东西，而是通过流经它的东西来获得和积累财富、控制权和权力。因此全球城市通常是用网络的流动水平、频繁程度、密集程度等连通性指标来进行动态的衡量。

第四，从经济功能转向多元城市功能。"四个中心"主要描述其空间的经济属性特质以及在世界经济体系中的战略性地位，但全球城市是有多重纬度和多元功能的城市。如今的全球城市已经是经济、政治、科技、文化全球化的原因和结果，因此上海未来的发展趋势是具有多元功能、全球网络联通的节点城市。

我想讲的第二个问题是上海迈向全球城市的驱动力及其逻辑结论。这个驱动力，刚才肖林主任已经做了很好的说明，我这里不具体展开，点一下题。

第一，全球化进程将进一步深化，世界格局会发生重大变化。特别是世界经济重心东移，其导致的逻辑推论是城市空间地位更加突出，全球城市网络更加密集，全球城市的世界体系空间表达的作用更加显著，全球城市的种类更加多样化。

第二，世界重心东移，亚洲地区引领世界。从中可以推导出来的逻辑结论是亚洲地区更多城市融入全球城市网络，亚洲地区将崛起一批全球城市，亚洲地区的全球城市将在世界体系中发挥更大的决定作用。

第三，从中国层面来讲，中华民族伟大复兴。从中国在全球的领袖地位可以推导出中国绝大多数城市将融入全球网络，中国将形成若干全球城市区域，中国将有数个全球城市崛起，并将在世界体系中起决定性节点作用。

第四，从上海层面来讲，上海具有全球城市的内在基因，并代表和体现国家战略。从中推导出的是上海有望崛起为全球城市，上海将成为全球城市网络中的一个世界级、综合性的全球城市，上海将是一个代表新时代文明的全球城市。

最后我想讲一下上海建设全球城市的目标取向。总体而言，这个目标取向是以中枢功能为核心，集多元门户通道、广泛多样平台为一体，基于全球网络广泛交流联系，具有全球资源配置战略性地位、全球科技文化交融和群英荟萃的、有强大吸引力的、在全球治理和国际事务协调中具有重大影响的、对人类文明高度引领和具有广泛传播力的全球城市。所以第一，上海不仅仅是打造平台经济，也不仅仅是构建门户网络，而在于类似于网络中的服务器，它是由强大的服务器、路由器和终端构成的。第二，它对世界资源的配置不是一般配置，而是要处在战略性的地位。第三，经济、金融、科技、文化的高度融合是未来城市发展的方向，所以上海在这个方面是典范，而在这个背后更核心的是基于信息和知识的高智力、专业人才的流动和交融。第四，随着全球治理的变化，国际组织、非政府组织在全球治理中的角色越来越重要，所以上海在参与全球治理、参与国际事务中也要成为一个重要的平台。

城市始终是人类的中心和社会文明的标志。人类文明的每一轮更新换代，都密切联系着城市作为文明孵化器和载体的周期性兴衰历史，换言之，一代新文明必然有其自己的城市，离不开城市的根本反思和进步。因此，未来上海崛起成为全球城市将显示人类文明的历史演变，成为新一代文明的典型代表，上海将是一个新一代文明高度引领和广泛传播的新型城市。

世界银行咨询顾问爱德华·李孟
在全球城市论坛平行分论坛一上作专题演讲

Edward Leman, World Bank Consultant,
delivers a speech at Parallel Forum Ⅰ of
the Global City Forum

基于大都市视角的
上海发展战略

爱德华·李孟

世界银行咨询顾问

今天我要讲的不只是上海市市区，而是一个与之不同的、更大范围内的概念。实际上，既然需要思考 2020 年到 2050 年的上海，那么我们肯定需要以大都市的视角来看待它。

在过去 20 年对中国和亚洲其他地区大都市的研究中，我们建立了这种大都市区域的模型结构。我们对大都市的定义是，一个城市内以地区作为集团的区域，并且该区域拥有 100 万非农业居民，拥有 1 小时行程所能覆盖的卫星城市和城镇（图 1）。

图 1
对大都市区域的定义

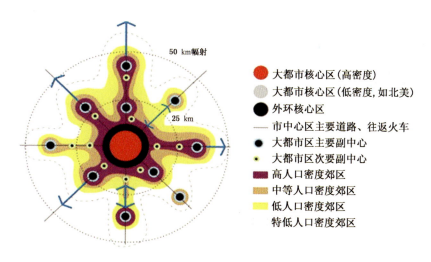

现在中国有 49 个这样的大都市区域①，它们都因其规模之大而受益于

---

① 这 49 个大都市区域包括：保定、北京、长春、成都、重庆、长沙、常州、东莞、大连、福州、贵阳、广州、哈尔滨、邯郸、合肥、衡阳、杭州、吉林、昆明、福州、洛阳、临沂、宁波、南京、南宁、南通、青岛、泉州、上海、石家庄、汕头、深圳、苏州、天津、唐山、太原、武汉、无锡、温州、西安、厦门、徐州、宜昌、盐城、烟台、淄博、漳州、郑州。

难以置信的集聚效益。其中上海拥有约 2 300 万人口，是最大的大都市区域（图 2）。从图 2 可以看出，大都市区域在过去十年内急剧扩张。

图 3 中，最左侧就是上海。图中，黑色显示 2000 年的城市建设用地，红色表示 2010 年的城市建设用地，这十年内的增长是显而易见的。图 2、

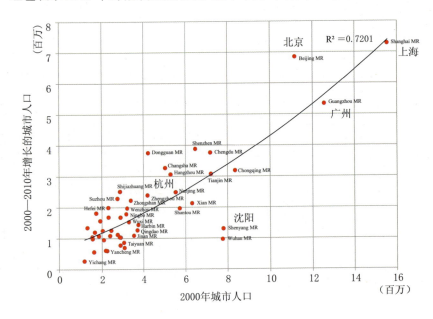

图 2
2000—2010 年大都市的路径依赖及增长

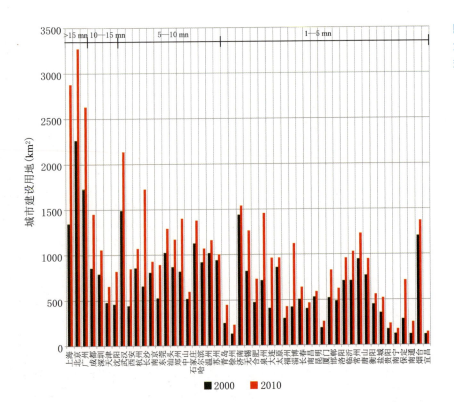

图 3
大都市区域的占地规模

图 4
上海城市区域在长三
角经济带中的状况

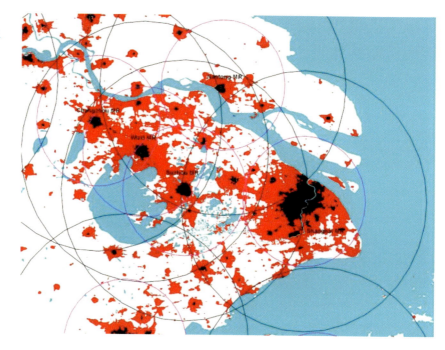

50 km r
100 km r
inh/km², 2010
■ 1000-5000
■ >5000

图 3 显示，不仅仅是上海，北京、广州、杭州、沈阳以及其他大城市区域
的建设用地在这十年中都是急剧增长的。

从图 4 中大家能看到上海在长三角区域内的状况。图 4 显示的是人口
密度，可以很明显地看出，大都市区域已经超越了城市的边界，并覆盖了
周边邻近的城市和地区。当我们观察从市中心出发的单位行车时间所覆盖
区域的变化时，就能明显感觉到城市的这种变化（图 5、图 6）。

图 5
上海 1990 年的出行
时间分析

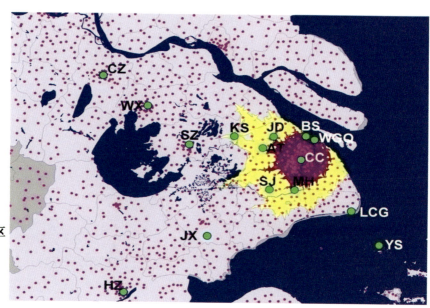

• 城镇、乡镇、街区

■ 1 小时出行时间
■ 2 小时出行时间

0   25   50 km

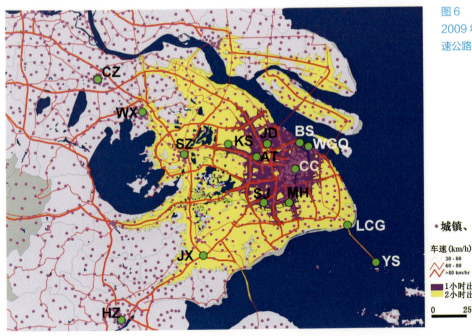

图6

2009 年的上海：高速公路建设的影响

我们看一下出行时间的变化。图5是90年代的图，紫色部分是1990年的1小时出行时间所覆盖的区域，而黄色部分是2小时出行时间所覆盖的区域。接下来的15—16年内，不断延伸的高速公路网络大大扩大了1小时出行时间所能覆盖的区域，并涵盖了加上昆山在内的更广阔的区域（图6）。而现在的2个小时出行时间能够到达的区域扩展至苏州、无锡，甚至到达了嘉兴。这使得很多企业名义上建在上海市区，但实际上可以从昆山、嘉兴、苏州以及无锡等周边地区获取廉价的能源和劳动力。

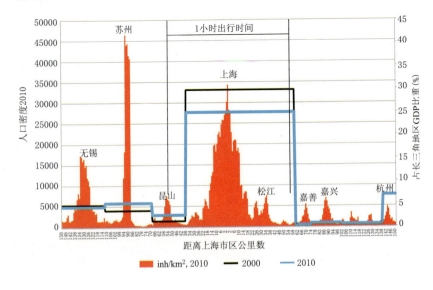

图 7 红色线条显示上海 2010 年的人口密度，黑色线条表示各地区在 2000 年长三角地区 GDP 中所占的比重，蓝色线条是 2010 年的比重。从这张图中可以看出，上海在长三角地区中所占的 GDP 比重下降了，然而周围区域如昆山和苏州等地区所占比重有所增长。这明显说明，周边地区仍然可以从上海获取很多的集聚效益。

从现在到 2050 年间的某一时刻，上海和其他地区的政府将不得不意识到设立地方机构的必要性，这种新型的地方机构有助于大都市地方管理，这样就可以启用周边地区的服务业，并减轻经济中的聚集等给两者所带来的危害。这个方法世界其他地区也在使用，称为单层合并管理方法（图 8），即周边的几个区合并管理，例如，20 世纪 50 年代松江县合并到上海。

此外，多级治理模式也在国家和地方政府的治理中起到了协调作用，运行良好，比如伦敦就曾试图运用二级城市治理方法（图 9）。

最后，我想给大家看一些具有特定目的的专用机构（图 10），在底特律、温哥华和首尔等大都市，这种机构能够起到提供服务、规划以及监控的作用。

图 8
单层合并/混合模式：多伦多，约翰内斯堡

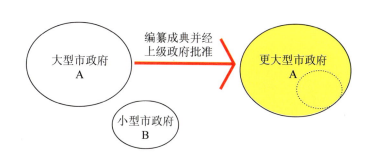

图 9
二级城市管理模式：伦敦

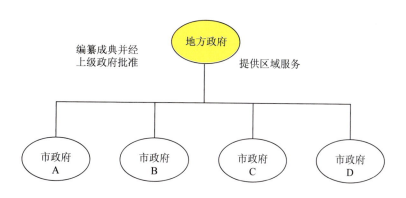

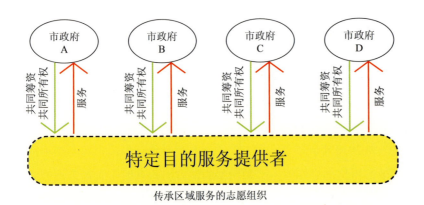

图 10
特定目的专用机构：
马德里、温哥华、首
尔大都市区域

传承区域服务的志愿组织

接下来我要讲的是首尔的两个例子。第一个是中央政府成立了区域交通运输委员会，首尔、京畿道和仁川道均为其成员（图11、图12），它可以协调大都市区域内的交通。第二个是汉江水质管理委员会，主要任务是加强污水管理，而中央政府和地方政府都在其中发挥重要作用。这两个委员会都可以说是特定目的服务机构，收效甚佳。

人类从起源时开始便是群居生活，正是大量人口和经济集中在一起才形成了集聚经济，而这种集聚经济又会将人类引向难以置信的经济繁荣。

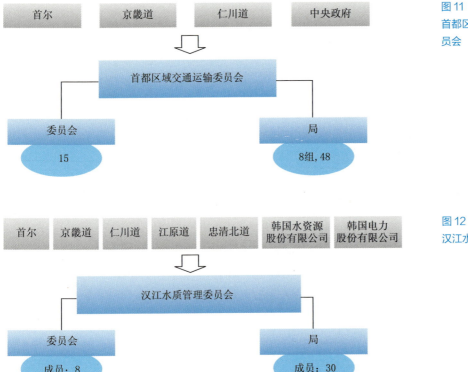

图 11
首都区域交通运输委
员会

图 12
汉江水质管理委员会

因此，与其考虑限制上海城市的规模，还不如将重点放在引进先进的实践经验上，使城市的区域规模转变成更好的优势。正如我们看到的，目前上海大都市区域发展中，从有效的区域管理中获取集聚效益将发挥其至关重要的作用。在建成全球城市的过程中，上海已经迈出很大一步，但在促进高密度、高质量核心城市的发展上还需要付出更多努力。这一点说起来容易，做起来并不容易。

世界银行咨询顾问塞尔日
在全球城市论坛平行分论坛一上作专题演讲

Serge Salat, World Bank Consultant,
delivers a speech at Parallel Forum I
of the Global City Forum

城市竞争力的空间规划策略

塞尔日
世界银行咨询顾问

有关文化爆炸、多元经济、交通拥堵的书很多，在某种意义上它们都传达了一个简短的信息，即空间是政治决策的一个重要因素。对城市来说，设施、技术、经济要素在空间上的集聚会产生许多重要影响。比如，纽约中心区域的生活成本很高。韩国、日本 GDP 的空间分布也清楚显示了这一点。伦敦的能源密度也是这样，越是经济活动密度高的区域，单位面积能耗也越高。

我想重点谈谈关于城市网络的问题，这种网络包括国际、国内以及区域范围的网络。连接了杭州、上海和南京的三角形区域内有 8 500 万人口，相当于德国的人口总和。上海是个外向型城市，因为它拥有一流的港口和连接全国其他地区的便捷贸易网络。

网络内部是什么呢？是空间。那么我们如何创造空间呢？可以在土地利用方面采取措施，通过构建综合性网络，创造区位价值。比如，金斯堡（Kingsburg）如今在英国甚至整个欧洲都具有区位价值，因为无论你在哪里，你都可以乘坐全世界最快的飞机抵达这座城市，航线很多，并且除了飞机以外，还有最快的火车直达。但是，以往 20 年金斯堡曾经没有任何区位价值，后来该市投入了 20 亿英镑来建设公共空间，建设了大量的建筑物、广场和公园，提升了空间价值，还吸引了英国及其他地方的人来投资建设大学。这里人口密度极高，许多人愿意来金斯堡工作、生活和学习，预计未来每平方公里内会有 20 万人口。

我们再看看北京和上海的情况。北京的地铁网络非常畅通，上海一些地方略逊一筹，不过上海地铁在前五名内，而且到 2020 年会建成和伦敦一样级别的网络。总体上看，中国的交通网络密度有待进一步提升。

下面谈谈多样性。多样性是提升竞争力的重要因素。在曼哈顿，不同性质的土地在功能上适度混合，这对于提升城市活力和宜居程度十分重要。总体上看，城市越具有竞争力，多样化程度越高，同时，竞争力又依托于多样化程度。

空间可达性也很重要。举个例子，在北京要去公园的话平均要走三公里才能到达，所以人们不大愿意去公园。而在其他地方，如伦敦和纽约，由于距离很近，人们喜欢去公园漫步。这就是两者在空间可达性上的差异，它对城市便利程度和吸引力会产生直接影响。因此，在公共场所的设计中，要注重与人口规模、交通衔接、区域功能等有机结合。

以上我们对城市网络的空间策略进行了讨论，这些都与2050发展战略有很大关联。上海2050发展战略研究具有相当的前瞻性，让我们共同期待上海未来的发展前景。

Long-term Development Strategy for Shanghai Based on Lessons from the World

Somik V. Lall

Lead Urban Economist

In 1987, Shanghai has officially homed 12.65 million people, and on average everyone made about 1 166 dollars per year, and at this time, started a process of many mansion. Over the past thirty years, you see companies such as Shanghai Volkswagen that led the regional industrial revolution, they have great incomes across the metropolitan area lifting incomes of billions of workers and attracting a lot from the countryside. In fact, when we think about 2011, Shanghai Volkswagen made a million and half automobiles.

Now let me pass forward to Shanghai today, which is a vibrant urban economy. Over the past thirty years incomes increased from two thousand dollars per capita to about twenty thousand (Fig. 1). This is comparable to what we see in OECD countries. And what this does is that it reflects prosperity the city has brought to its residents, and you see structures behind such as Atlantic, Shanghai Tower, which is going to be China's tallest building and world's second tallest skyscraper at about 600 meters high. Along with this growth, you see that Shanghai has been growing well at 10% over the past twenty years. It has now over 24 million people, about double of what its population was in 1987 (Fig. 1).

Building on its success, all of you in Shanghai are now talking about another transformation, which I think is a fundamental transformation. For the last thirty years, Shanghai has been a buzzing name across the world for the products made in the city. But for the next thirty years Shanghai should be known across the world for the products, ideas and services that are created in the city. This transformation from making to creating can help Shanghai become

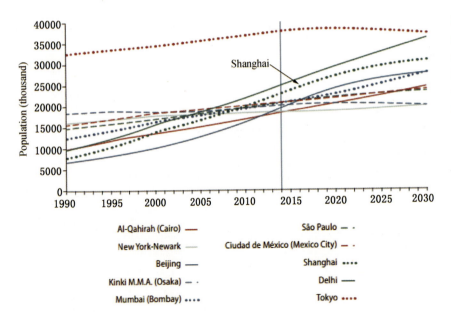

Fig. 1
Growth patterns
of the ten
largest urban
agglomeration in
2014

Al-Qahirah (Cairo) ——
New York-Newark ——
Beijing ——
Kinki M.M.A. (Osaka) — ·
Mumbai (Bombay) ••••

São Paulo — ·
Ciudad de México (Mexico City) — ·
Shanghai ••••
Delhi ——
Tokyo ••••

a high-income, incredibly competitive economy, and help Shanghai's residents make the city not only a great place to make a living but also a great place to live.

So what needs to be done to enable such transformation? Let me tell you about a simple framework. I'm an economist, so I'm going to tell you from perspective of that plans.

On the one side, I have stuff that economists call the urban wage premium, which is all about enhancing productivity, about getting innovation, and attracting and nurturing skilled talented workers, and creating an urban environment that enhances management capabilities. This premium is what economists and a lot of others call agglomeration economies.

On the other side is what we call the urban cost penalty. These are costs that cities generate when urban form is not well managed, when the cost of transporting increases, pollution becomes a problem, access to reliable services starts failing and many people in the city don't have access to affordable housing. If these costs are not managed, it'll chip away at agglomeration economies and city productivity. The challenge of all of your government, is to think about how we strike a balance between the urban rage premium and the urban cost penalty.

So what does this mean in practice? The economic role of Shanghai and

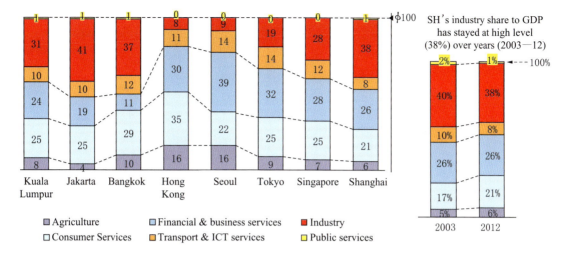

SH's industry share to GDP
has stayed at high level
(38%) over years (2003—12)

Kuala Lumpur Jakarta Bangkok Hong Kong Seoul Tokyo Singapore Shanghai

- Agriculture
- Consumer Services
- Financial & business services
- Transport & ICT services
- Industry
- Public services

2003   2012

Fig. 2
Shanghai's share
of economy,
business and
financial services

large metropolitan areas of China are to connect China with the global economy. This is best done with producer services and financial services that Shanghai exports to the rest of China and across the world. And here Shanghai faces a challenge. Its share of economy and business and financial services is smaller than global cities such as Tokyo, Seoul, Hong Kong (Fig. 2). And the share of such services has not really increased over the past ten years (Fig. 3). Further the large share of Shanghai's economy is anchored in industry while most global services have dominance of services that are traded vibrantly with the rest of the world. Beyond the issue of economic potential is a rather more important issue on innovation and technological upgrading. Here China has an advantage. What you see here is that the Chinese economy has been investing more in research and development as share of GDP than countries such as India, even more than countries such as Korea and Malaysia when they were at China's level of income. (Fig. 4)

Fig. 3
Industry share to
GDP in Shanghai
has been
decreasing, while
services share
has been
increasing
(1997—2011)

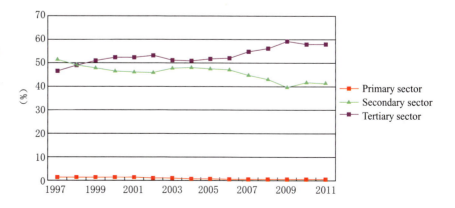

- Primary sector
- Secondary sector
- Tertiary sector

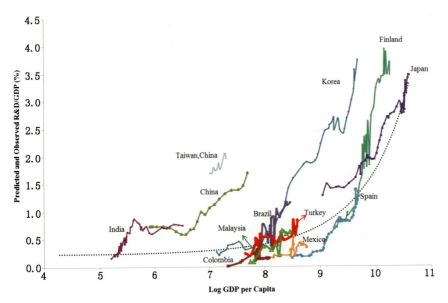

Fig. 4
China's R&D
over-performance

However, the challenge is that stepping up investment in R&D is only part of the solution. The translation of scientific knowledge into product enhancement is the key. And here China faces a major disadvantage. Research by World Bank staff Bill Maloney shows that China's management quality is not sufficient to manage R&D (Fig. 5). That's a major issue that needs to be addressed and management capabilities need to be upgraded.

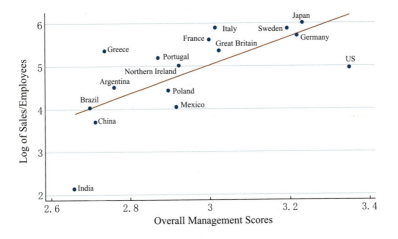

Fig. 5
The management
quality of
China's R&D

There's a lot of good news here. There're examples from around the world how this can be done. Lots of companies have built management capabilities like Toyota, which uses the 5S[①] methodology to help managers sustain production

_____

① 5S is the name of a workplace organization method that uses a list of five Japanese words: *seiri, seiton, seiso, seiketsu,* and *shitsuke.* Transliterated or translated into English, they all start with the letter "S": Sort, Straighten, Shine, Standardize, Sustain.

processes and increase productivity. This model has been adopted in America and in many other sectors. (Fig. 6)

Fig. 6
Examples for
increasing
management
capabilities

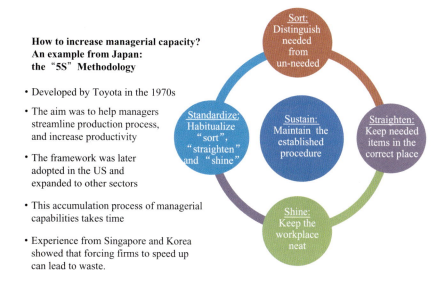

**How to increase managerial capacity?
An example from Japan:
the "5S" Methodology**

- Developed by Toyota in the 1970s
- The aim was to help managers streamline production process, and increase productivity
- The framework was later adopted in the US and expanded to other sectors
- This accumulation process of managerial capabilities takes time
- Experience from Singapore and Korea showed that forcing firms to speed up can lead to waste.

Sort:
Distinguish needed from un-needed

Standardize:
Habitualize "sort", "straighten" and "shine"

Sustain:
Maintain the established procedure

Straighten:
Keep needed items in the correct place

Shine:
Keep the workplace neat

Now let me tell you about urban cost penalty. Increasing evidence such as congestion and pollution is becoming a major issue in shanghai and they're eating away at Shanghai's productivity. This is making it costlier for families who want to live in Shanghai. What I found in the data was that families in Shanghai spend about 8% of their total consumption expenditures on transport. In contrast, families in Hong Kong and Tokyo spend 4%.

Part of the problem is that transport is not well managed. That is, it does not provide a mix of private and public options for families to get from work to home or from work to recreation. And just as important is that the use of land is not well coordinated with the placement of infrastructure and transport is not priced as a social cost. What's of real concern to all of you is that when land use and transport decisions are made, they live with you for 100 years or more. So the mistakes we make today are going to be very costly when Shanghai is an 80 thousand dollar economy. Urgent action is needed now.

Global cities around the world are rapidly responding to such challenges. In New York, former mayor Bloomberg proposed a congestion pricing program and he looked at the ideas from London and Stockholm, and he tried to figure out how to increase the cities revenues, reduce congestion and promote a healthy lifestyle. While he did this congestion pricing, he also exhilarated the rehabilitation of subway stations and he increased bus services and provided for new transit services. The point here was a judicious mix of pricing schemes accompanied by options for improving public transport.

London used to be a manufacturing center, but has become a leading global financial center, something that Shanghai would like to be. But what happened in the 1980s? The land use plans in London were very dysfunctional, but at that time London was entering global markets and a lot of capital from outside was coming in and being concentrated in the region. At that time, authorities in London thought about new ways of urban redevelopment by changing the zoning of planning and by levering transport infrastructure at the same time. And it led to a multiple complex center of economic activity. What happened in this process were low value activities moving out of the city and high values activities coming into the financial center. Today if you think about London's competition, it's no longer based on price issues. It's based on innovation and it's a place where ideas are exchanged.

So let me leave you with a final thought. Shanghai today stands at a turning point and inflection point. It has an opportunity to move from being a producer to becoming a creator. Not only do you need efforts to enhance and upgrade productivity and innovation, you need to reduce the cost of living and working in the city. This transformation will be very painful. But hopefully if you do it right it will be worth the pain.

Strategy Positioning and Implementation of Core Competitiveness of Global City for Shanghai

Zhou Zhenhua

President of Shanghai Economics Society

I'd like to start with a global city, an upgrade version of future Shanghai. After being built into a city of Four Centers and a modern metropolis by the year 2020, which direction should Shanghai go in next 30 years? Shanghai's upgrade version is a global city, however, it is not a simple transformation of the concept. When upgraded to a global city, metropolis has a deep realistic content. Metropolis has long been used to describe a big city which plays a dominant role in the world economy. But global cities are indeed products against the specific backdrop of interaction between modern globalization and informatization, which is a new type of spatial expression in the world system. So these two concepts completely differ from each other. To be specific, the following four fundamental changes are necessary for Shanghai when it comes to upgrade from a metropolis to a global city.

First is the transformation from a central city to a node city. Metropolis was originated from the theory of central space distribution in traditional urbanology, emphasizing the concept of "central position", i.e. it plays the role of trade sites, ports, financial or industrial centers. This "central position" is "space of place" which has territorial boundaries, so it emphasizes concentration of goods and services, vertical connectivity, one-way mobility and traffic cost. While a global city extends within global cities network and among this network it is the major node city, which features a wider and closer interaction with other cities. So the concept of "nodes" means that there is not only a strong non-local contact, but also the establishment of smooth internal connections which keep interaction between cities. Thus, the global city is not simply a place of space, but also the space flows of "network nodes", which stands for a kind of double spatial structure including the "address space" and the "space flows".

Second is the transformation from a competitive metropolis into a synthetic and cooperative metropolitan. An international metropolis to the cities surrounding it is what "the center" to "the periphery", namely a kind of master-slave relationship. Hence, an international metropolis is at the top of the urban system which is vertical hierarchical structure. As the "center-periphery" is a completely competitive relationship of zero-sum game of space, international metropolises which occupy a disproportionate amount in the world of commercial activities, gather resources and wealth disproportionately like a "black hole". And the "black underneath the lamp" phenomenon usually occurs in the cities surrounding international metropolises. However, based on the global urban network, global cities are changing the relations between its domestic and regional cities, forming a "non-zero-sum" cooperation and collaboration relationship on the basis of equality. Super global cities, New York, London, Tokyo in particular, are fully integrated into all levels of regional, national and global economy throughout urban networks. One important aspect is that we can build a strong internal relationship with cities surrounding them by intensive regional exchanges and cooperation, including the mobility of highly developed capital, information, and human resources, and integrate them all into the global economic system. Thus, the world's global cities could rely on the development of urban area.

Third is the transformation from interior structural function to exterior linking function. The concept of Cosmopolis stems from functionalism and structuralism, that is, reveals its interior features and functions and in turn defines the characteristics and status by an analysis of urban structure. In empirical analysis, some primary parameters based on standards including economic strength, market scale, competitiveness are used to evaluate the Cosmopolis. Therefore, Cosmopolis features the control and influence on the basis of material power and scale. The nation of Global City comes from urban network analysis by which to disclose its exterior linking features and functions, and in turn to define the characteristics of the city and confirm its status. As a node of the global urban network, its nature is connectivity. Thus, the importance of a city in the network relies on how it relates to other nodes and "what it exchanges with other cities rather than what it has".

Therefore, what global cities are interested in is the pathway for flowing through and out, as well as the contraction and expansion of the acceleration and deceleration. It doesn't rely on its possession, but gains and accumulates resource, control power and rights through what flows through. Therefore, to get and accumulate fortune, control and power, global cities rely on what flows through rather than what they have possessed. Global cities usually use the connectivity index such as the level of net work flow, the level of frequency and the level of intensity for dynamic measure.

Fourth is the transformation from primary economic functions to multiple urban functions. "Four Centers" mainly depicts features of its space economic property and its strategic role in the world economic system. But the global city is the node city which boasts multi-dimension and multiple functions in the global urban network. Currently the global city has already been the reason and result of economic, political, scientific and cultural globalization. So, Shanghai will be a global city which possesses the multi-functional global network connectivity.

The second aspect is the driving force and logic consequence of Shanghai's advancing towards the global city. Concerning the driving force, Dr. Xiao Lin has already made a good explanation. Here I'd like to skip the concrete expansion and only bring out the theme.

Firstly, the first obvious driving force is that the process of globalization is further deepened and the world situation is largely altered, especially the movement of the world center towards east and Asia. The first logic consequence is that the urban space position is becoming more prominent, the global urban network more intensive, the expression and function of global city's world system more influential and the global city more diverse.

Secondly, the world center is moving towards east and Asia is leading the world. The logic consequence is with more and more Asian cities having access to the global urban network, there will be a bunch of global cities springing up in Asia. The emerging global cities in Asia will play a more indispensable role in the world system.

Thirdly, from the perspective of China, the great rejuvenation of Chinese nation and China's leadership in the world can derive that with an increasing number of cities in China getting involved in the global urban network, a couple of urban regions will be formed in China. There will be a bunch of global cities regions springing up in China and they will play a decisive role in the world system.

Fourthly, from the perspective of Shanghai, Shanghai has the internal genes of becoming the global city, a representation and embodiment of national strategy. The logic consequence is Shanghai is expected to be a global city Shanghai will become a world-level and comprehensive global city in the global urban networks which stands for a new civilization.

Finally, I'd like to discuss about Shanghai's objective in building the global city. Generally speaking, the objective is to be a global city on the basis of center functions by integrating multiply channels and various platforms. It has strategic role in global resources with the extensive exchanges in the global network, the alluring power for the global science and technology, culture and talents, and the profound significance in global management and international affairs coordination. It will lead human civilization and exert tremendous impact. A high integration of finance, technology and culture is also a major development trend for the future global cities. Therefore, Shanghai is a model in this aspect. What lies behind is high intelligence of information and knowledge, exchange and integration of professionals. It needs to be a city that full of intellects, wisdom and innovation. With the changing of the global governance system, the role of international organizations and non-government organizations is becoming increasingly important in handling global issues. Therefore, Shanghai needs to congregate large numbers of influential international and non-government organizations to enhance its ability in participating and coordinating global affairs.

Cities are always the symbol of human civilization. In any period of history, cities are the brooder of human civilizations. That is to say that any civilization cannot come into being without the existence of cities. And no progress in human history would be made without the existence of cities. Therefore, Shanghai will be a vivid reflection of the evolutionary history of human civilization on its way of becoming a world city in the future. It will ultimately become a symbol of our new civilization. What's more, it will be a symbolic city where human civilizations are converged and spread!

Shanghai Development Strategy
—From the Perspective of Metropolis

Edward Leman

World Bank Consultant

I would like to talk about a different spatial scale than only the municipal area of Shanghai. Actually when thinking about Shanghai in the year 2020 to the year 2050 we must be looking at it in terms of a metropolitan region.

We have developed in the course of about 20 years of research on metropolitan regions in China and elsewhere in Asia, this model of the structure of metropolitan regions. And we define its own regions as the area in groups within in a city of at least 1 million non-farming residents, and the satellite cities and towns within a one-hour travel time (Fig. 1).

Right now there are forty-nine metropolitan regions in China that are benefiting from these incredible agglomeration benefits afforded by cities

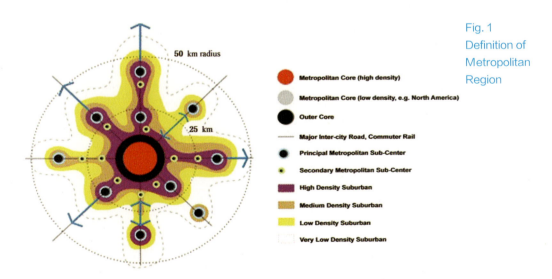

50 km radius

25 km

Metropolitan Core (high density)

Metropolitan Core (low density, e.g. North America)

Outer Core

Major Inter-city Road, Commuter Rail

Principal Metropolitan Sub-Center

Secondary Metropolitan Sub-Center

High Density Suburban

Medium Density Suburban

Low Density Suburban

Very Low Density Suburban

Fig. 1
Definition of
Metropolitan
Region

Fig. 2
Path Dependence
and Growth of
Metropolitan
Regions,
2000—2010

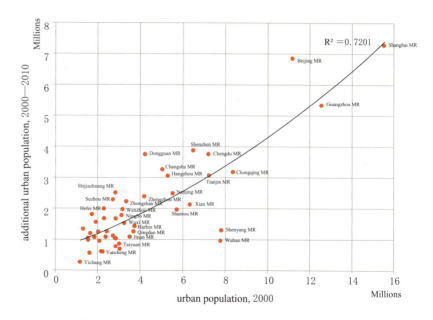

of large size[①]. Shanghai is the largest at around 23 million people (Fig.2), and there's been a huge expansion of metropolitan areas within the last 10 years.

You can see on the left hand side is Shanghai (Fig.3), with the area built up in black in the year 2000 and a huge increase until the year 2010 shown in red. Fig. 2 and 3 show that other than Shanghai there's been a huge expansion in Beijing, Guangzhou, Hangzhou, Xi'an and other metropolitan regions (Fig. 3).

Here we can see Shanghai metropolitan region in the context of the Yangtze belt megalopolis (Fig. 4). This shows the population densities (Fig. 4). What this clearly shows is that the metropolitan region has extended beyond the municipal boundary to encompass the surrounding and adjacent municipalities. And that is clearly shown when you look at the changes in travel time or drive time from the centre of the city (Fig. 5 & 6).

---

① These 49 metropolitan regions include: Baoding MR, Beijing MR, Changchun MR, Chengdu MR, Chongqing MR, Changsha MR, Changzhou MR, Dongguan MR, Dalian MR, Fuzhou MR, Guiyang MR, Guangzhou MR, Harbin MR, Handan MR, Hefei MR, Hengyang MR, Hangzhou MR, Jilin MR, Kunming MR, Luoyang MR, Linyi MR, Ningbo MR, Nanjing MR, Nanning MR, Nantong MR, Qingdao MR, Quanzhou MR, Shanghai MR, Shijiazhuang MR, Shantou MR, Shenyang MR, Shenzhen MR, Suzhou MR, Tianjin MR, Tangshan MR, Taiyuan MR, Wuhan MR, Wuxi MR, Wenzhou MR, Xi'an MR, Xiamen MR, Xuzhou MR, Yichang MR, Yancheng MR, Yantai, Zibo MR, Zhangzhou MR, Zhengzhou MR.

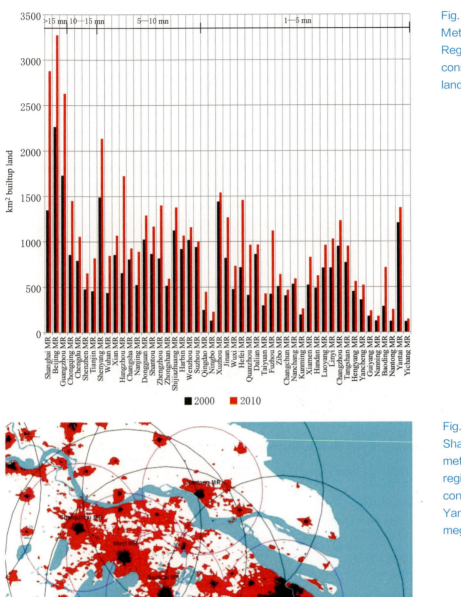

■ 2000　■ 2010

50 km r
100 km r
inh/km², 2010
1000-5000
>5000

   This is 1990 (Fig.5), and you can see the purple is the one-hour travel time in the year 1990 and the yellow is the two-hour travel time. In the course of the next 15-16 years the construction of these extensive networks of express ways

Fig. 5
Travel-time
Analysis:
Shanghai 1990

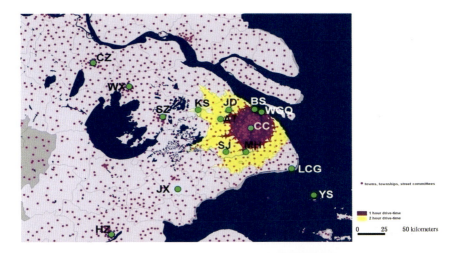

Fig. 6
Shanghai
2009: impact of
expressways

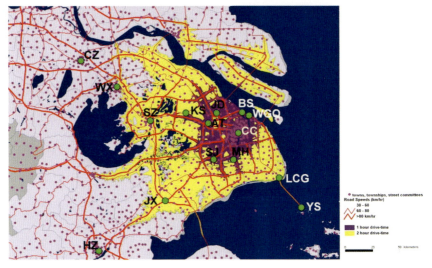

has considerably expanded that one-hour travel time to encompass Kunshan, a much broader area (Fig. 6). The two-hour travel time now extends beyond Suzhou to Wuxi and back to Jiaxing. This has enabled firms to be located nominally in Shanghai municipality but to have access to cheaper energy and cheaper labour in surrounding areas, such as Kunshan, Jiaxing, Suzhou and Wuxi.

The red bars show the population density in 2010 (Fig.7). The black line is the share of the GDP of the Yangtze delta in the year 2000. The blue line is the share in the year 2010. You can clearly see that Shanghai's share of the Yangtze delta's GDP has gone down while the surrounding areas of Kunshan and Suzhou have gone up.

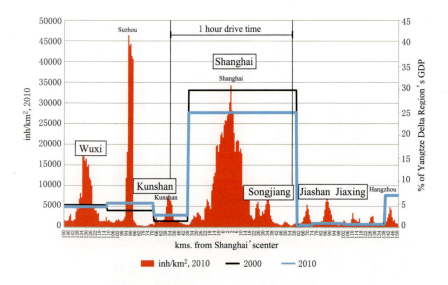

Fig. 7
red bars show the population density in 2010; the black line is the share of the GDP of the Yangtze delta in the year 2000; the blue line is the share in the year 2010

Now at some point between now and the year 2050, Shanghai and other governments are going to have to recognize the need to put in place institutions that enable metropolitan regional governance to occur so that regional services all over it can be enabled and the harm of economies such as agglomeration to both are reduced. Some of the ways, this and across the world is one-tier (Fig. 8) consolidated governance, where surrounding municipalities are annexed as in the 1950s. Songjiang county were annexed to Shanghai.

Other models of much smaller region governance are where national or subnational governance plays the coordinate role and works well. Places like London have tried to introduce two-tier systems of governance. (Fig.9)

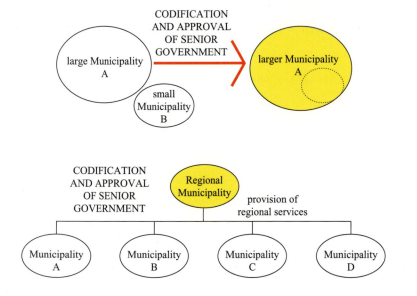

Fig. 8
One tier consolidated: Annexation/ amalgamation model: Toronto, Johannesburg

Fig. 9
Two tier government model: London

Finally there are special purpose agencies (Fig. 10) like in Detroit and Vancouver and in Seoul metropolitan region that take on this metropolitan role of delivering services and planning and monitoring.

Next, these are two examples of Seoul where a central government set up the Regional Transportation Commission with Seoul, Gyeonggi and Incheon provinces as members (Fig.11 & 12).

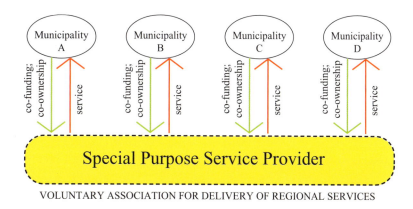

Fig. 10
Special Purpose
Agencies:
Madrid,
Vancouver, Seoul
Metropolitan
Region

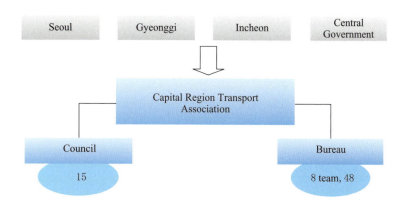

Fig. 11
Capital Region
Transport
Association

Fig. 12
Committee for the
Management of
Han River Water
Quality

It coordinates metropolitan regional transport and includes the management of the Han River water quality which is essentially post water treatment, where again the central government plays a key role as do other provinces to which it's a special purposes service provider. And it works quite well in the context of Seoul.

From the beginning, human start group living that large population and economic concentration can create the agglomeration economies that lead to incredible economic prosperity. Rather than thinking about limiting the size of Shanghai, the focus should be on introducing practices that make it a much better advantage taking from the region scale. Productivity is essential as we've seen in the development of the Shanghai metropolitan region so far. Shanghai has taken important steps which we discussed in the course of the day today, but more needs to be done including the developing of core cities and higher densities and quality which as my colleague said is a lot harder than it sounds.

Spatial Planning Strategies for Urban Competitiveness

Serge Salat

World Bank Consultant

So many blue paper books are about cultural explosions, dizzy economies and congestions. To some extent, they deliver a very brief message: Space is one of major elements for political administrators. The elements of facilities, technology and economy have significant impact on a city. For example, the living cost in New York is very high. It is the same with Japan and Korea. If you look at the rates in London, the rate values are extremely spiky. If you have a lot of economic activity density, you have a lot of energy density.

My focus is on urban network, which includes international, national and regional network. Inside the triangle that links Hangzhou, Shanghai and Nanjing, there are 85 million people, which is the demographic size of Germany. Shanghai is a very open-connected world with the first-class ports and the fast trade linking to other places of China.

What is inside connectivity? Space. So how can we create space? If you look at Kingsburg, it is the highest node value in the UK and probably among the highest ones in the Europe. You have the fastest plane coming here. You have six or seven lines. You can transform everywhere in the UK. The fast train comes from Europe. So it should be the key place like the city of London, like all of this. Of the twenty years in the past, there was totally nothing, because actually there was no placed value. And they had come here and invested 2 billion pounds in the public space, creating twenty square meters of buildings, ten squares, gardens, which created a place of value. Now, this has attracted the partners in the UK and others to start a university. Look at the high population density. 45 000 people are going to work, live and study in Kingsburg. That is two hundred thousand people per square kilometers.

Beijing has a very flat network of subways. Shanghai is not so flat at some parts but the very one to take note which are very useful values and the subway is in five top. Shanghai is moving by 2020 towards London. Inside China, there was not enough density of connectivity.

Diversity is a strong base force for competitiveness. In Manhattan, fine grain mix use is very important for urban vitality and livability. The most competitive global city displays high diversity rate and the development rate depends on the diversity.

Space accessibility is also important. We took that because in Beijing people have to walk 3 km on average to get to the park, so people are reluctant to go to the park. In other places like London and New York, people would love to go to the nearby park, because it is close. People would love to walk through a public park. Therefore, through the differences, we can see that space accessibility has direct effect on urban convenience and attractiveness. So, in the design of public places, population size, traffic condition and regional function need to be taken into account.

That's one of the key issues we've talked a lot about planning 2050. Let's look forward to the future development of Shanghai.

FORUM II

分论坛二

Innovation and Competitiveness Enhancement of Global Cities

全球城市创新与竞争力提升

全球竞争力联盟创始人、主席皮特·卡瑞·克里塞
在全球城市论坛平行分论坛二上作专题演讲

Peter Karl Kresl, Founder and Chairman of Global
Competition Union, delivers a speech at Parallel
Forum II of the Global City Forum

全球城市竞争力和
上海的未来

皮特·卡瑞·克里塞
全球竞争力联盟创始人、主席

大家都在说创造力，世界城市必须具有创造力，成为创造性活动的中心。很多年来，已经有很多心理学家和其他学者研究过创造性活动。哈佛大学心理学家霍华德·嘉德纳（Howard Gartner）研究了创造力中与城市发展联系最为紧密的那部分。他提出了创造概念化理论，认为我们有七种或者八种不同形式的智能，而不是通常认为的两种：语言和数理智能。这些智能包括空间表达、音乐思维、制作（机械工具、木工）、对他人的理解（如何在社会环境下发挥自身功能）、内省智能（对我们自身的理解）等等。大部分国家的教育都只重视语言和数理智能，而忽视了其他智能的重要性。创造性思维可以理解为发散式思维，这种思维可以突破常规思维的限制。对于一座要成为创新中心的城市来说，必须有人能够以全新的方式开展经济活动。这些具有创造性意识的人应当不受任何限制，可以完全跟着自己的想法行动，不受具体的目标和条条框框的影响。

上海要提升自己作为世界城市的地位，要成为一座创新型城市，就应该看看一些创造中心的城市情况。我们来看六个创新型城市：19世纪末期的维也纳，第一次世界大战前的巴黎、柏林，20世纪20年代以来发生文艺复兴运动的哈莱姆，四五十年代的纽约，几十年前的硅谷。虽然情况各有差异，但有四个主要原则对这些城市是普遍适用的，并且对现在也有指导意义。第一，每座城市都接纳外来人口，例如维也纳的哈布斯堡帝国和拥有来自全世界人才的硅谷。第二，这些城市里的艺术家、物理学家、计算机专家拥有能挑战现有秩序的新观念。第三，这些有新观念的人往往遭到反对或者排斥。印象派画家被禁止在艺术沙龙里展览自己的作品，所以他们不得不建立自己的"拒绝沙龙"，意为被拒的作品。第四，每座城市都有一些资助人，愿意在经济上资助这些有创造性思维的人。这四个因素促进了印象派绘画、量子物理学以及爵士乐的发展。其他经济体，例如英国的米德兰地区等没有这四个因素，因此就在竞争中败下阵来。一些城市通过产业更新重构竞争力和活力，芝加哥和匹兹堡就是非常好的例子。上海面临的挑战在于如何避免上述问题的发生，提升自身的国际地位和竞争力。上海是一个相对开放的城市，不仅有国际人员流动，也有大量的国内人口迁移。中国的天才政治家邓小平在向世界逐渐开放中国的同时，也掌控着改革步调，以防止过度现象。因此，很多跨国公司带来了最新理念和技术，虽然发展中遇到一些阻力，但这些阻力有希望在未来逐渐减弱。在中国，一大批在新体制下获得成功的人们积累了大量财富，其中包括不少对创新性技术成功至关重要的风险投资者。

上海不是一座首都城市。这是不是劣势呢？上海的优势之一就是它不是首都城市。许多大都市都是首都，如伦敦、东京、巴黎等等，但也有很多不是，像纽约、多伦多、米兰不是首都，但也非常成功，具有竞争力。首都城市仅仅因为政治上的影响力拥有天生的优势。很多公司在那里设立机构，是因为可以更好地获得与政府的国防、运输、卫生、住房、通信、科研等机构的采购部门的联系机会。因此，首都城市不需努力争取便可拥有竞争力、实现经济繁荣，它只需要依靠自身的地位来获得发展。而像上海这样的城市就必须不断努力，来保持自身的竞争力和对经济主体的吸引力。在上海能完成的工作，在其他地方也能完成，因此上海必须创造一个人人都想来上海而不是去别的地方工作的环境。非首都城市要想生存和繁荣，就必须灵活变通且富有创新力，这种特质必须成为上海未来战略的重要组成部分之一。

城市竞争力的另一个重要因素是建筑。高素质人才希望生活在有吸引力的城市里，拥堵少，污染少，氛围好。但许多首都城市的建筑风格缺乏创意，充满官僚作风，缺乏优雅美感和想象力。华盛顿特区有一栋建筑，即胡佛大厦（联邦调查局大楼），因为外形实在过于有碍观瞻，所以被拆毁重新建设，新的大厦有望不像胡佛大厦那么难看。伦敦、巴黎和罗马拥有许多历史上传承下来的建筑，这些建筑具有令人艳羡的美丽和优雅。上海有很多令人叹为观止的建筑和公园，融汇了法国、德国、英国等不同的风格，这使上海成为对游客、企业和劳动者来说充满吸引力和竞争力的城市。理查德·迈克尔·戴利任芝加哥市长时，芝加哥每栋建筑的建造工程报告都需要经过一般官员的许可，最终呈现在市长的办公桌上，然后他会亲自决定这是否与城市的风格相协调。因为非常关注建筑，芝加哥成为了世界上最美丽的有趣城市之一。上海也应当如此。

我认为，上海应当通过提升其创新城市、科技城市地位的战略来成为世界城市。创新型城市应该是开放的城市，能够接纳新的思想，新的人群，新的工作方式，而不仅仅是跨国公司。拥有丰富的文化氛围、经济生活和教育条件的城市更容易吸引有创造力的人才。就竞争力来说，软实力比硬实力更加重要。另外，上海必须将自己定位于创新型世界城市活动中，定位在最适合、最成功的结构体系中。制造业和电子产业等集群结构已经展示出其非常有益的一面，未来经济发展充满着与其他城市的激烈竞争，这些城市都灵活多变而且积极进取。在竞争中，精益、灵活和创新比规模庞大更为重要。

世界银行驻华代表处项目负责人彭勃
在全球城市论坛平行分论坛二上作专题演讲

Paul Procee, Project Leader of World Bank
Office in Beijing, delivers a speech at Parallel
Forum Ⅱ of the Global City Forum

建设富有创新力的
宜居城市

彭 勃

世界银行驻华代表处项目负责人

　　众所周知，上海已经成为中国经济的驱动力，很大程度上已经是全球的领袖城市。因此，当上海市政府发展研究中心要我们就从现在到2050年的全球城市发展战略研究做报告时，我就在想，到2050年全球城市会发生什么样的变化呢？毫无疑问，上海近些年来所取得的成绩使这座城市在全球城市中脱颖而出，成为全球最发达、最具创新力和最有竞争力的城市之一。世界银行在全球各个地区包括美洲、非洲、亚洲等都有研究机构，在我们看来，上海和北京已经成为全球许多城市的发展楷模。

　　今天主要讨论城市创新和竞争力提升问题。我们一直在讨论中国经济的结构性调整。很显然，中国正处于一个十字路口，就是如何将现在基于工业和出口的经济模式转化成更依赖内需和自主创新的经济模式。我相信，上海在这个过程当中一定会扮演至关重要的角色。我们对上海今后的发展思路十分清晰，就是要把"中国制造"、"上海制造"，变成"上海创造"。这是一个根本性的发展目标，也就是说从过去生产大量产品，到现在要慢慢变成在上海创造，也即要强调创新力，强调新的经济模式。这对中国而言将会是至关重要的改变，上海会为实现这一改变发挥重要作用。

　　我们来看图1，它显示了1970年以来全球前25位大港口的分布情况，非常直观。我想从1987年到2014年，没有哪一座城市发生过像上海这样翻天覆地的变化。如果将浦东过去和现在的规模进行比较的话，我们会发现变化是多么惊人。长江三角洲现在已经完全互相联通了，上海是该城市圈的中心，而且扮演着非常重要的角色，在过去十年建设了很多的基础设施，从而可以加强与区域的相互联系，并且把这个区域和全球联系起来。

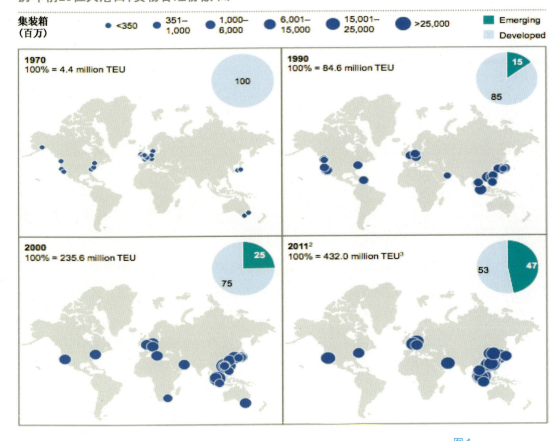

历年前25位大港口;货物吞吐份额(%)

集装箱
（百万）　●<350　● 351–1,000　● 1,000–6,000　● 6,001–15,000　● 15,001–25,000　● >25,000　　■ Emerging　■ Developed

1970
100% = 4.4 million TEU　　100

1990
100% = 84.6 million TEU　　15　85

2000
100% = 235.6 million TEU　　25　75

2011[2]
100% = 432.0 million TEU[3]　　53　47

图1
全球前 25 位大港口
分布状况

　　基础设施的建设在城市发展过程中起着至关重要的作用。如今，上海和世界已经高度联通了，在基础设施建设方面做得非常不错。但如果往深层方面去看，便会发现其中存在的问题。举一个我自己的例子，昨天我从北京飞到虹桥机场用了一个半小时，然后从虹桥机场到酒店也同样花了一个半小时。这就是说城市内部的关联性存在很多问题，而这点恰好是城市竞争力的关键要素之一，我们不但要加强城市区域之间的关联性，也要加强人与人之间的关联性。上海将发生一些转变，将着重加强基础设施建设，满足人们的需求，同时提高生产力和创新能力。

　　再来看图 2。其中黑色区域是 2000 年之前上海的状态，红色区域是 2000 年到 2010 年的发展状况。可以看出上海城市扩展很快，随着人口不断增加，城市用地面积也在飞速增长，这是上海面临的巨大挑战。在建设一些大型基础设施时，城市可用土地非常有限。

　　下面我们来看竞争力。上海 2050 年要成为全球最有竞争力的城市，

图 2
2000—2010 年上海
城市的扩张

仍然面临很多挑战。图 3 是不同城市产业结构的比较，它显示上海和东京在生产力方面有一定的差距，今后上海在提高生产力、调整产业结构方面还有提升空间。

中国城市存在很多问题，尤其是生活成本偏高。上海、北京已经成为居住成本最高的城市，我相信大部分上海人会有这种感受。我住在北京，北京市民也觉得房价异常昂贵，甚至许多中产阶层都买不起，这确实是亟须解决的大问题，这里不过多探讨。从上海与其他大都市比较的指数来看（图 4），上海还有很大的进步空间。还有一点就是城市污染，我们都很关

图 3
上海的产业结构及其
与全球大都市的比较

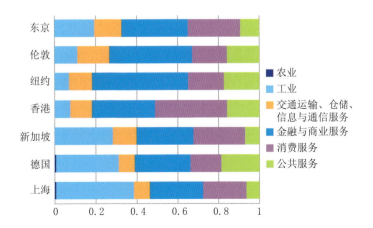

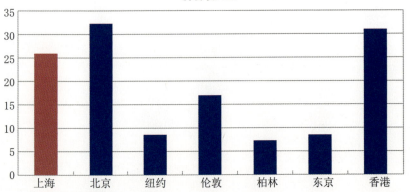

房价收入比

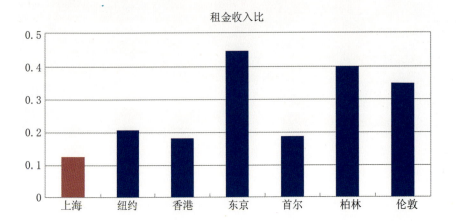

租金收入比

图 4
全球大都市房价收入
比与租金收入比

注城市污染问题，因为城市宜居性关系到城市的吸引力，对引进高端人才
至关重要。

下面这个话题很有意思，上海学生的受教育情况从全球来看都是非常
好的。在一些国际性评估测试中，他们的表现甚至比新加坡和东京的学生
都要好。上海人才资源利用得很好，但若要达到香港、伦敦、纽约的水
平，还需不断努力和提升。由此可见，上海机会多、人才多，但是怎样充
分开发人才资源是一个值得思考的问题。

最后，我想再提一些关键问题，城市如何提升创新能力，如何留住更
多人才，如何更好地利用人才资源？在此我想强调，教育对城市保持创新
力、提高连通性的重要性不容小觑。昨天在上海师范大学，我们就城市连
通性问题进行了一些有趣的探讨，我觉得增强城市的连通性不能一味强调
基础设施的连通性，更重要的是人才资源要流动，人尽其用。另外，良
好的管理机制和政策是非常重要的，因为它能够有效推动城市发展，而
这其中最重要的便是私营企业的参与度。我们在这一环节中应该营造良

好、宽松的环境，让企业家和私营企业找到最适合自己的发展方式，取得成功。

我们如何科学预测未知事物？世间变幻莫测，难求尽善尽美，中国的城市规划人员面临严峻挑战，需要因势利导，殚精竭虑。

世界银行高级经济学家南洛希
在全球城市论坛平行分论坛二上作专题演讲

Nancy Lozano Gracia, Senior Economist of
the World Bank, delivers a speech at Parallel
Forum II of the Global City Forum

宜居城市的未来

南洛希
世界银行高级经济学家

一个城市如何走向成功与繁荣，如何变得富有竞争力？这些是我们时常会提及和探讨的问题。对此，可以在当今许多发达国际大都市的实践中找到答案。

我想和大家一同分析目前国际大都市中的就业率和居住密度等关键问题。从图1、图2可以看到，伦敦、纽约与香港三个国际大都市在就业率上和居住密度上，都呈现出令人印象深刻的特征。在未来城市发展中，我们应如何连接居住密度和就业率这两个峰值，从而更好地提升城市功能呢？我们知道，不同城市密度的结合将最终带来城市的多样化，但这同时也会带来另一个问题，就是城市管理成本的提升。为什么会有成本的提升呢？我们都知道空气污染在上海和中国其他一些城市都是一个比较严峻的问题，不可否认，为了解决这一问题，城市必须承担额外的管理成本。此外，城市的飞速发展也会带来交通拥堵等情况，这些都是亟待解决的问题。

那么，对于这些问题，如何找到正确的处理方法？如何能够在促进城

图1
伦敦、纽约与香港的
居住密度

城市形态：居住密度

伦敦
27100人/km²

纽约
59150人/km²

香港
111100人/km²

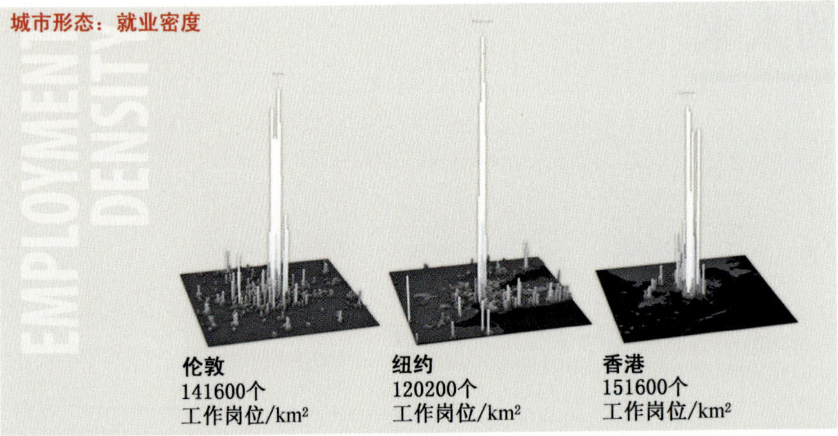

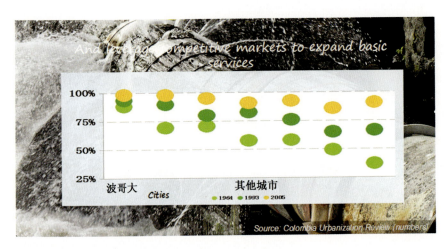

城市形态：就业密度

EMPLOYMENT DENSITY

伦敦
141600个
工作岗位/km²

纽约
120200个
工作岗位/km²

香港
151600个
工作岗位/km²

图2
伦敦、纽约与香港的
就业密度

市发展的同时又将管理带来的成本最小化？要做到这点，我们需要保证城市管理的充分灵活性。比如纽约在城市规划和管理上就有很高的灵活性。当我们谈到如何连接不同的居住地、如何更好地利用城市功能时，我们应试图做好城市节点间的协调连接。我们必须根据城市的具体规划，然后再去判断如何加强基础设施建设。除此之外，不同因素之间的协调也非常关键。

我想举一个巴西的例子。在巴西，城市发展速度也非常快，就连圣保罗郊区小城镇的发展也很快，这些小城镇的快速扩张给圣保罗发展带来了一系列问题，原本是重要集水区城市却面临缺水问题。因此，在研究制定该城市发展战略时，我们考虑到各方面影响，并寻找了不同的解决方案，包括增加人口流动性、完善交通运输体系、不断扩展绿化面积等。随着水质的改善，城市宜居性得以提升，生产力也不断提高。

除了基础设施建设和合理利用之间的协调、不同干预方式之间的协调

图3
哥伦比亚城市1964—
2005年水资源供应
情况

之外，发挥市场的作用、通过激励机制改变人们的行为同样重要。

最后这张图显示的是哥伦比亚不同城市的水资源供应情况（图3）。一个城市的供水能力不仅仅依赖基础设施的建设，还需要通过立法去强化监管，改变居民的用水观念和行为。我们必须完善这种管理机制，并在一定程度上采取干预措施，这样才能指导市场做出正确的反馈与激励。

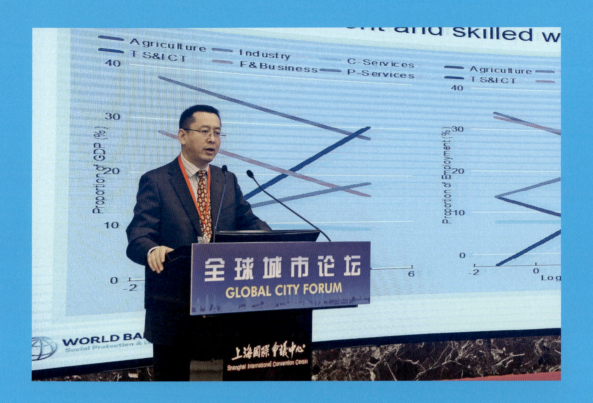

世界银行社会学家王德文
在全球城市论坛平行分论坛二上作专题演讲

Wang Dewen, Social Specialist of the
World Bank, delivers a speech at Parallel
Forum Ⅱ of the Global City Forum

吸引与全球城市需求
相适应的人才

王德文

世界银行社会学家

如果我们要从上海制造转变为上海创造的话，怎么吸引高端人才和熟练工人非常重要。我们对全球 700 多个城市 GDP 的构成进行了研究，发现随着城市经济的快速发展，两个大的产业比重不断上升，一类是交通运输和信息科技产业，另一类是公共服务类产业，而制造业和农业所占比重大幅度下降。同时，随着产业结构的变化，就业结构也在变化，于是在城市化过程中，城市之间对高端人才和熟练工人的竞争就会日趋激烈。

为什么城市和国家之间都在相互竞争吸引高端人才和熟练工人呢？有两方面原因，一方面，高端人才和熟练工人本身就是人力资本，是保持经济增长和提高生产力的重要组成部分；同时，它也是智力资本，与整个创新和发明创造密切相关。从这个意义上讲，吸引高端人才和熟练工人就变得非常重要，这也是为什么目前世界各国都在不断地实施各大方面的战略措施和项目去吸引人才。之后我会举例说明。

全球的经验告诉我们，这些高端的人才和熟练工人自愿地全球流动，他们的流动性是非常高的。那么怎么样吸引他们是每个国家都共同面临的问题。这里面有两个重要因素要考虑，一是它的就业机会，或者经济机会，就是说，他是否去一个城市，比方说如果考虑是否留在上海，他就要看上海是否有好的就业机会，给他工资的报酬高低怎么样，未来的职业生涯发展怎么样。对于企业家来讲，例如如果到上海去投资，那么上海社会、金融、劳动力、税收这些环境是否有助于他来投资创业。所以从这个意义上来讲，这是一些主要因素，决定他们是去上海还是去北京等其他城市。

另外很重要的一点就是生活成本。近几年随着中国生活成本的不断攀升，有不少高技能人才在考虑往国外移民，这是一个很令人头疼的问题，它与这个城市的生活质量是密不可分的。生活环境包括不少方面，还有社会环境，如一个城市是否多样化，是否具有包容性，这些非常重要。还有一点很重要的是公共服务怎么样，他可能不是只身一人，有可能是整个家庭过去，那么他孩子的教育、家人的健康、医保状况怎么样，这些因素实际上也是很重要的。好的教育体系有利于培养人才，也有利于吸引人才。

从全球经验来看，不同国家或城市为了吸引和培养人才采取了许多措施。简单地来说有这样几个方面：一是制定一系列战略与规划来吸引人才。比方说中国香港和新加坡，它们有专门的政府机构来制定和实施计划。二是采取相应的移民政策措施来吸引高端人才和熟练工人。比方说，新加坡会把高端人才和一般移民区分开来，伦敦采取积分政策来决定你是不是能够到英国或伦敦去。实际上从所有全球城市来看，移民政策大部分倾向于有技能的，高技能人才更易于全球流动。三是很多国家和城市都会提供教育、培训或就业服务，主要帮助高技能人才（高端人才和熟练工人）减少劳动力市场中匹配错位的问题。比如，为不知道哪里能找到就业机会的人才提供一个就业顾问。还有许多城市和国家在大学和研究机构做一系列项目，予以大量投资，鼓励大学、企业和研究机构合作来吸引人才。上海也在做。四是很多城市和国家采取一系列税收、金融服务方面的商业环境改善措施来吸引人才的流入。有很多种做法，但是不同国家有不同的做法，不同国家有不同的系统性，有些国家或城市可能会采取某些单项。

我们来看一看上海在满足未来发展的人力资源方面面临哪些挑战。客观地看，上海跟全球很多大都市相比还有一定差距。有数据显示，从一个城市的人才多样性、全球流动性和商业环境来看，上海基本上是倒数两三位。唯一稍微好一点的就是劳动力资源获得方面，因为中国人口数量非常庞大，这也是理所当然的事情，从这点看，上海是有短板的。上海的人口老龄化在中国城市里是最快的。如果以上海本地人口来看，每四个上海人之中就有一个老年人。但如果把外来的劳动力加上，上海的老龄化没有那么大的挑战。紧接着的问题就是，上海的落户是非常难的，而且门槛非常高，外地人获得上海户口非常困难。上海的房价是北京以外最高的了，人才来了怎么样定居也是个问题。还有一点，税收非常高，社会消费很高，劳动力成本高，上海未来城市在全球是否真正有竞争力？这是个很大的问号。还有培训体系，教育和培训不对外来劳动力开放，这个问题随着未来产业升级变得越来越重要。更重要的一点，虽然在全国上海首次全面提出发展终身教育体系，但是究竟实际效果如何，我们尚不清楚。另外一点，在整个教育体系和整个劳动力市场衔接方面的质量和针对性，我们不是很了解，但我感觉到上海也在考虑这些事情。这些就是我们所能看到的一系列挑战。

The Future of Shanghai and the Competitiveness of Global City

Peter Karl Kresl

Founder and Chairman of Global Competition Union

Everybody is talking about creativity. World cities have to be creative places, centers of creative activities. The creative processing, creative thinking have been studied by a variety of psychologists and others for many years. The approach to the issue of creativity that is most relevant to cities has been done by Howard Gartner, psychologist from Harvard University. Gartner developed a conceptualization of creativity that is based on the notion that we have seven or eight different intelligences. Not the two, linguistic and mathematical, of which we usually think. He also included spatial representation, musical thinking, use of our body to solve problems and make things (machine tooling, woodworking), understanding of other individuals (how you function in the social environment), straight smarts (understanding of ourselves). The educational systems of most countries tend to stress the first two, linguistic and logical, mathematical, but short-change the other ones. This narrow focus tends to prepare students to fit into existing places, but what sort of thinking is required for one to take a leap into the unknown? Is it just linguistic, mathematical and logical? Creative thinking can be thought of divergent thinking, thinking, as they say, outside the box of conventional thinking. For a city of urban economy to become a center of creativity, it must prepare individuals to take radical new paths to economic activity. The creative individuals must be given a free rein to go wherever their thinking takes them. There should be no specific objective and restrictions that constrain their actions.

As Shanghai seeks to enhance its position as a world city, and thereby as a creative city, it's worth looking at the experience of some other cities that were centers of creativity in the recent past. I have examined six of these creative cities: late nineteenth century Vienna, Paris and Berlin before the First World War, the Harlem Renaissance since the 1920s, New York in the 40s and 50s, and Silicon Valley during the past decades. While each is distinctive, there are four principal factors that are common to all, and may provide guidance to urban leaders today. First, each was open to inflows of people, whether it was the Habsburg Empire for Vienna, and the entire world for Silicon Valley. Second, these emerging ad artists, physicists, computer specialists had new ideas that challenged the existing order. Third is the consequence of this: they were opposed, or excluded from existing institutions. The artists who were (not all) the impressionists were not allowed to exhibit at the Salon de beaux-arts. They had to create their own Salon des Refusés, known as refused. Fourth, each had a patron that was willing to supply the new creative people with financial resources. These four factors facilitated the growth of impressionism, abstract impressionism in painting, post-Newtonian quantum physics, and jazz music. Other urban economies did not have these four factors such as the Midlands in England, and they failed to meet the competition and suffered a decline in their economic activity in status. Some of these cities in these areas have been able to reconstitute their economic competitiveness and vitality. Chicago and Pittsburgh are good examples of what can be done to resuscitate a declining manufacturing sector. Shanghai's challenge is to avoid this difficulty and to develop and to enhance its international position and competitiveness. Shanghai is a relatively open city, with China's immigration laws in some ways being more welcoming than those in the United States and Europe. There's recently been substantial internal migration in addition to its international flows of people. A genius of China's politicians Deng Xiaoping has begun a gradual opening of the economy and society to the rest of the world while maintaining control of the pace of the change to avoid excesses. Thus while the presence of many foreign multinational corporations has brought access to the latest new production ideas and technologies, there is still some resistance to full access, but one can only anticipate that this will be gradually reduced in coming years. In China wealth is being accumulated by a large number of people who have succeeded in the contemporary economy. These individuals will probably most likely to be a cohort of the population that will supply the venture investors who will be crucial to the success of Shanghai's creative technology and economy.

Shanghai is not a capital city. Is that a disadvantage? One of the advantages of Shanghai is that it's not a capital city. While many of the great cities are national capitals: London, Tokyo, Paris, among others of course, it's also true that many others are not: New York, Toronto, Milan are not capital cities but they are very successful, competitive cities. In comparison between Shanghai and Beijing, we see how these advantages and disadvantages come into play. Capital cities have nice things happen simply because of the political cloud or power of the individuals and institutions that reside there. Firms established offices and plants there because of the better access they have to procurement offices of the ministry such as defense, transportation, healthcare, housing, communication, scientific research and social policy. The city does not have to work to become competitive, to have its economy. It simply has to rejuvenate in its capital city status. A city such as Shanghai has to work continuously to maintain or to enhance its competitiveness and its attractiveness to private sectors, economic actors, most of whom are highly mobile. Everything Shanghai can do can be done somewhere else. You have to create an environment in which people want to come to Shanghai to do those things instead of going somewhere else. Non-capital cities have to be agile, innovative and creative if they are to survive and flourish. The maintenance of this character must be one of the principal elements in any strategy for the future economy in Shanghai.

Another competitive element in a successful city is architecture. The talented want to live in attractive cities with low congestion, low pollution, low traffic hustle, et cetera. Many capital cities have an architecture that is uninspired and bureaucratic and lacks beauty, gracefulness, imagination or inspiration. In Washington D.C. one building, the J. Edgar Hoover, Federal Bureau Investigation Building, is so hideous that it is soon to be demolished and replaced with one that will hopefully be less so. Capitals such as London, Paris and Rome that are blessed with architecture from an earlier age do have an enviable beauty and elegance. Shanghai has a marvelous combination of buildings, neighborhoods and parks from foreign communities (French, Germany and English among others) that makes it such an inviting therefore competitive city for tourists, firms and organizers, and for skilled workers. When Richard M. Daley was the mayor of Chicago, every building project had to declare all of the usual bureaucrats but it then landed on the major's desk at which he would look and declare this is or this is not a Chicago building. This attention to architecture has made Chicago one of the truly beautiful and interesting cities of the world. Shanghai has apparently taken the same approach and must continue its beautiful city.

I assume here that Shanghai seeks to become a world city through its strategy of enhancing its position as the city of creativity, and as the city of technology. Creative cities have to be open cities, open to movement of ideas, people, new ways of doing things, not just capital multinational firms. Creative individuals will be attracted to a city that has exciting cultural, economic life, educational facilities and so on. Hard determinants are less important than soft determinants of competitiveness. Shanghai will have to be situated in its creative world city activities, be situated in structures that are appropriate and most conductive to their success. Cluster structures such as manufacturing or electronics have been shown to be very beneficial. In the economy of the future with its intense competition among many other active and aggressive cities, agile, innovative will be more important than large and dominant.

Constructing an Innovative City with High Livability

Paul Procee

Project Leader of World Bank Office in Beijing

It is well known that Shanghai is a big driver for Chinese economy and to some extent a leader city of the world. Thinking through strategy going from now to 2050, I really wonder about what we are going to say about 2050. Shanghai is the most developed, most innovative and most competitive city, excelling other cities in the world. We work in Africa, America and all over the Asia, and actually you know, Shanghai and Beijing are the cities that we look at to use as examples for a lot of cities in the world.

We will focus mainly on how to enhance innovation and how to improve competitiveness of our cities. We have long been discussing about the economic structure adjustment of China, and it's clear that China has come to a cross road in terms of the current model of industrial-based, export-based colony to a model that is now more related to internal consumption and more productivity. I also believe Shanghai will have to play a pivotal and essential rule in the new Chinese economy. We are actually going to move from "made in Shanghai" to "created in Shanghai", the fundamental change from what China has been doing so far, which is basically producing all of the products in China and in the world, and now basically becoming the place where these things are created and innovated. This will be kind of fundamental change in Shanghai and it will play an important role.

Let's take a look at Fig. 1. I want to speak to you because this shows you the general location of 25 major global port after the year of 1970. I do not think any city during 1987 and 2014 can show a bigger change than Shanghai. It is an incredible change physically speaking if you look at the Pudong before and what

Top 25 ports each year; share of volume shipped by top 25 ports (%)

Container TEU¹
Million   ● <350   ● 351–   ● 1,000–   ● 6,001–   ● 15,001–   ● >25,000   ■ Emerging
                        1,000   6,000   15,000   25,000   Developed

1970
100% = 4.4 million TEU
100

1990
100% = 84.6 million TEU
15
85

2000
100% = 235.6 million TEU
25
75

2011²
100% = 432.0 million TEU³
53   47

Fig.1
Location of 25
major global port

it is now. The Yangtze River belt now is completely connected to Shanghai. And Shanghai is definitely in the middle of the enormous metropolitan region. Actually China did the right thing in the last ten years. It built all of these infrastructure that is needed to connect the region and the region with the rest of the world.

Infrastructure plays a significant role in terms of the city's development. Shanghai is doing extremely well in terms of that. But then, if you look a little bit more carefully, there are problems. I give you one example about yesterday. Coming from Beijing, within one and half hours, I flew to Hongqiao airport, and it took another hour and half to make myself from Hongqiao to this hotel. So we have a lot of issues about connectivity within our city. I think that is one of the important aspects of innovation and competitiveness that we have to focus on. It is about how we connect place and also how we connect people. There will be a shift from the focus that Shanghai has had, to the focus on developing its infrastructure in meeting people. We need to now increase productivity and create innovation. And in that we need to attract talents and skilled workers and make them stay in our place.

Let's take a look at Fig. 2. So the black side is what Shanghai was in 2000, and the red side is what it has grown between 2000 and 2010. So you see the long increase of sprawl of the cities, and all the cities connected to the metropolitan region. While Shanghai is growing in term of population, it has grown even faster physically, especially the land use that has grown tremendously. It has fragmented the city to certain extent. So while it has connected with the big infrastructure, the land used by the metropolitan region is limited.

If Shanghai wants to be the best and most competitive city in 2050, we need to overcome enormous challenges then we have to compete with place like Tokyo. Fig. 3 shows us the comparison of industrial structure among different cities. It indicates that Shanghai still has a long way to go in terms of increasing productivity and adjusting industrial structure.

One of the biggest challenges that cities in China face is the affordability. The cost of living in cities like Beijing and Shanghai is extremely high. Shanghai

Fig. 2
Sprawl of
Shanghai from
2000 to 2010

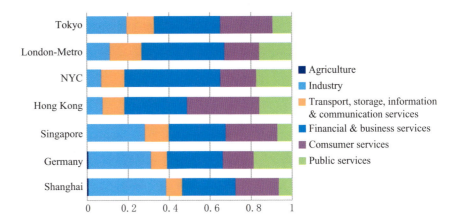

Fig. 3
Comparison of
industrial
structure among
Shanghai and
other
metropolitans

nowadays and Beijing are already among the most expensive places to live, and I am sure most Shanghainese agree with that, because when I ask people the same question in Beijing where I live now, they say it's extremely expensive and it's even difficult to find an affordable house even for the middle class. This is going to be a big problem. I am not going into this, but the whole index (Fig. 4) when we compare Shanghai with different cities, again, there are still room for improvement. And it comes to spiral pollution that we all talk about. The livability of the city is extremely important for attracting skill workers and to keep them there.

The following topic is quite interesting. When you look at the education record of Shanghai graduate students, they do very well internationally. They are even higher than students in Singapore and Tokyo in terms of international assessment test. When it comes to human capital, there is still a lot of space. Shanghai is not doing bad on this, but if they really want to go up to the Hong Kong, London and New York level, there is still a lot of room. So on one hand, this is the message that there are a lot opportunities in shanghai, a lot of human capital in shanghai, but it's not just coming out of. Therefore, this is an issue that really worths considering.

Finally, I just want to pick up key questions that we have to ask ourselves. How do we maintain productive growth in innovation and human capital? I will kind of emphasize more about significance of our education in creating connectivity. We had some interesting discussion yesterday at Shanghai Normal University that connectivity is not only about infrastructure connection, it's a lot about abilities of people to relate and connect to each other in different

Price to Income Ratio

Rent Income Ratio

Fig. 4
Price to income
ratio and rent
income ratio of
metropolitans

ways, and it is not only about infrastructure. We also need to do much better in creating sufficiency within the city. One of the big drawbacks in large cities is that they are not managed well and that's all reasons of congestion and pollution and so on. So if we want to be a competitive city, once we deal with the issue of efficiency, we need to think about spatial structures. Finally is basically about creating institutions and policies and more participation of private business, and especially highlights investment. On top of that, less restrictive planning and more guiding for entrepreneurs and private business who can succeed and who can find themselves a way.

How do we preview an unforeseen, unknown thing in the future? You can never predict the future perfectly. And one of the greatest difficulties that planners and planning institutions have in China is how you are able to change your plans, how you can adapt yourself for unforeseen changes, not only your resilience in terms of natural disasters but also economic downturns.

The Future of a Livable City

Nancy Lozano Gracia

Senior Economist of the World Bank

How does a city become rich, competitive and prosperous? This is a question that we discuss occasionally but yet could not find one correct answer. As far as I am concerned, the answer of the question can be found from the development experiences of our major global cities today.

So I would like to make a brief analysis about the employment rate and residential density in major global cities. From Fig. 1 and 2, we can see the general feature of employment rate and residential density of New York, Hong Kong and London. So how can we achieve the power by connecting these different spikes? The connectivity to different sources of density can bring about the diversity of cities. But with the duty that density brings, we see costs. Why are there these costs? These costs are pollution. We all know about the air pollution in Shanghai, and we also know that one of the big problems in large cities is congestion. So what is it that matters when you think about managing

Fig. 1
Residential density of New York, Hong Kong and London

Urban form: residential density

RESIDENTIAL DENSITY

LONDON
Peak 27,100 pp/km²

NEW YORK
Peak 59,150 pp/km²

HONG KONG
Peak 111,100 pp/km²

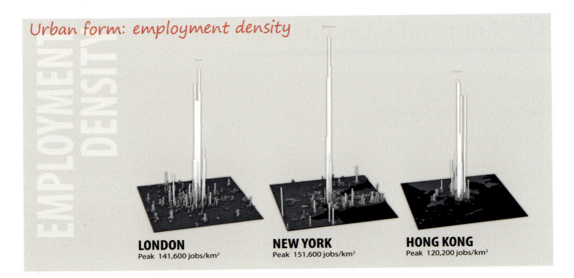

Urban form: employment density

LONDON
Peak 141,600 jobs/km²

NEW YORK
Peak 151,600 jobs/km²

HONG KONG
Peak 120,200 jobs/km²

Fig. 2
Employment
density of New
York, Hong Kong
and London

this cost that comes with cities? How is it that we can get the best of our cities while managing the cost? Thinking about the flexibility in our regulation is important.

Here we have one example, very flexible. Among these regulations, you can see the variations here. On the other side, you see New York City. Its ability in terms of regulation is very flexible. So when we think about connecting the spikes to achieve high-power cities, infrastructure is not enough. Coordination between those flexible regulations and infrastructure is important.

Coordination is not only important between land conservation and transportation. Coordination between different interventions is also important. There is a city that is located in the outskirts of San Polo. And that actually grew in what was one of the most important watersheds of the city. So once it grew, it brought large water problems to the whole city. A specific intervention has been made upon the city which invested on improving the search system, improving mobility on the settlement, but also bringing green areas that acted as marinas that absorbed extra water. Actually, not only the livability of the residents of this area was improved, but it actually helped improve the productivity of the city because people who worked here were able to move more easily. And the livability of the city was improved because the water quality of the city as a whole was improved.

Another important thing we said, coordination between infrastructure and appropriate use, coordination across different interventions, but also efforts to leverage market forces and allow incentives to change behaviors. Here is an example of Columbia (Fig. 3), which achieved universal coverage in water across the cities, not only through expansion of infrastructure, but actually through changing its regulation that changed the behaviors of water consumers. So coordination between transport and different interventions are allowing the market to provide the right incentives.

Fig.3
Columbia's households with access to water from 1964 to 2005

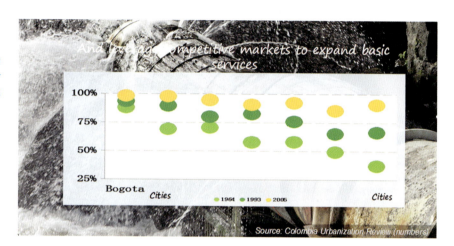

To Attract the Talented Needed in a Global City

Wang Dewen

Social Specialist of the World Bank

Attracting talents and skilled workers is quite significant if Shanghai wants to transform itself from MADE IN SHANGHAI to CREATED IN SHANGHAI. The changes of GDP in more than 700 cities around the world tell us the changes of the proportion that each industry takes in overall GDP. So we can very obviously see the fact that, the spiral increase of urban economy is largely attributed to two major industries, which proportion in GDP has been steadily increasing. For example, compared with manufacturing and agriculture, the information technology and public service's proportion in overall GDP has been declining. The structure of employment is changing with the changes in industry structure. Consequently, the competitions among cities over talents and skilled workers are intensifying.

Why do the countries and cities compete for attracting top talents? There are two aspects in this regard. The first one is, the group of the top talents and skilled workers is a significant labor capital which maintains economic growth and improves the productivity of a city. Besides, they are also a intellectual capital which is closely linked to the overall innovative competence of a city. In this sense, it is very important to attract top talents, and nations around the world are constantly implementing strategic measures and projects to attract top talents. I will talk about some individual cases on this later.

From the experiences of global aspect, it tells us that the top talents are voluntary global liquidity with high mobility. So how to attract them is a common problem nations are facing. There are two important factors to consider for top talents. One is the job and economic opportunities, employment opportunities as we say. If he went to a city, for example, to Shanghai, he will consider if there are good jobs in Shanghai and how high the salary will be. On top of that, the other factor he might consider would be opportunities for career development. As for the entrepreneurs, they would consider more on if the investment environment and the social, financial, labor, taxation policy of Shanghai could help investment and business. So in this sense, these are the major factors that impact their decisions to remain in Shanghai or to go to somewhere else.

Another very important point is the cost of living. As cost of living keeps increasing in recent years in China, many highly skilled workers have been considering migrating abroad. So this is a very tough problem since it is closely associated to the overall live quality of the talents in the city. While other aspects are also important, such as social environment and the diversity of the city. The quality of public service is also quite significant, as most international top talents may probably move into a city with their family members. In this context, enormous attention would be paid to their children's education, family health, and the quality of the health care situation of the city.

All in all, we can sum up those aspects mentioned above as the life quality. Last but not the least, the local educational development is very important in attracting global talents. On the one hand, developed education helps attract global talents. On the other hand, a good education is conducive to training local talents.

According to the global experiences, nations and cities use various methods to attract talents. Generally, there are several following methods: one is to make a series of strategies and plans to attract talents as Hong Kong and Singapore did. Another thing that Hong Kong, Singapore did is that they established special government agencies to develop and implement these plans so as to better attract top talents and skilled workers. For example, Singapore and the United States differentiate between the ordinary migration and the global talents, whereas London takes integrating immigrant policy in determining whether you are able to go to London or not. In fact, immigration policies in major global cities tend to encourage the inflow of global talents. Moreover, many countries provide education, training or employment services for global talents to help reduce the labor market dislocation problems among them. Let's say that there is a talent who does not know where to find jobs. So we gave him a job consultant.

Another point is that, in many nations and cities, universities and research institutions are responsible for engaging in a series of projects that encourage universities, businesses and research institutions to attract global talents. Shanghai is doing pretty well on this.

Besides, many nations and cities optimized their policies in taxation and financial services to attract more global talents inflow. Of course, nations and cities around the world apply various approaches to fulfill their goals on this.

Shanghai is remarkable if we compare it with other international cities on high school students' performance on PASSA exam. But if we take the comprehensive capital of the city into consideration, we will see the big remaining gap between major global cities like Seoul, London, Hong Kong and Shanghai. Obviously, there is still much work to be done.

From the perspective of attracting talents, Shanghai is lagging far behind. Shanghai ranks at the bottom among global cities when it comes to diversity, global liquidity and commercial environment. It is only slightly better in obtaining labor resources since China has extremely large labor resources. Therefore, from this point of view, Shanghai has its weakness.

Finally, based on the researches that we have done on Shanghai, it is taken for granted that Shanghai will confront with various challenges in attracting and training top talents.

Shanghai has a fastest rate of aging population among Chinese cities. If we only consider local population of Shanghai, we will find that one fourth of the population belongs to aging population. Once the non-locals are included, Shanghai's aging population is not that challenging.

The next problem is that it is extremely difficult for non-locals to become registered residence of Shanghai. Moreover, high real estate price of Shanghai is also a great challenge for talents to settle down. Besides, high taxation, social consumption and high labor cost are posing great challenges to the future competence of Shanghai among global cities.

From the point of training talents and workers, educational and training sectors cannot be able to fully be exploited. This is a big issue. These issues will be more and more pivotal in the process of industrial optimization, and migrants should be given more access to cities' social resources.

One last critical point, we still do not clearly know that though Shanghai is the only city in China which is proposed to promote lifelong educational system, we still could not see the practical effect of such a system. Most importantly, we do not know how the current education system is linked to the labor market. Nevertheless, I take it for granted that Shanghai needs to give its concern on this issue.

The above are the challenges that we observed.

FORUM III

分论坛三

Brand Building and Attractiveness
Strengthening for Global Cities
全球城市品牌建设及国际吸引力提升

上海师范大学副校长康年
在全球城市论坛平行分论坛三上主持会议

Kang Nian, Vice President of Shanghai Normal University,
chairs Parallel Forum Ⅲ of the Global City Forum

上海师范大学校长朱自强
在全球城市论坛平行分论坛三上致辞

Zhu Ziqiang, President of Shanghai Normal University,
addresses at Parallel Forum Ⅲ of the Global City Forum

上海市人民政府发展研究中心副主任严军
在全球城市论坛平行分论坛三上致辞

Yan Jun, Deputy Director of the Development Research Center
of Shanghai Municipal People's Government, addresses at
Parallel Forum Ⅲ of the Global City Forum

全球城市论坛平行分论坛三的与会代表

Delegates attending Parallel Forum Ⅲ
of the Global City Forum

面向 2050：上海超大城市的发展方向

皮特·卡瑞·克里塞

美国巴克尼尔大学教授

　　首先，我想提一个令人深思的问题：未来的上海将向什么方向发展？这个问题涉及许多方面。比如，2050 年的上海会不会由于规模过于庞大、人口过于密集而失去现在的竞争力？我们的超大型城市会重蹈恐龙的覆辙，还是会保持原来的灵活性、活力和创造力，从而继续维持在全球的领导地位？在一个人口达到 4 000 万甚至更多，并且大部分人口从农村流动到城市、缺乏足够教育的城市里，社会将变成什么样子？到 2050 年，上海肯定会成为一座超大型城市，几个重要的不确定因素会对这座拥有众多人口的城市带来巨大影响。接下来，我将对这些因素及其对城市竞争力和民众福祉造成的影响作一剖析。

　　要成为一座世界城市都需要什么？在 2011 年北京举行的一次会议上，北京市规划委员会主任黄艳提出，世界城市有三个要素：第一，人均收入超过 15 000 美元；第二，在政治、经济和文化领域具有全球影响；第三，具有国际组织总部中心的地位。中国有两座城市的人均收入达到了 15 000 美元左右：北京和上海。北京在世界范围内具有政治影响，上海则具有经济影响。中国的文化形象代表，例如郎朗等许多音乐家、艺术家都具有全球影响力。上海确实已经具备了作为企业和国际组织总部中心的地位。因此，借用黄艳的标准来看，上海有资格成为一个世界城市。

　　萨斯奇娅·萨森认为世界城市应具有决策和领导职能。约翰·弗雷德曼在他的著作中提到新型国际分工的空间组织形式，也注意到了社会阶级、移民、极化现象的增加。彼得·泰勒关心世界城市所提供的具有刺激作用的因素，这些因素体现为信息知识和创造力，并与新型服务商品的生产相融合。还有什么呢？几十年前人们对于一个 2 000 万人的城市都感到担忧，也许现在我们应该考虑一下 4 000 万甚至 5 000 万人口城市的可行性。东京超过 3 700 万人口，由于种种原因，企业和国际组织都认为在东京设立办事处很有必要。如果上海的人口是现有的两倍，又会怎么样？我们很可能看不到平均收入的增加，收入分配的可行化，全球经济和文化影响力的增加，以及在环境、人口、福利、流动性等方面的可持续性。

这里有两点是非常值得注意的。第一是 20 世纪 70 年代之前在工业国家里曾经处于领导地位的城市的经历。美国的工业核心区在 20 世纪 70 年代之后变成了"锈带"，这主要是因为关键的工业进口原油价格发生了变化。德国鲁尔区和英国米德兰地区也都遭遇了同样的境况。第二是运输、通信和生产技术的变化导致了许多城市往积极或者消极方面转化。制造业曾经从美国往中国转移，现在又由于生产技术和劳动力成本的变化逐渐回流到美国、墨西哥等国家。而且由于通信技术的发展，小规模的城市也可以和许多大城市一起参与全球性活动。约瑟夫·熊彼特曾提出"创造性毁灭"的概念，技术、价格的变化，例如油价、通信和运输技术的变化会完全改变世界经济格局。这种创造性破坏的力量能摧毁旧经济体制，然后新的经济体制就会取而代之。

于是，我们可以问一个有深度的问题：上海在 2050 年的竞争地位会变得如何？原先的一些促进上海成功的因素，例如要素价格、技术革新等会趋于恶化吗？上海会由于变得太大而失去竞争力吗？一座城市最佳的规模是多大？多出的数百万人口对上海会产生什么负面影响？3 700 万人口的东京对其他城市是一个好的样板吗？波戈维奇提出最优城市规模约在 50 万人以下，最近 OECD 的研究显示最佳城市规模应该在大约 600 万人，总之没有研究表明 3 000 万居民可以作为一座城市的最佳规模。从《经济学人》杂志的报告《热点 2025》中可以看到，最具竞争力的十个城市，从世界最大的城市东京（现有人口 3 700 万）到世界上最小的城市之一瑞士苏黎世（人口约 140 万）。确实，一座城市的规模与其竞争力之间并没有太明显的关系。我在对美国城市的研究中发现了这一点，而李平飞发现这也适用于中国的城市。

我认为上海采取与东京在城市规模方面匹敌的政策是不明智的。上海应当将注意力集中在提升城市核心竞争力上。作为中国第一个自由贸易区，上海自贸试验区的建立就是往正确方向上走出的一步，但很多部门仍然受到限制，而且自贸区到现在的进展仍然有很大改进空间，需要在制度创新上继续付出不懈努力。因此，这个举措或许不像 20 世纪 80 年代建立经济特区一样具备改革性的效果。要发现上海的绝对与相对优势，以及在全球经济中扮演的角色，就需要进行实证研究，并且需要花费更多的时间。

2050 年上海全球城市吸引力
建设及领军企业的作用

里奥·凡登伯格

荷兰鹿特丹伊拉斯谟大学教授

　　我第一次来到上海还是在十年前。在上一个十年，上海已经成为了一座大都市，在世界上最具竞争力的五百座城市排行榜上名列前茅。现在，上海是中国最大的港口和工业基地，在技术创新、全球化接轨和文化多样性等方面也相当出色。上海在包括南京、扬州等在内的城市群发展中还发挥了重要推进作用。2010 年世界博览会在上海举行，口号是"城市，让生活更美好"。在我看来，上海的目标显然是在生活、工作、旅游和投资等方面成为世界上最具吸引力的城市之一。

　　现在，上海已经成功地完成了工业化进程，进入一个新的阶段，当然也面临着新的挑战。上海必须在更多方面注入活力，以实现"城市，让生活更美好"这个目标。首先是加强人力资源建设，未来上海的劳动力素质必定会比现在高得多，这样才能满足不断增长的对高素质人才的需求。其次，实现产业集群的融合发展也同样重要。第三，上海要成为一座安全的城市，并能够提供住房、医疗、教育等完善的公共服务。一座城市要想吸引高素质人才，生活环境的吸引力是重要因素之一，而安全的环境，良好的住宅、文化、教育、娱乐设施和清洁的自然环境都是城市吸引力的重要组成部分。能否在这些方面大力改进将成为未来几年上海遇到的最大挑战之一。最后是加强基础设施建设。为了更好地实现在全球与区域城市网络中的枢纽功能，上海需要不断提高自身的交通可达性，还需要提高通信等基础设施的质量。

　　增强上海的可持续吸引力，关键在于和利益相关者建立伙伴关系。这就需要决策者在各个层次上具备相应的眼光、领导力、沟通策略以及社会和政治上的支持。这一点对于城市管理的不断改善是不可或缺的。而在建立伙伴关系以实现可持续竞争力方面，上海的龙头企业应当承担关键职责。跨国公司越来越多地在本地和全球同步实现可持续发展以确保自身利益。因为初期环境中的投资以及本地供应商、客户和合同关系的存在，或者仅仅因为所处位置的地理特点，导致了很多跨国公司的发展确实主要以本地为基础。同时，社区、劳动力市场和政府机构也依靠从在当地进行国际化运营的商业团体的可持续发展中，获得就业机会、税收、附加价值、知识转移和投资机会。不论是跨国公司还是地方上的利益相关者都面临着新的游戏规则。从全球上来看，就可持续发展方面来说，二者都需要确保自身在本地所依靠的基础。

事实上，我们正在经历公共利益与私人利益的交融。城市福利取决于发展良好的私人部门，而私人部门需要在秩序井然而且能够可持续发展的城市中生存。把城市里商业团体的利益、当地政府的利益以及其他利益相关者的利益融合在一起，就能创造一个双赢的格局。一般公司可以担当重要职责，促进其所在城市的可持续发展。而一些典型的、以赞助当地动物园、音乐厅等公共设施的方式从事慈善事业的公司，则应该通过与城市其他利益相关者进行战略性接触、建立战略伙伴关系的方式共同承担职责。所承担的职责范围不仅包括城市区域和更长远的全球商业网络，还包括全球供应链。这样一来，各个龙头企业就能把世界范围内的城市的可持续发展有效地联系起来。

但是有一个实际问题依旧存在：龙头企业如何在不同环境下支持可持续发展？这样做的动机是什么？最近我们进行的一项欧洲城市比较研究院的研究工作探讨了在上海及其姊妹城市鹿特丹两座港口城市的可持续发展中公司所扮演的角色。实现可持续发展的动力给予了港口城市打破其封闭状态的新机会。港口城市拥有在环境技术方面成为新城市集群中领导城市的潜力。一些老工业区就有过类似的情况，比如德国鲁尔区从欧洲的重工业核心地区转变成为德国领先的环境技术中心。值得注意的是，鲁尔区的新型产业分支的出现，例如环境技术，是由各个公司自发努力的结果。市场迫使公司走多样化的道路并向新的产业分支投资。不仅如此，当地政府和北莱茵威斯特法伦州也不再支持传统工业，转而支持新型工业。港口城市的公司也因严格的政府规定和变化的市场需求而不得不转而投资新型产业分支和更为清洁的技术。港口城市相比于其他地区有更多的竞争优势，因为在港口城市中已经存在对于新兴技术中清洁技术的相关了解和认识。不仅如此，在污染最为严重的活动中存在大量利益相关群体，他们的利益各不相同。由于对清洁技术的了解和认识每年都会进一步更新和深化，因此这种了解和认识有助于解决实际问题。

为了分析龙头企业的战略行动，我们建立了一个理论框架。在这个框架中设立了四种环境。在这四种环境下上海和鹿特丹的龙头企业可以促进可持续性的发展。这四种环境是区域、供应链、集群和网络。我们的研究表明，上海与鹿特丹的相似与差异都可以通过这两座城市巨大的背景差异来解释。

从区域环境方面来看，除了一些为了改善劳动力资源和吸引潜在客户的战略性投资，两座城市的龙头企业都向社区和环境工程投资。在地域环境下的可持续投资主要由慈善投资来完成。投资的驱动力和动机在两座城市中是有区别的。在上海，由于起步点较低，为了得到政治上和社会上的支持，就必须进行区域投资。在鹿特丹，基本需求（例如清洁的水源）已经得到满足，投资主要是为了获得社会支持，并且以间接的方式促进商业发展。

在供应链环境下，龙头企业的战略行动或多或少都是相似的。在两座城市中，供应链领导者都意图自始至终在各个维度实现可持续性。龙头企业对它们的客户和供应商使用软硬兼施的方法增加可持续行为的发生。许多有关可持续预测的努力都由供应链领导者发起，他们意在开发能获得巨大市场份额和增生新市场的新型产品。

在集群环境下，两座城市就存在很大的差异。在鹿特丹，龙头企业推动其他企业和政府决策者对CCS，即碳捕捉和储存技术，进行投资从而在短期上达到京都议定书的相关要求。而在长期上，他们希望发展新技术，创建新产业。上海化学工业区就是个很有说明性的例子。上海化学工业区是一个新兴的化学工业园区，有着严格的环境和安全标准。上海的市政部门是一个很有作为的团队，领导着发展的进程。它利用一个龙头企业来创造最佳实践经验，并且将各个龙头企业和当地的公司联系在一起，共同解决问题，分享经验。上海和鹿特丹处于它们各自发展进程中的不同阶段，这就影响了在这两个城市的龙头公司的行为。大部分公司的可持续性政策具有全球视野，但是执行政策的背景却因地点不同而不同。这就导致了全球性政策要适应大量的地方性情况。

下面是我的结论。在研究中，我们探讨了鹿特丹和上海的龙头企业的行为。大部分公司似乎主要将关注点放在减少污染和减少二氧化碳排放上。在鹿特丹和上海的龙头企业都认识到了自身在地区可持续性上所肩负的职责，这也是它们政策中的二级目标。对区域可持续性的投资也就是对生存环境、生活和教育质量的改善。从上海和鹿特丹的管理思维上来说，对可持续性的看法没有什么不同。很明显，又是背景导致了两个城市的公司所采取了不同的行动。在这个关于公司主动行为和被动行为的讨论中，不同公司采取的行为有很大差异。

真正主动面向可持续性的战略并不多见。许多公司针对可持续性问题采取主动方法，然而却以社会团体的需求为导向采取行动。一个公司采取自行设立标准、发展新的途径和新的伙伴关系以改善一个地区的可持续性，这种采取主动策略的公司依然很少见。然而，现在主动策略已经成为一种趋势。很多公司把从欧洲和美国得到的关于可持续性的经验和教训在上海的背景下用于实践，这促使龙头企业共同影响整个上海地区的可持续性政策和实践。我们的研究结果说明，上海未来进一步提升宜居和城市吸引力的前景十分广阔。

城市数据全球委员会：
标准化城市数据的国际平台

帕特里夏·麦卡尼

加拿大多伦多大学教授

城市数据全球委员会总裁兼首席执行官

我想侧重介绍一下城市数据全球委员会的演变，以及新的 ISO 即城市数据国际标准化组织的建立，我们称其为 ISO37120。这是第一个关于城市的标准，这项标准是从国际标准化组织中衍生而来。我很高兴和中国国家标准化管理委员会、国际标准化组织以及 20 个国家进行合作，以推进这个标准的发展。今年（2014 年）这项标准已经出台。

很重要的一点是，为什么城市需要国际指标。当然，城市的经济实力是很重要的一个因素。当你将城市的人口分布优势与其经济实力结合起来考量，你会得到一个城市在世界舞台中的表现，而这一种考量方式在过去几十年中很少有人使用。考虑到这一点，我们迫切需要得到城市的数据。举个例子，城市基础设施建设的需求量和合理投资规模，需要进行科学的计算。我们要合理地投资这些基础建设，因为这些基础设施至少会维持 50 年。比如北美那些城市，它们基本上都是战后建成的，大部分投资是在交通干线和公路上，而这些设施现在仍在使用，它给城市留下了长久的印记。所以，现在我们更需要得到一系列完备的数据，因为只有这样，我们才会准确把握未来城市的需求，并且以此为依据进行合理的投资。

接下来我要讲的是关于我们如何建立城市数据的全球标准以及如何最终形成 5 月发布的 ISO 标准这一过程。在城市数据方面，我们面临着很多挑战，这里我列出了其中四个，当然还不止这些。其中一个很主要的挑战是，当你把城市放在一起做对比，如果你要在一篇论文中建一个表格，如果这个表格左侧纵向所列的城市多于一个，横向所列的指标多于一个，可以肯定的是，你的表格将要有 15—20 个脚注，这些脚注的作用就是把这个小表格无法囊括的例外予以解释。这些例外与以下我要提到的四个因素有关，通常情况下，只是城市边界这一个因素的影响即可以让我们意识到，城市研究富有挑战性。其他三个因素分别是：对需要衡量的对象缺乏标准定义，衡量数据的方法缺乏统一的标准，缺乏世界各地城市分享数据的机制。当然，在城市数据方面还存在着其他一些挑战。如果我们关注非洲、亚洲、北美的一些城市，这些城市数据的无规律性也是一项极大的挑战。关于这个问题，我的同事本（Ben）正在研究，目的就是建立我们称之为"非正常地区"的城市数据。

因此，我们开始对数据进行标准化，同时建立标准化的定义和方法。我们和世界银行一道，从9个城市入手，这9个城市是我们在2008年初选定的。那段时间，我们仅对这9个城市进行研究，然后我们重新制定城市研究的方法，各种定义，城市的边界等，随后我们将这个网络体系推演到82个国家和255个城市。我们之所以可以如此迅速地从对9个城市的研究发展到把255个城市作为研究对象，其原因在于我们的城市、城市管理者以及市长都极其需要城市数据。越来越多的市长会问这样的一个问题：从全球范围来看，我们所做的事情和其他城市有何种关联。所以，我们的研究显得十分迫切，需求非常大。

我们后来去日内瓦，希望与ISO即国际标准化组织合作，建成一个ISO的标准体系。ISO是一个标准化组织，通常做的是对诸如灯泡、电脑零件、手机中的部件、拖拉机、汽车零件等这类物品进行标准化定义，但是一直以来，它都没有对城市以及城市指标进行过标准化的定义。所以我们到日内瓦，询问他们是否可以对我们6年来所做的工作进行标准化的认定，但当时他们对此并不感兴趣。之后，我们这群加拿大人回去以后，认定我们还需要一些努力，才能使得我们所做的工作在ISO得到认证。当时，日本政府找到我们，说他们可以和ISO谈谈对基础设施的数据化问题。随后，法国政府也去日内瓦，与ISO探讨了关于管理系统的城市化标准问题。所以，最后我们将这些系统并在一起，构成了ISO TC268，自此ISO TC268诞生了。我主持第二工作组的工作，我们和20个国家、很多工作伙伴和国际机构进行会谈，自2012年起，在过去的两年里我们一直在建立这个标准。诚如各位所见，TC268的成员中包括中国，中国是我们这个大家庭中的一员。我们有20个有投票权的参与国和17个观察国。这是我们的工作组。我们每3到4个月见一次面，讨论城市指标的问题，也会对一些问题进行界定和制定新的研究方法。我们这个工作组做出了很多的努力，也做了一些妥协，最终我们为这个标准的制定也达成了共识。我们一共历经6次国际会议，形成5个草稿，收集了来自全球各个国家的选票中的300多条评论。最终我们成功了，ISO37120出版了，这是关于城市指标的第一个国际标准。

那么什么是ISO37120呢？它包含100个标准化指标，其中的46个是核心指标，也就是说，如果某个城市想要得到ISO37120的认证，首先至少要汇报这46个核心指标的内容。这些指标都是围绕着城市服务和生活质量来设定的，所以这100个指标也包含了各种主题。一般来说，大多数城市都有衡量生活质量的数据，因此在最初阶段这项工作并不是特别困难，对大多数项目而言这些城市是可以汇报的。这46个核心指标是对城市进行标准化的第一步。用户可以是任何城市、自治区或是当地政府，它也可以成为城市管理者、规划者、企业领导、设计师、市民、研究员、教授和其他专家的工具。其次我还想提到的一点是，在我们建立这个标准的过程中，许多国家和城市在投票的时候都一直要求我们再添加一些指标。我们本来想要把指标数目控制在75个，但是最后还是有100个。我们会对此加以限制，是因为我们认为如果指标的数目超过100个，ISO标准将起不到什么作用，因为对于城市而言，汇报如此多的指标是不大实际的，所以我们将其限定在100个。但是，每次有国家投票，他们都会问我们，为什么不添加生物多样性这个指标，为什么不添加植树情况这个指标，为什么不添加PM10指标，基于空气质量的考虑，为什么不添加微小颗粒的指标，如PM2.5，还有应急反应指标，飓风中城市发生洪水灾害的情况等。所以我们开始关注，在投票过程中一些国家和城市要求添加的这100个指标外的一些其他指标。我们形成了一个计划，即形成一个新的关于城市恢复能力的技术报告，就是现在我们正在建立的ISO37121。我们现在关注的新主题包括应急准备和危机处理的各个方面。

接下来介绍城市数据全球委员会的建立。正是由于ISO标准的形成，城市数据全球委员会也在这样的环境下应运而生。在ISO37120通过以后，我们便成立了城市数据全球委员会。现在，这个委员会作为一个世界中心，为各国建立共同学习的伙伴关系，进行信息收集，并且报告给ISO37120，以便对信息进行数据化。这个委员会也将作为一个开放的数据平台，所以对我们这些研究者而言，它将成为一个极佳的工具，帮助我们对比城市之间的数据。这个工具已经投入使用，我也将在接下来的演讲中提到目前的进展程度。因此，我们在全世界的一些奠基城市建立机构来开始这个项目，我们邀请了20个城市作为城市数据全球委员会的一部分。上海也是其中之一，同时这项工作是由上海市人民政府发展研究中心开展。我们希望在兼顾城市规模的同时，这些城市的地理位置也要有所不同。所以我们选取的城市有伦敦、阿姆斯特丹，在西亚、中东地区选取了迪拜、圣城麦加、约旦的安曼，在拉丁美洲有布宜诺斯艾利斯、波哥大和圣保罗。在欧洲也有很多国家，比如巴塞罗那和鹿特丹。我们选取的城市中也有墨尔本、波士顿和多伦多。这些城市在地理位置和规模上都存在着差异。所以，以非洲为例，我们选取了较大的城市比如约翰内斯堡，也有诸如尼日利亚的米纳这样比较小的城市。也是由于这项标准的通过，我们能够有 255 个城市参与其中，才会有这么多的合作伙伴，因为我们为世界各国的城市，建立数据化的平台，为其提供了展现发展进步的世界舞台。所以，就像我刚才所讲的那样，我们才会在过去的 6 年中建成这个全新的也是充满活力的城市数据全球委员会。关于这个委员会，我会在结论部分跟大家谈一谈我们下一步的计划。

我要说明的另外一点是，很多人问我为什么城市需要全球标准化的数据。这些城市代替我们做出了回答。其中一个答案是，通过数据分析作出明智的决定，设定最佳策略与目标，计划可持续发展计划，为其建立新的框架，同时获得高级政府部门的资助。这一点也已经引起了一些与我们合作的北美城市的关注。除此以外，评估城市基础建设项目对城市综合表现的影响，建立信用度和保险安全，这对飓风和海啸等自然灾害高发的城市而言尤为重要。另外，建立智慧城市和可持续发展城市，学习并与全球其他城市分享经验也是很重要的一个原因。这种城市与城市之间进行的、有关数据标准化的知识交流，可能是最重要的一项贡献。对于全球城市的利益相关方而言，有多个原因可以用来解释我们为什么需要将标准化的数据纳入考虑的范畴。其中之一就是，依据标准化数据来决定该城市市场投资的入口点，设定最佳投资计划，建设智慧城市和可持续发展城市，在一段时间内评估投资项目，以及加强城市管理的效率等。

我们如今已从千年发展目标进入联合国可持续发展目标的阶段，因此这一系列的城市标准化数据也将为联合国可持续发展目标建立一个基础，让我们更好地定位何为联合国可持续发展目标。这些数据也可以让我们以此来衡量各项发展，监控发展过程以最终达成目标。我们把这些数据放在一起进行比较，在多伦多大学建立了机构来研究其中一些问题，比如城市与繁荣、城市与老龄化以及城市与可持续的基础设施问题。我们的网站上提供了关于这些问题的报告。

我们再来谈谈城市和老龄化的问题。我们在全球范围内追踪了老龄化如何影响世界上的城市。这在撒哈拉以南非洲以及北非地区尤为明显，可以看到其老龄化人口以366%的速度增长，这是一个很惊人的数字。我们以年龄组为分类标准，对世界范围内的一些城市进行数据收集和统计。北京和上海在这方面的表现还不算太差，老龄组即65岁以上的人口仅分别占到9%和10%。

我们也与总工会一道对儿童友好型城市指标进行调查，在未来6个月内也将形成一系列新的指标。基于已收集的数据，我们做了很多对比的图表来进行可视化处理。例如，你可以关注健康指标或一些其他的主题，以及不同地区的数据集中情况，我们可以清楚地看到健康指标是如何变化的。你也可以变换主题，例如教育，然后用不同的教育能力来追踪这些城市的情况。因为有了城市数据，我们才能第一次做到这些工作。

除此之外，我还要谈一个重要的问题，即城市边界问题。我们尝试了一种聚集的方式，把城市边界扩展到地区，到城市中的经济功能区，无论我们将其称作大都会还是聚集地，还是大城区，这都是对城市数据进行比较过程中最大的挑战之一，因为每个人划定的边界都不相同。我们尝试设计了一种数据总和的工具，并以多伦多作为案例进行研究。这种工具是由我们政府的高层提出的，他们要求我们去划定城市的边界。他们划好的区域实际上是城区地带，之后，我们开始调查多伦多地区的情况。我们关注这些划定的地区之外，还留意区域边界是什么样的。但问题是多伦多城区周边有很多不同的城市，他们分别把数据汇报给我们，而关键在于我们如何对数据进行整合。因此，我们开始自己划定城市边界，然后观察夜晚灯光的俯视图，来验证我们的工作是否正确。因为如果我们划定的区域的确是多伦多建筑物聚集的城区，它在地图上的轮廓将和灯光俯视图的轮廓非常接近。接着，我们把这个聚合结果与世界其他地区的聚合情况做一个对比，包括大芝加哥区、圣弗朗西斯科湾区、沪宁走廊等，试图探究如何在标准化的基础上，对更大的城区进行数据整合。

以高等教育程度为例，通过这个研究最后进行的数据整合工作，我们可以明显看出，多伦多城区的高等教育程度与硅谷所在地旧金山湾区相比，也是很有竞争力的，而这一点，在多伦多也没人知道，直到我们拿到数据进行了整合以后才了解了这一现象。后来，我们也通过整合数据，研究了收入中位数、在国外出生的人口、选用大众交通工具的通勤情况等。边界问题是一个很困难的问题。以2010年城市市长网站上的数据为例，上海位列第二，城市人口达1 490万，都市人数达到1 920万；而卡拉奇位列第一，因为从城市规模来看，它是最大的城市，但是如果看它的都市人口，其实是位列第九的。也正是因为我们对于边界的看法不同，在这些统计呈现中会有很大的差异。如果我们再次以上海为例，来看这个标题，是城区聚合而非城市聚合，也不是都市聚合。所以在对全球城市进行比较之前，先要解决的一个最大问题就是边界的界定。

另外，许多城市，比如布宜诺斯艾利斯，已经开始利用 ISO37120 作为基准来衡量其发展目标和国家规划策略。在多伦多的例子中，我们运用 ISO37120 更多地是为其选定更有竞争力的投资位置。我们目前也在与上海合作来规划 2050 年的发展策略。

现在，要成为我们认证的城市首先要签署意向书，然后我们会对该城市予以批准，之后要提交关于 46 个核心指标的数据，随后可以登记入册。我们与奠基城市以及国际机构合作，目的是在未来的 5 到 10 年里，把这项工作再向前推进。希望在中国会有 100 个，甚至更多的城市和我们一道来庆祝这项标准化数据工作。

产业集群创新与
城市转型

斯蒂芬·科拉特克

德国奥德河畔法兰克福欧洲大学教授

上海是中国经济强有力的区域性引擎，也是世界城市网络中崭露头角的大都市。主要想谈谈大城市产业集群的创新能力及其与全球都市制造业网络的关系。通过对德国的观察，逐渐形成了这个独特的研究视角。德国制造业丰富，科技水平高度发达，创新能力强，但其劣势是，经济的发展主要集中在金融产业和商业服务业。今天，对于全世界的城市而言，全球化进程对其经济发展的影响越来越大。我们如今面临着这样的形势，全球经济网络日益扩张，有越来越多的城市，无论是否处于同一地区，属于南方城市还是北方城市，它们都已成为这一网络中的一分子。这也是为什么我更倾向于用"正在全球化的城市"这一表达形式，因为这正说明了这些城市在全球网络关系中的特殊地位，是它们将对未来经济发展起到决定性作用。

城市创新能力对经济发展具有重要战略性的意义，而城市集群则是创新活动开展的中心地带。从地理位置上看，创新活动的中心大部分位于大都市聚集的地带。区域性集群的形成也是经济发展过程中的一个重要特征。谈到区域性集群，我们会把它和一系列发展因子的聚集联系起来，这些发展因子包括行业中的领头公司、供应方等，而这种聚集是由于它们相互间进行的业务联系或合作关系而逐渐形成的。需要特别指出的是，城市集群可能会被视为一种超级集群，它可能包含多种下位集群，比如金融和商业服务行业集群、媒体产业集群和一些制造业集群等。这些不同的集群之间不必互相关联，但是如果它们之间可以相互作用，那么这种互动将会促使新的产业的形成，多媒体产业和洛杉矶城区就是通过这种方式而逐渐形成的。

近年来，关于区域性集群创新能力的争论，大多集中在知识网络的问题上，这是由于创新多依赖于科技性知识和组织性知识的创造与整合。与上述不同的是，集群知识网络是在特定行业的公司以及科研机构的基础上建立起来的，是一个集群生命力的源泉。简而言之，创新的最大刺激因素源于知识资源的网络化过程，而这种网络化会成为一个地区经济发展的关键因素。基于这些观点，一个区域性创新系统可以从三个方面进行概念化，进而整合为一个完整的结构：第一，区域内公司的内生创新能力，这种能力与公司本身及其正在开展的研究有关；第二，这个地区与创新有关的基础设施，包括公共研究中心、私人研究中心、大学、技术转移机构等；第三，地区知识的网络化，这种网络化会使参与者之间产生正式或非正式的关联，从而促进组织内部知识的流动。在这三个方面中，知识网络起的作用尤为重要，因为它比市场的联系更具有交互性且持久性更强。创新与公司间的合作以及知识的交流有关，而这些因素反过来也会生成新的知识，形成良性的循环。

下面再谈谈产业集群和全球城市网络形成之间的关系。从我的角度来看，某些规模较大的城市集聚本身即是一种创新能力的体现，是在产业进行国际转移这一背景下，在全球范围内和地区间进行互动的结果。全球性的公司正在建立一个由子公司组成的跨国网络，某些城区则选择这些子公司作为零售服务业和制造业的活动方。从地方层面上讲，这些全球公司的机构也是个别城区工业集群的组成部分，而大部分的这种集群还会包括当地的一些公司。在各自的城市工业集群中，全球公司的下设机构和地方公司之间形成的这些网络的发展，也是知识交换和整个集群内部公司日益增强的创新能力的重要来源。

以上海的汽车产业集群为例，德国制造业巨头大众公司在上海建立了一个大型合资企业，它的制造活动是在一个有着500多个周边供应企业组成的网络中进行的。从地理位置上看，这个合资企业已经与其他企业一道，融合成了一个城市的产业集群，促进了知识的交流。同时，在各自区域内工业集群所开展的创新活动也会得到刺激，从而得以加强。这一方面也通常被看作是国际城市网络形成所带来的最重要的经济影响。

在此基础上，谈谈我此番讲话的最后一点，即在全球城市网络结构中制造业所扮演的角色。在当今的全球城市网络中，城市之间的连接包含着众多城市，既有小城市也有全球化大都市，覆盖范围极广。多年来，关于全球城市布局和全球城市网络的研究始终集中在全球服务供应商上，可事实上运营范围遍及全球的制造公司所选择的城市也不尽相同。举例来说，德国大众汽车的全球制造网络覆盖三个城市——圣保罗、墨西哥和上海。我做了一项分析，研究全球范围内，制造行业如何对不同城市进行联系和组织，范围涵盖了汽车行业、信息行业及医药与生物科技行业的120家顶级全球化企业。

制造业全球城市中心的分布和全球服务中心的分布可谓有着天壤之别。这也正是我们需要对全球城市网络的多种全球化模式保持清醒认识的原因。此网络所包含的城市区域以其具体的经济功能为特色，覆盖一些拥有先进生产商服务以及金融部门的公司，同时还有其他一些涉及全球连接活动的城市。

我研究观察的是不同制造行业的全球生产网络有何具体的城市定位。在分析中，我们区分了以资金流向为标准的城市收入以及以区域资源和资金流出为尺度的城市支出。收入环节也可解读为是一种城市区域引进的功能，即运用国外市场和相关知识能源来扩大自己原有的生产能力。支出环节则可被解读为一种城市区域的控制能力。

再给大家展示一些我们在汽车这个传统行业里的发现。我们以节点的集中能力为标尺对城市进行排布，发现了下级分部中340个城市的排布情况。拥有强大支出供应的城市，诸如东京，在汽车行业中处于掌控地位。当然也有一些城市展现出的是相对平衡的支出与收入水平，我们无法从中得出明确的功能定位。以汽车行业城市的支出关系为基准，东京和底特律应该可以被排在前两位。

排在后面的是斯图加特、密尔沃基、名古屋、沃尔夫堡和慕尼黑。从整个排布来看，欧洲国家拥有的一些全球化企业在该行业处于霸主地位，如美国和日本。然而我们应该注意到的是，其他一些拥有全球化资源的城市区域也已经占据了相对较高的排位，比如印度的孟买和浦那。中国的上海也占据高位，巴西的圣保罗也已名列前50。这些迹象都表现出中国、印度和巴西正在加速迈进生产网络全球化的大军中。

除此以外，亚洲城市在上述三个行业的全球生产网络集中力的排布情况也表明，在中国，有越来越多的城市正在进入全球化生产网络。特别值得关注的是，中国城市区域的高收入表现也证明了其在全球制造业网络中的强大吸引力。

最后，我想谈谈节点网络、全球服务和制造业之间的相对排位。通过比较全球服务中心排位的几个版本，一个是彼得·泰勒的版本，另一则是全球化城市研究小组的版本，还有一个是全球生产中心在过去提供的版本，我区分出了三类城市。第一类是在生产行业上排名特别靠前的城市，同时它们的排位远超其在全球化服务领域的排名。属于这一类城市的有汉诺威、名古屋、密尔沃基和斯图加特。第二类是在服务领域和制造行业排位均衡的城市，如多伦多、曼谷和圣保罗。第三类城市则是在服务与金融领域的排名超过了其他领域的名次，这些城市普遍拥有强大的全球化服务集合力，且这种能力远超它们在制造业的表现。属于这一分类的有一些著名的全球化城市如香港、北京和上海。总而言之，如果以经济活动为衡量标准，我们可以发现全球化城市各有特点。

总结一下，我首先强调的是城市间持续的联系对工业创新产生的影响。其次，我也强调了对于创新来讲，最重要的外在刺激是经济活动中产生的地区或本地的知识资源。此外，我们还可以把创新描述为，通过本土网络和全球知识交流所产生的知识创新。这样一来，创新能力较强的特大城市和大型城市之间的独特联系就伴随着地区集群的工业活动间联系的建立而生成。本土公司和全球化公司在城市工业集群中的建立和发展因此也会起到交流知识、加强集群整体创新能力等积极的作用。还有一点，我一直在强调全球制造网络结构中制造业的重要作用。许多城市正在扮演着制造业全球化网络价值中地域节点这一角色，这实则也是城市全球化的一个相关方面。许多城市在制造业全球化网络中的参与也展现出了全球经济中城市所起到的重要作用。总之，我认为城市拥有许多进入全球化的渠道与跳板，这对于全球化经济发展战略可能有重大价值。

世界城市网络中的
上海定位

本·德鲁德

比利时根特大学教授

对世界城市网络问题，我们可以用多种方法研究。我今天要介绍的是一种叫做 GaWc 的方法。对这一方法大家最熟悉的就是，借助它来研究城市和生产服务类公司分支机构选址的关系问题。我收集了很多相关数据进行研究。今天我想重点谈谈如何以中国城市为样本，研究其在国际网络中的地位。

首先，我向大家简单介绍一下我们采用的方法。GaWc 实际上是萨森最早开始研究的，在很多著作中，她都强调了城市在知识产出过程中所扮演的角色，而这些知识可以用来运作迅速扩大的国际生产网络。因此，像我们在科拉特克教授的演讲中看到的那样，全球生产网络仅仅是第一步，接下来我们还需要创造知识来操纵和控制这个全球生产网络。公司通常都很大，需要在不同的地方设址，而我们需要具备某种知识，能够从某种程度上组织这种情况。萨森在其著作中指出，全球城市包括像伦敦和纽约这样经济崛起的城市，但是，我们也能注意到，如果我们以全球化城市作为衡量标准，世界上越来越多的城市可以在这幅图中有一隅可寻。出现这种现象是由于生产的规模已不再局限于个人，而是通过服务达到的知识生产，也就是一种群体生产，当然，信息技术的发展，以及经济全球化的影响等也起到推波助澜的作用。我们注意到高级生产服务业在近年来的兴起，这类服务业通常是公司和机构用来组织全球生产网络的。举个例子，大公司到处做广告，但是它们绝不会每到一个地方就换一家广告公司，它们会选用一家有国际竞争力的广告公司，让这家公司帮它们缓和国内外的文化冲突，而方法就是，让国际产品适应本地标准。所以会存在兼具国际影响力和地方意识的广告公司所构成的国际网络，这些公司的总部一般都设在某几个城市中，而这些城市就是我们所说的世界城市或全球城市。

我们从 GaWc 这个方法入手，对全球网络中的城市定位进行评估和检测，为的就是对高级生产服务公司办公点所构成的网络进行系统的分析。我今天不会把这些数学模型都展示出来，但是，我的演讲中还是会涉及一些模型。有一点我希望大家明确的是，整个研究的出发点还是很简单的。我们具体的工作就是，对全球服务公司进行系统分析，观察它们在城市中的选址，从而通过这一分析发现城市间的互动模式。

我觉得这是一个很好的开始。这里有两张我 10 年前在阿姆斯特丹的史基浦机场拍摄的照片，是德勤的广告展板。德勤是一家很有代表性的服务公司，它在广告中所要传达的意思很清楚，它是要对潜在的顾客们讲：你想知道你在哪里吗？其实你知道你在哪里。你不需要上网搜索，因为在阿姆斯特丹，在纽约，在上海，在圣保罗以及世界上其他地方，德勤的国际声誉无人不晓。借助这一方法，我们发现最有意思的是，如果你把这张城市列表往下拉，会看到一些稍小的城市，比如南京、武汉等，然后结合这类公司的国际竞争力，你会了解到这些服务公司是如何在全球网络策略中运用城市这一决定性因素的。

以安立国际为例。安立是一家人力资源公司，它在中国有三个办公点，一个在北京，另外两个分别在上海和广州。在澳大利亚，它的办公点设在墨尔本和悉尼。一家公司有多少个办公点，一般由这家公司是何种行业决定，会计师事务所通常在上千个城市设有办公点，律师事务所一般会在 20 个多城市有办公点，所以说具体行业也会产生地理分布的偏向。但是如果许多公司聚在一起，呈现集聚发展模式，那么在考虑选址问题时，就要从这个集聚模式入手进行分析了。有趣的是，如果我们考虑这样一个问题，安立要在中国设第四个办公点，它会选在哪里？成都、武汉、南京还有一些其他城市都可能成为它的最终选择。因此，只有通过系统的分析，我们才能知道它所呈现出的模式和分布模式。

再具体谈谈我们的做法。首先我要特别指出的一点是，我们低估了这个模型的分析力。此外，我们也观察了办公点对于一座城市有什么样的重要性，因为不是所有的办公点都是一样重要的。这些办公点中，有的是总部，如果是总部选址在此，肯定是这座城市对于这个公司而言意义重大。也会有一些是一般的或者较为典型的办公点，但还会有亚洲总部这种办公点的存在。所以，我们首先要做的就是，运用标准化方法量化一家公司对于某个城市的重要程度，这样我们可以对不同公司的情况进行比较。我们用的是一种 6 分制的量度方法，我们叫它服务值，意思就是一家公司对于某一座城市的重要性。这 6 分是从 0 记到 5，每一个数字都有不同的含义。0 代表这个公司在这座城市没有办公点，而 5 则代表这个公司的全球总部设在了这座城市，4 表示在这座城市有一个地区性总部，3 则是说有多个办公点或者是某国总部在这座城市。接下来我们看一看这些数据，你会看到很多的城市以及公司，同时对应着相应的 0 到 5 之间的服务值，然后我们就可以借助这些数据进行下一步的研究了。

那么借助这些数据我们又能做些什么呢？我们不是把这些值进行简单相加，那样得出的数据仅仅说明这座城市是有多重要。我们做的是，运用科拉特克教授研究城市网络的方法，这种方法可以让我们明确公司网络中各元素的互动关系。我稍后会用例子为大家做进一步讲解。我们得到了 CDC（城市并向连通度），这个数值表示任何一组城市间的关系，具体算法就是把城市对应的服务值相乘。也就是说，如果一个公司在纽约有一家全球总部，在伦敦有一个地区总部，那么这两者之间潜在的连通度就很大。如果一座城市没有什么竞争力，那么它的服务值是 0，同时还有一座城市的国际影响力一般，服务值是 2，0 乘以 2 还是 0，这两座城市间就该公司的活动来看不存在交流，因为这家公司在第一座城市中没有任何活动。

所以说，城市并向连通度表示的是城市间的关系，如果将这些 CDC 值都相加，就会得到一个 GNC 值，即一座城市的全球网络连通度。它的基本含义是说，如果把这个城市与其他城市的关联值都相加，那么就可以知道这座城市在整个关联网络中的地位。CDC 和 GNC 是两个我们需要关注的参项。我们的研究大体上就是通过这种方式进行的。当然，如果要研究任意两个城市的连通性，还有一些其他方法可以选择。比如说，如果研究 A 公司在纽约和上海的发展情况，这两者之间是相互联系的，具体的联系可以对比这两个城市的 CDC 值。所有的公司间比较都可以使用这一方法。所以，如果把 5 乘以 2，4 乘以 2，5 乘以 0，3 乘以 5 都计算出来，我们即可以得出这两个城市间的联系情况。纽约与上海的 CDC 关联值是 33。这里只列出了三个城市，如果我们把这些值都算出来，把 33 和 15 相加，得到的 48 这个值就是纽约在世界网络中的联系度。这个数值本身并没有什么意义，只有在城市间进行对比的时候，这个数值才可以作为考察城市间联系度和不同服务公司对城市的联系程度的一个指征。

我们从 2000 年开始做这个项目，今天我向大家展示的是 2013 年收集的最新数据。表 1 中，我为大家展示的仅仅是 3 个城市和 4 个公司的情况，实际上我们研究的对象是所有超过 200 万人口的城市以及经济绩效良好的城市。我们选取了526座城市、175个不同行业的服务类公司，包括75个金融服务公司、25个管理咨询公司、25个广告公司、25个律所以及25个会计事务所。这些公司都是相关行业中规模最大、影响力最强的公司。以我们选取的银行为例，这75个银行不是随意选择的，是最大的75家银行。

表1

$CDC_{纽约-上海, A公司}$
$=5 \times 2=10$
$CDC_{纽约-上海}$
$=10+8+0+15=33$
$CDC_{纽约}=33+15=48$

	A 公司	B 公司	C 公司	D 公司
纽　约	5	4	5	3
上　海	2	2	0	5
约翰内斯堡	2	0	1	0

最后，我要向大家解释一下我们是如何得到这些城市和公司的数据的。我们搜索了这些公司的网站。服务类公司在哪里设立总部、分公司和办事处很清楚，因为这是它们的广告策略之一。所以，如果搜索德勤的网站，我们就会看到有专门一个版块是关于办公点位置的，进入以后便可以知道德勤的办公点在哪些城市。如果还能得到更多的信息，那么这个公司的服务值也可以求出来。以律师事务所为例，有许多专业和行业知识会影响到办公点地址的选择。这也就是为什么在北京和布鲁塞尔会有很多的办公点，因为所有与欧盟有关的办事处等都设在了布鲁塞尔，所以设在布鲁塞尔的那个办公点可能对于那个律所而言是比较重要的。也就是说，526个城市，175家公司，最后我们还收集了9万条信息，然后就得出了这些服务值。我在刚才的展示中也用到了这些数值，这些数值也是大家在以后研究中可以用到的。

接下来，我要着重展示一组关于中国城市的数据结果，这里的排名仅仅针对中国的城市。如果从谷歌进入GaWc的网站，我们还可以看到全世界所有城市的排名。在这个表里，这里的GNC实际上是以世界上连通度最强的城市伦敦的GNC值为基准算出的百分比。以伦敦为基准，是因为伦敦最有连通性，也是主要的服务类公司办公点网络的中心。纽约在连通性方面紧随其后，香港和新加坡分别位列第三第四。在榜单上还有其他一些城市，但这些城市都至少占到了伦敦GNC的10%才可上榜。从这些数据中可以看出，香港是中国连通性最强的城市，在世界城市中连通性排名第三位，在中国榜单上，上海和北京位列香港之后。从全球连通性以及服务业公司的办公点网络分布来看，中国有三个表现很突出的城市，但是这并不说明上海和北京比中国其他的城市大，它们之所以突出是因为如果一个服务类公司要在中国选择一个办公点，它更倾向于设在北京、上海这样的城市。在中国城市榜单中，台北位列第四，然后就是广州和深圳。

显然，这种研究最直观的结果就是得到个别城市的全球网络连通性，但是一旦得出城市并向连通度，基于这些数据，我们还能做很多其他的研究。比如可以研究空间模式，因为两个有着相似连通度的城市也会与差异性很大的城市有联系。例如，多伦多可能和欧洲的城市有相似的连通度，但是这些城市间的空间联系却有很大差别。这是我们可以用CDC进行研究的一个角度，可以把某个城市的CDC值与其他525个城市的值做比较。我们还可以把这些CDC值求和，这样可以得到某种城市模式。我们也可以比较中国城市与中国城市之间，以及中国城市与欧洲城市之间的连通强度，看会得到什么样的结果。

这些都是我们可以做的研究，从这个角度我们还可以理解城市全球化这一议题。城市全球化可以理解为，一个城市是如何与世界上连通性最强的10个城市进行联系的。因为并不是所有的联系都有着同样的重要性，所以，我们关注的重点应该是像上海这样的城市如何与纽约、伦敦、芝加哥等城市发生联系。表2很好地说明了这一点，它的数据指的是该城市与其他主要城市连通程度的平均水平。这里的数值，比如0，表示的是没有特别的模式或集群形成。它不代表联系度很强或者很弱。如果数值很小，它仅仅说明这个城市没有和像芝加哥和纽约这样的城市有联系。同样，如果某一个城市得到一个很高的正值，说明该城市与那些大都市的联系度很高。在深入研究后，我们也会发现其模式会有所不同。以深圳为例，它在中国城市中算是一个很有连通性的城市，但是深圳更像是一个地方化的城市，不具有全球化的典型特征。在这里，香港、上海和北京再次位居榜首，这几个城市不仅仅与国内城市连通性高，与国外大城市，比如伦敦和纽约，联系也很多，同时这三个城市也是服务类公司办公网络的覆盖点。运用这一模型，我们还有很多可以开展的课题，比如，如果大家有兴趣，可以研究中国城市与欧盟、非洲或其他城市的联系程度。

我们再来看看地方化的情况。我们要研究的是一个城市与同一区域内其他城市的联系程度。虽然对于地区的定义有所不同，但是比较普遍的是指本国的范围。所以，如果地方化这一栏的值很高，说明这座城市与本国其他城市的联系度很高，这是与全球化相反的一个效应。我们来看看武汉的情况，武汉是一个与国内其他城市关系很密切的省级城市。它也与全球网络有关，但这里标识的全球网络连通性实际上也是与中国其他城市的联系，是由于中国公司的榜上有名才会出现这种情况，比如中国最大的银行也是世界最强的 75 家金融机构之一。所以，尽管这里的数据呈现的是全球网络，但像武汉这样的城市真正与其建立联系的并不是国际公司，而是中国的公司。所有中国的公司都有一种本地化的倾向，这很正常，同时这也表现出中国公司强大的国际影响力。此外，从这个表中也可以看出一种有内在关联性的模型或集群，因为这种集群的存在，世界上主要的城市都会愿意与中国城市建立联系。同样，通过这些联系我们也可以看出，台湾城市与大陆城市的联系还是比较少。

表2

排名	城市	全球化值	排名	城市	全球化值
1	香港	3.2	10	深圳	0.2
2	上海	2.9	11	大连	0.2
3	北京	2.9	12	青岛	0.2
4	台北	1.3	13	杭州	0.1
5	天津	1.3	14	西安	-0.3
6	重庆	0.8	15	厦门	-0.4
7	广州	0.8	16	南京	-0.5
8	武汉	0.7	17	澳门	-1.1
9	成都	0.3	18	高雄	-1.4

我们从 2000 年开始收集数据，在这一过程中也做了很多分析。我们可以比较城市在国际排名中的变化。以上海为例，它现在是前 10 位的城市，但是 2000 年的时候它还未挤进前 10，所以我们可以得出城市不同的发展轨迹。除此之外，在这些表中都可以发现，2000 年至今，每一个中国城市的连通性都呈上升趋势。这一点都不奇怪，但奇怪的是香港、上海和北京一直位列前三。南京和上海都变得越来越国际化，但上海作为一个发展很快的城市一直表现出众，与其他城市的联系也更广泛。北京和大连也是如此，都发展很快，但北京的表现更让人称道。同时，许多分析家预测，香港在未来将会经历一个过渡期，它的发展可能会有所停滞。但实际情况并非如此，尽管自 2000 年起香港就一直表现出众，但如果与它现在的国际地位相比，香港仍然在国际连通和交往中获益颇多，且表现越来越好。

上面简要介绍了关于这个议题我们可以开展的研究工作，主要集中在中国城市的连通情况，如果研究跨国城市间的联系也可以采用这种方法，选取一个生产服务性公司作为切入点进行分析。

城市跨文化交际能力：
全球城市的重要标杆

陆建非

上海师范大学校务委员会主任、教授

　　今天的话题是全球城市，或者叫世界城市，这改变了我们原先的一个说法，就是上海是国际化的大都市，但今后我们试图要建成一个全球城市。我今天要跟大家交流的，就是如何从跨文化交际的角度来看待建设全球城市。

　　上世纪 50 年代，美国人类文化学家爱德华·霍尔在其里程碑的著作《无声的语言》中首先提出了 "intercultural communication" 这个词，就是跨文化交际或者交流，来自不同文化背景的个人和群体之间进行交流。今天到了全球化的时代，我想城市的跨文化交际能力应该进一步提出来。城市的跨文化交际能力，首先是市民的跨文化沟通能力，包括语言交往能力、非语言交往能力、文化能力。此外还有城市本身，涉及城市的硬实力如地理位置、自然环境等，还有软实力如对外宣传、公共服务等。

　　市民的语言交往能力肯定是非常重要的，所以我觉得是跨文化交际能力的一个基石。上海的外籍人员覆盖了 214 个不同的国家和地区，这是最新的数据，而外籍常住人口超过千人的国家达到 20 个。我觉得全球城市的衡量指标既包括对高素质外语复合型人才的要求，也包含对普通市民外语水平尤其是强势语言英语的交往能力的要求。英语作为一个世界通用语言，在国际交往中起了很大作用，所以通过市民英语水平的提高，就可以更好地为来沪外籍人士提供便捷的学习、工作和生活环境。当然专业人士如果精通英语，也可以及时了解和交流各个领域的前沿动态。这里我想谈一点，就是从全球城市角度来说，我们的语种不能太单一。现在最多的就是三种话：上海话，普通话，再加上英语，显然是不够的，也要有其他很多语言如法语、西班牙语、葡萄牙语、日语等等。要在市民中普及英语，我觉得基础需要在学校里面夯实。以前有一个争论，英语该不该退出高考，最后结果是英语不但没有退出高考，在上海地区，英语和数学以及语文紧紧地捆绑在一起，继续在 6 月考。上海到 2017 年还要把口语测试、听力测试和笔试捆绑在一起，我觉得也是一个巨大的进步。另外还有一点，在语言交往当中，我们经常讲叫 "understand and be understood"，你懂人家，但现在更重要的是，中国的智慧如何用世界的表达来传播，我们民族的故事如何讲给世界各国的人听，让他们听得懂。这不仅仅是语言的问题，其实是跨文化交际当中，你对对方的语言文化以及外国人对我们的语言文化的通晓程度。

我觉得市民的非语言交际能力也是非常重要的。一切不使用语言进行交际的活动统称非语言交际。在日常交往中，其实肢体语言所占比重要超过一半，其余 38% 是有声音的，8% 是真正的文字、书面语。这些非语言交际方式比如手势、身势、面部表情，对空间的使用，审美情趣等，如果处理得不好，会发生一些文化误解、文化冲突。我觉得上海市民在公共空间所展示的文明素养，实际是上海城市形象的一个窗口。如果市民有一些不文明的行为，就会给城市形象蒙上阴影，使域外者产生一种不适感。这在日常生活当中也是挺常见的，比方大声喧哗，无适度的体距感，公共场所吸烟，乱扔垃圾，随地吐痰，随意拍照，车不让人，乱鸣喇叭。我觉得上海在全球城市的建设过程当中，要强化市民的法制观念和公共道德意识，要提高跨文化交际能力，充分发挥广大市民的主体作用，就要从具体抓起，比如提高公共空间的意识，这是一个非常关键的环节。

文化能力如果用的好的话，实际上体现了城市交际者的灵活性和适用性。这种交际能力是指交际者与不同文化和社会经济背景的人进行有效沟通和互动的能力，包括交际者对自我文化、本族文化、异域文化的感知，对本族文化和外来文化的认知水平，特别是对待文化差异的态度以及出现一些文化上的碰撞、休克时如何去适应、去理解和适当处理。我觉得上海在建设全球城市的过程当中，一定要提升城市的亲和力，使域外的人到了上海感觉好像到了家乡。上海在城市跨文化交际中，需要积极主动地推介和传播富有个性的城市品牌。上海有很多的优势，包括地方特色、人文的积淀，城市规划做得相对也不错，但是我们在个性方面、在特质方面的构建显然还不够，给外国人留下的印象还不是十分深刻。在传播地域特色文化的同时，我们既要关照和兼容人类的共性、城市的共性，也要产生或者制造一些惊喜、惊奇，这样就会使外来客油然而生一种亲近感和归属感。

宜居性和亲和性是城市环境的硬实力。上海四季分明，地处海滨，但污染情况不容乐观,经常困扰着上海。这方面我觉得有不少工作要做,特别是治污规划和一些指标体系要超前,不能和内地相比较,因为我们要向全球城市迈进。此外,在气象预报方面要进一步完善指标体系,比方说紫外线指数,夏天的旅游者对此是非常关注的,还有出行指数、旅游指数、洗晒指数,包括水质状况、污染指数等等。

规范化和国际化是城市公共服务的软实力,我觉得它决定了生活在这座城市的各个文化群体的认同感和幸福感。如果一些做法违反了通常的国际惯例,人们可能就不太接受,甚至有一些局促不安。比如城市的标识翻译,上海的情况总体上还不错,但不少公共标识尤其是路牌、路标、门牌和指示牌破旧、损坏的比较多,符号不清晰的也比较多,尤其是翻译不恰当的更多。我们喜欢用"WC",但在国外很多地方基本上看不到"WC",因为它的意思就是"water closet",即抽水马桶,按照国际惯例我想可以用更委婉的词"restroom"取代"WC"。再举几个例子,中国在标识语方面经常讲"禁止什么""严禁什么""不许什么",是不是也可以委婉一点呢,像顾客止步可以用"Staff Only"。有些甚至是误解,像"当心碰头"翻译成"Look after your head"的非常多,特别是在旅游景点,非常好笑。我觉得还是要规范,要得体,要按照外国人的习惯来表述。比如"老、弱、病、残、孕者专座",这在国外是很少看到的,因为给人贴标签,显然是不礼貌的,当然我们中国文化对这个很讲究。因此我觉得不要拘泥于我们的传统表达,可能稍微放开一点,翻译成"Offer seats for those who need help"可能更好一点。现在地铁上已经做到了,但是很多公交车、包括在很多其他的城市当中,给"老、弱、病、残、孕"贴标签,这种做法还是比较常见的。

我觉得,城市信息的对外速递也是很重要的,"速递"就要快,翻译是来不及的,现在上海就两种英文报纸,一个 Shanghai Star,一个 Shanghai Daily,还有 ICS 一个外语频道,这显然不够,和香港相比距离还是蛮大的。因此要创设更多的英语媒体,建设更多的英语网站,及时更新。在涉外写字楼、国际酒店、公共交通工具中电子屏幕也要用双语。另外要组织专人绘制双语的交通地图、文化地图,而且要有专门机构进行管理、审核、检查,这样就提高了国际化语言环境的纯度。像法语、西班牙等语言以后也应该在上海大力鼓励使用。

上海的公共服务设施基本还是可以的,但是在无障碍化服务方面还亟待改善,包括停车、行走、专座等等还是有一定距离。垃圾分类与东京相比也有相当大的距离。最近强生推出了英伦"土豪金"出租车，非常受欢迎，它好在什么地方呢？一是宽敞，二是及时，第三，司机穿西装、系领带、戴白手套，服务非常像英国出租车。因此大家除了惊喜之外，愿意付同样的钱或者稍微贵一点，来接受这种标准的国际化服务，从而有一种舒适的感觉。

关于城市跨文化交际能力，我觉得有四个重要的考量：第一是顺畅，就是到了这个地方办事很顺，没有障碍，这个不仅仅是手续上的顺，还有情感上的顺，语言上的顺。第二是得体，不亢不卑，非常自如。我想这也是上海今后在市民教育中，在城市文化构建中要提倡的。第三是愉悦性，就是非常高兴，有一种回头再来访问的感觉，有一种回到本土的感觉，有一种憧憬，一种美好的回忆。最后一个就是有效性。我们很多服务设施其实有效性是不够的，例如，可能讲到厕所有点不登大雅之堂，但是上海厕所的规划，有些地方偏密、太多，有些地方又非常少。

总之，在城市跨文化交际中，提高自身的文化竞争力和文化亲和力是两重性的问题，但又是一脉相承、相互关联的问题。我们一方面要讲文化竞争力，和欧洲、和美国、和域外的竞争，另外一方面又要提升中华文化亲和力，给人的感觉不是咄咄逼人的，而是能够回头再来访问、能够接受的。因此我觉得在城市跨文化交际能力上要进行深入研究，这是建成全球城市的一个标杆，对于提升城市品牌非常重要，也有助于城市亲和力的形成。

城市知识创新生态系统

威廉·凡温登
荷兰阿姆斯特丹政府首席顾问

    城市化是经济发展的引擎。像上海这样规划良好的城市可以促进经济增长和创新，但是要想成为全球城市，还有更多方面的考量。城市的建设不仅仅在于土地和人口的扩张，更在于城市的智能化。我认为除了扩大城市规模、建立新的交通体系等，我们需要新的城市发展方案。如何将城市市民、公司以及大学等更好地关联在一起，促进城市经济绩效的提升，这是一个很大的挑战。我们做了很多这方面的研究。如何使一个城市更加智慧？这个"智慧"本身不仅仅是指应用更多的高新科技，更多的是指能够将城市所拥有的各种资源更好地关联在一起。

    首先，我想回到最基本的一个话题，那就是规模经济。对城市而言，城市规模的益处也可以叫集聚经济的益处，换句话说，就是相较于居住在一个小村庄来说，居住在一个大城市集聚经济体所带来的好处。不管是公司也好个人也好，如果你居住在一个大城市中，那么你就离各种活动更近一些，离最新的事物更近一些，也能更快更好地了解这个世界正在发生什么样的变化，这将会帮助你成为更有创新能力的公司或个人。另外一点，在大城市中，跳槽是普遍现象，人们带着自己的知识和经验更换工作，就使得知识信息和新事物能够快速地从一个公司传播到另一个公司。因此，大城市的各种人才和大的人口密度能够为新关联的建立提供可能。正像著名经济学家熊彼特所说，大城市为新的组合和创新提供了条件。

    那么问题是大城市应该多大，多大才够大？我想这对于上海来说也是一个关键问题。有的人可能会强调正在进行的城市化的消极影响，觉得城市化使更多的人涌入城市，会造成诸如贫民窟等问题，就像拉美国家的一些城市一样。但是我们也应该看到其积极的一面，在人口流入城市的同时，大批的企业家等也会涌入城市，因为他们看到了大城市的各种机会，在那里他们可以发挥自己的才智。另外，更多的人口迁移到大城市会抬高土地价格，那么这就迫使土地不够用的工厂迁出城市，被服务性产业和低污染产业所取代。我们看到许多大城市都是这样发展的，包括曼哈顿、东京、首尔和许多其他城市。像上海和东京这样的大都市会吸引许多富有创意的人。有人可能会拿各种负面影响来当作限制人口流入的借口，但是我们应该看到，这同时也是在限制各种城市新动力的输入。

另一个城市化的积极影响就是，如果城市化进程控制得好的话，资源配置会得到优化。大的人力资源市场能够达到一种更好的供需平衡。另外，人口密度大的城市通常会比无计划一味向外扩张的城市污染性更小。在这种城市中，私家车逐步被公共交通工具取代。另外，就像之前我所提到的，由于地价的上涨，许多工厂会被迫移出城市，由服务性行业等取而代之。因此，大城市会更加专业化，为新的商业活动和新型投资提供更多支持。

说到这里，我想如何管理城市发展对于任何国家来说都是至关重要的问题。发展许多小城市的同时适当限制一些大城市的规模是明智之举吗？还是应该集中力量发展像香港、北京和上海这样的大城市？关于这类话题，不仅在中国，在其他国家也已经掀起了热烈的讨论。我们已经看到自从改革开放以来，中国城市尤其是大城市的经济取得了飞快的发展。这还是在中国限制增长的情况下，因为中国对移民有所限制，许多外国人拿不到他们需要的居住许可，享受不到社会福利等，就无法在中国工作。与此同时，我们这有证据来证明集聚经济和城市密度大的积极一面。例如经济合作与发展组织最新的一个研究非常有说服力，它表明，在中国像上海和武汉这样人口密集的城市污染度要远小于其他城市。此外，就业密度越高，城市的薪资水平就越高。事实上，中国许多大城市的密度还没有像东京或首尔那么大。

这就是现在人们一直在讨论的问题，像各种技能的集聚、城市的大小等。实际上我想强调的就是城市密度固然重要，但是城市建设远不止于此。要想知道如何提高一个城市的经济绩效，我们就必须得更深入地了解刺激经济增长的重要因素：创业和革新。它们是如何在这些大城市中起作用的？知识是如何从一个公司传播到另一个公司的？工业种类彼此不同，那么在不同种类的工业环境中该如何创新？最重要的一点是，我们如何组织和建设我们的城市，才能促使更快更好地创新？这不仅仅是每平方米有更多人口或公司的问题，而是要将城市发展成一个创新的平台。我觉得"平台"这个比喻更为恰当，因为我们知道公司的创新过程已经发生了较大变化。我们可以看斯蒂芬·乔布斯的例子，他独自一人在自己的车库里研究出了新电脑，这是一个比较传统的做法——一个研究者独自在自己的实验室里面发明新东西。但如今，这已经不是新事物产生的方式了。如今的创新，实际上是一个非常开放的过程，在这个过程中不同的人、不同的公司共同合作，形成了许多网络。因此，它实际上是一个网络化的活动，我们把不同的知识相结合，把不同的人才相结合，把公司中各种技能相融合。因为如今科技的发展速度太快了，我们只能选择合作的方式来研发创新。我们知道亨利·切撒布鲁夫关于开放式创新理论的著作极富影响力，他向我们展示了高科技公司不再是闭门造车，而是越来越多地参与到这个开放式创新的网络中来，与其他公司合力创造新产品。这个开放式创新理论不仅适用于规模大的公司，也逐渐渗透到一些小企业甚至是服务业。

你可能会问：这个开放式创新模式对城市发展和规划有什么启示？我觉得启示之一就是我们已经看到，富有创新精神的人才和公司都更喜欢能轻易找到合作者的创新环境。当然，可能有人会说，现在这个全球化的环境下我们有一个全球性的网络，找合作者可能不是问题。但是就像我解释过的，同一地区的合作者是非常重要的。那么创造一个这样的环境需要什么呢？我们需要这个环境能够有助于网络的发展，有助于面对面的交流和沟通。因此我们可以看到在许多城市中建立了一种新型的创新区，将公司、酒吧、住宅、娱乐场所等集于一处，实现区域的多功能。因为这就是这些新型知识工作者所需要的，这就是创新所需要的环境。这种新型的环境需要我们精心计划，它不仅仅是将办公楼或办公大厦建在这里建在那里，它真正需要的是一个非常详尽的规划方案，能够将这些建筑与周围多功能场所融合在一起。这种新型的城市创新区正在成为城市知识经济的热点地区。我们知道我们以前建的科技园功能非常单一，只有大学和各种建筑，生活在其中也有点乏味。由于这种新的创新模式的驱使，新的创新区比科技园的装备更良好。一个很棒的例子就是在瑞典的斯德哥尔摩有这样一个新的创新区，它坐落在城市中心以南的瑟德港区。最初，并没有计划将它打造成一个科技园，然而现在它却成为了瑞典一个主要的科技中心。其实许多新创办的公司都汇集于此，像 Minecraft 和 Sportyfy 这样的公司也是出自这个区。它是一个非常好的混合性创新环境，拥有许多便利的设施、有利的条件以及高质量的公共空间。

对于城市来说，一个关键的问题就是如何去创造这种人口密度大又多样性的环境来迎合创新的需要，如何增强不同的合作伙伴之间的协同作用？我再次强调，这不是建各种工作大厦的问题，这是如何组织规划的问题，是如何用更智慧的方式将不同的人才汇聚在一起的问题。我将会向你们展示几个案例，它们都是来自我曾经研究过的城市，我认为也是在这方面做得非常棒的城市。第一个例子是关于德国的亚琛，位于德国西部的一个小城市，它有一所非常著名的科技大学，正在建一种新型校园。我们知道经典的校园建造方式就是建立许多教学楼，然后让所有教职工和学生在里面办公、学习。但是在亚琛却不是如此，他们创建了一个新的理念，使大学在伊始就能更好地与公司联系在一起。那么他们是如何做的呢？首先，他们定义几个觉得自己大学做得好的研究课题，比如说汽车工业。然后他们会邀请有关这方面的公司进驻这个汽车工业校园。因此这个大校园实际上是许多更小的迷你校园的一个集合，每个小校园都有自己的专业。每一个迷你校园又是公司、中小型企业和研究机构的一个集合，将它们集中于一个建筑楼，都能够使用相同的研究设备和实验室。并不是随便什么公司都能进驻的，在这之前公司必须与学校签订一个协议合同，商定在接下来的十年里致力于这项研究。因此，公司员工在与大学的合作过程中都勤勤恳恳。另外，公司还必须承诺派其老板来学校当客座教授，作为回馈，公司的员工也可以交比较少的学费来大学修研究生的课程。所以从一开始他们就致力于建设这种新型的校园商业与研究的结构性协作。这种新型校园的结果已经表明是非常好的。这所大学已经吸引了100家公司前来合作，许多来自慕尼黑、斯图加特，也有不少来自国外。这些公司对这种新型校园非常感兴趣，因为他们知道一旦进驻，就会离一流的学生、一流的人才更近，所谓"近水楼台先得月"。同时他们也对这种合作研究兴趣浓厚。我想说建设这样的环境在于有一个好的观念的引导，而不是盲目建筑。

第二个例子就是芬兰坦佩雷的例子。坦佩雷也是一个非常小的城镇，它拥有三所大学。这个城镇一直致力于将学生在大学里的功课更好地与城市的需要契合。他们创造了一个叫 DEMOLA 的结构，实际上可以把它看作是一个中介机构，它将大学和公司、城市联系在一起。我来讲一下它的运作模式。这个城市里的公司可以提出问题，表达陈述自己的问题或者他们想要做的事情。例如英特尔，芯片制造公司，他们想做一个系统来记录公交车的行驶轨迹。他们就提出了这样的问题，想要做一个这方面的调查研究。然后学生可以申请来解决这一问题。他们可以组成一个团队，融合不同专业的学生，共同撰写论文来解决这个非常实际、具体的问题。从这个实践过程中，学生可以学到很多知识，英特尔公司能从学生的论文中得到自己想了解的东西，坦佩雷这个城市更能从中受益，因为这个工作为城市发展增添了动力。实际上，他们是将大学看作一种非常有价值的资源并且很好地利用起来了，我觉得这是非常智慧的一个举动。在坦佩雷，他们不仅将大学看作是一个教育的中心，更是将其看作公司盈利和解决城市问题的一个有效资源。有趣的是，做这些工作的学生都是有着聪明潜质的，一旦成功，可能会变得很富有，实际上他们中有些人的确已经变得很富有了。

第三个关于我所说的智慧城市的例子就是创客空间。你会在越来越多的城市中看到它的身影。它是一个有着许多机器、各种设备的地方，任何喜欢创造创新的人都可以走进那里，创造出一些新东西。这也是让普通大众参与到知识经济建设中来的一种好方式。我举一个来自巴塞罗那的例子。有一个孩子每天都得给养的植物浇水，他的妈妈总是叮嘱他每天记得浇水。他觉得天天浇水很乏味，就想做一个自动化的浇水系统。于是他来到了创客空间，并把这一想法告诉了那里的负责人。然后创客空间就联系了一个大学退休教授以及其他一些专家，共同来想办法。最终，他们利用空间的机器设备，设计出了一个小型的自动浇水系统，满足了这个孩子的想法。这是一个非常简单的事情，现在越来越多的人走进创客空间，因为非常有趣，也非常有吸引力。

最后我想做个简单的总结。我们讨论的是集聚现象和人口密度等问题，根据集聚理论，城市密度越高，集聚程度越高，就越能产生积极效应，也可能减少拥挤现象，因为许多制造业会被迫移出城市等。但是对于想要城市持续发展和繁荣的城市管理者来说，该做的不仅仅是扩张城市、建设交通运输系统等。如今的开放型创新趋势要求城市变成一个创新的平台。我提到的一些例子也说明了这一点。我想亚琛大学的校长懂得一个好的校园并不只是大学各个部门的集合，他将大学校园设计成一个商业和科学有效交流的平台，硕果累累。芬兰坦佩雷的例子让我们看到简单又经济的干预既能释放大学生创意的潜能和创业的力量，又能够帮助机构创新。创客空间的例子告诉我们创新并不仅限于学术领域和高科技公司，每个平凡人都能成为创新者，每个人都能参与创新，无论老少。这种民众参与创新的景象真是激动人心。因此，我认为城市繁荣和创新依赖于这种新的观念。只有鼓励这种组织创新或软创新，城市才会有光明的未来。

世界旅游城市建设与品牌形象

张 辉

北京交通大学教授

"上海 2050 年"这个题目对我们来讲是个很尴尬的题目。因为对于我这个岁数的人而言,身体好一点能活到,身体不好一点就活不到。活不到的时候可以预测,因为身后自有人去评价。但如果能活到就不好去预测,因为作为一个预测来讲,它是有风险的。世界旅游组织曾经云集了一大批专家,包括旅游、市场、经济、社会等领域专家,在预测世界旅游发展趋势的时候,他们认为到 2020 年,中国是继美国、德国、日本之后第四大出境国。结果这一预测发表不到几年,2002 年我国就超越了日本,2005年超越了德国,并在 2008 年超越美国成为世界第一大出境国。所以在很多情况下,做预测是比较困难的。就今天的主题来说,2050 年上海到底是一个什么样的状态?由于城市的发展是各种力量博弈的结合,因此这里我不想做这个预测。

我们首先思考一个问题,城市未来发展方向是什么?刚才很多专家学者都对城市进行了描绘,包括经济学家、社会学家还有城市规划师都在考虑城市的发展方向到底是什么。从我的观点来看,未来城市发展的方向就是一个旅游化的方向。可能这一讲大家都觉得很突然,我们现在城市是朝着工业化发展的,你怎么提出了个旅游化?那么我就从城市的雏形开始谈起。我们从中文去理解城市,它是两个概念,一个是"城",一个是"市"。

"城"最早是一个防御的功能。在游牧社会以前没有城的概念,因为它是移动式的生产方式,从而会产生移动式的生活方式。成吉思汗曾统治了全世界三分之二的版图,但是成吉思汗的陵墓你是找不到的,因为他是一种移动式的生活方式。"城"的概念是人类社会进入到农耕社会之后才出现的,它是一个政治的象征。在中国的古代,"城"都有东南西北四个门，以"城"这个政治概念控制整个乡村，就是说乡村的各种资源包括人口都是通过城来控制的，谁占了这个城就等于占了一片疆土。所以，城在那时是一种政治象征，它的表面形式就是军事防御功能，而目的是控制整个乡村。当时的城市是没有很多人的，大部分是为整个周边乡村的人服务的。

再一个就是"市"，交换的场所。既然你为这样一个乡村服务，那么在商品经济的条件下，人们是需要进行交换的，所以城市的概念当时就这样逐渐形成了。农耕时代城市就已经出现了，但是功能主要局限在军事防御和举行祭祀仪式，它不具有生产功能，只是一个消费中心。每个城市和它控制的农村构成了小的单位，是相对封闭、自给自足的一种社会形式。

所以，从这点来看，早期的城市是一个以贸易和防御为核心的空间，它的主要功能是为周边乡村提供贸易服务，其生产功能是弱化的。

城市的最大变化是工业革命以后，工业化后城市化进程大大加快，大量农民涌向了城市，涌向了一个新的工业中心，所以城市获得了前所未有的发展。在第一次世界大战前夕，英国、法国、德国、美国等西方国家绝大部分人口都生活在城市里。到现在世界上二分之一的人口生活在城市。所以，它既是一个人口的集中地，也是文明的象征。这种情况下城市发生了两个重大变化。第一，城市的功能由原来的政治中心转向了经济中心；第二，城市为周边乡村服务转向了为城市定居者服务。这两个变化决定了未来城市的基本走向。这种变化会带来什么问题呢？由于工业化的挤压，城市成为一个工业化的空间载体。工业生产方式使整个社会的财富成几何式增长，这就为劳动时间的缩短创造了很好的条件。所以伴随着城市的发展，劳动者的劳动时间逐渐减少，而自由时间越来越多了。在这样的情况下再加上工业化生产方式使人们的劳动不具有幸福感，于是围绕人们放松和娱乐的休闲产业便产生了。

所以可以这样讲，休闲是工业化生产挤压下的一种定居者的生活方式，它是与工业化的生产方式相对应的一种生活方式。当工业化促进了城市化以后，人们对惯常环境产生了厌倦，也必然会产生对空间的消费，使城市进入一个旅游化时代。人类社会可以分为三个类别，一个是游牧社会，一个是农耕社会，一个是工业社会。三个社会的不同在于生产方式的不同，游牧社会是移动式的生产方式，农耕社会是定居式的生产方式，工业社会我给它起了个名字，叫"移居式"的生产方式。特别是在互联网和移动办公不断发展以后，这种移居式的生产方式和对应的生活方式将会进一步放大，于是城市就进入了旅游化时代。在这个时代，城市逐步从为定居者服务转向为移动者和定居者双重服务。比如像北京，如果用常住人口除绿地、公共厕所、广场等等，我们是绰绰有余的，因为北京只有两千万人口。但是北京一年的国内旅游者是 2.6 亿人，如果用 2.6 亿一除，我们会发现厕所不够了，广场不够了，停车场也不够了，什么都不够了。也就是说，这个城市原先是为定居者服务，而未来的城市应该朝着既为定居者服务也为移居者服务的双重职能发展。我想这是很重要的一个旅游化的表现。

我们总结一下，工业化创造了休闲，城市化创造了旅游。休闲是工业化发展的产物，旅游是城市化发展的结果。两者都是工业化生产方式下城市居民的生活方式。工业化越发达，城市化程度越高，居民休闲和旅游的生活方式就越普遍。这就是为什么上世纪 90 年代中期，旅游成为世界第一大产业的主要原因。进一步概括起来说，有这么一些观点。随着人类社会进化，城市的功能也在演化。城市功能是沿着军事化、商业化和旅游化方向不断进化和发展的，农耕社会的城市呈现军事化和商业化的形态，工业社会呈现商业化和休闲化的形态，后工业社会呈现旅游化的形态。所以农耕社会的城市是为周边乡村服务的，工业社会的城市是为定居者服务的，后工业城市是为移居者和定居者服务的。

从当前世界的发展趋势看，我们有很多数据去证明。一是服务经济在整个经济的占比不断提高，二是服务业的产值在整个 GDP 中的比重不断增强，三是服务业从业人员占比不断提高。比如，发达国家城市服务业的占比都在 85% 以上，第三产业人数在就业人员中的比重也都在 80% 以上，我们还有很大差距。所以这是一个旅游化的过程，我们的城市建设就要朝着这个方向不断调整城市功能，实现未来的进一步发展。

全球城市旅游目的地形象建设

诺埃尔·斯科特

澳大利亚格里菲斯大学教授

首先我想简单谈谈我个人在澳洲的一些工作经验，以及澳洲旅游业的几个例子。在我看来，上海可视为旅游城市中的一个典范。一个旅游城市的声望与形象是建立在城市自身基础之上的。因此，我们应该充分认识到造就一个良好城市的一些基本因素，这些因素包括：城市风貌、城市给予人们的体验、城市组织以及城市居民。

那么接下来，我们应该做的是如何寻找一个旅游品牌，并通过广告来吸引游客们的注意力。因此，我今天主要想通过一些例子来告诉大家我所在的城市及澳大利亚其他城市是如何在这方面取得成功的。就旅游业而言，我们需要明白以下几点；首先，旅游业是一个零碎的产业，它并没有太多规模庞大的组织。此外，大部分和旅游业挂钩的机构均为政府组织。例如在中国，主要的旅游机构分别为：中国国家旅游管理局、地区和地方旅游机构等。倘若想让旅游业成为一个高效率的产业，不同的组织之间必须相互合作。

打造一个共同的旅游品牌是让这些不同组织进行合作的最有效途径之一。同时，这也是提高一个城市、地区乃至国家声誉的最好方式。要做到这一点，我们必须和不同组织进行沟通，并加强各个层面的协调。在澳洲，我们有一个叫做澳洲旅游的机构，它等同于中国的国家旅游局。该机构致力于组织协调各州、各地区的旅游品牌打造工作，从而确保不同品牌相互衔接，这就是所谓的品牌构建。被打造出的品牌不仅要能够向游客展现澳洲的整体风貌，还要能够展现出澳洲人独有的求真务实、热爱友谊、幽默风趣、积极向上的特征。不管是对昆士兰，还是对布里斯班的黄金海岸做旅游宣传时，这些旅游品牌形象都会被包含在宣传内容之中。

为了说明协同的重要性，我举几个例子。比如，过去昆士兰有"昆士兰旅游局"和"昆士兰赛事"两家旅游机构，为了提高机构之间的协调性，它们最终进行了合并。合并以后，昆士兰旅游局不断通过举办各种赛事以提高自身影响力。再比如，旅游业和许多国家部门相关联，例如与农业部、交通部等。为了加强协调，昆士兰政府建立了一个旅游内阁，该内阁由与旅游业有关的各部门代表组成，定期召开会议就旅游业发展进行协调。

对于一个城市的旅游业发展而言，良好的基础设施也非常重要。似乎每一个大都市都有独特吸引力的设施，例如巴黎的艾佛尔铁塔、旧金山的金门大桥等。那么布里斯班有什么呢？布里斯班一直把自身定义为一个阳光明媚的休闲城市，于是我们就在想如何将这一理念传达给游客？应该建造什么样的基础设施以打造我们的城市形象呢？最终，我们在城市中央建立了一个免费沙滩。这样，游客们在沙滩游玩时，市中心的整个风貌都会映入眼帘。在我看来，这个市中心的黄金沙滩便是布里斯班旅游目的地形象。这一形象和品牌的打造并不是无意间产生的，它是有意识建设的成果。

当然，城市品牌的打造也可以通过举办大型活动。如同上海举办了2010年世博会一样，布里斯班也曾举办了"英联邦运动会"。这些大型赛事项目意义重大，因为它们会树立城市的形象。在这些赛事和项目的推动下，游客们会认识一座城市，从而去定义这座城市是属于体育氛围浓厚型还是属于文化氛围浓厚型的城市等。

除此之外，还要提到的一点是游客的感受和体会。我的同事珍妮和高教授正在研究"品牌承诺及品牌感受"，也就是当游客来到一个城市时的内心感受。布里斯班选择了和纽约相同的理念，这一理念就是，我们的品牌应该流露出一种真实的情感，去建造深受居民和游客喜欢的城市。那么，我们想让城市给游客留下什么样的感受呢？最近我们正在做一个研究，内容是什么样的旅游经历能给游客带来快乐的体验。记得很久以前，我和珍妮以及马博士一同在上海，当时去了一家餐厅，它给我留下印象最深刻的并不是美味佳肴，而是别出心裁的设计。如果你想打开饭店的大门，那么必须将你的手伸入门壁上的许多洞口中。如果你把手伸入错误的洞口，那么打开后你会看到一面镜子，这突然出现的镜子会吓你一跳。如果选择的洞是正确的，那么你便能毫无障碍地走进饭店。在旅游业中也是如此，我们要和游客一同开发新的体验，打造出像那家餐厅带给游客一样的全新感受。再举一个布里斯班的例子，在布里斯班原来有一座桥，可是一个富有创造力的企业家突然发现这除了是一座桥以外，还可以给人们带来冒险的体验。如今，你可以在那座高耸的大桥顶部一边行走欣赏布里斯班城市的风貌，一边感受高空行走带来的刺激。

在布里斯班，我们发现许多中国游客并不喜欢在大海里游泳，也不怎么喜欢在海上冲浪。但同时我又发现游客们是那么喜欢沙滩，几乎对所有的中国游客而言，当他们到达黄金沙滩时想做的第一件事就是在沙滩上漫步。那么我们如何适应中国游客的需求，创造新的旅游产品呢？一个办法是举办"沙滩文化节"。如此一来，一些不愿意下海游泳或冲浪的中国游客就可以通过参与这个活动在海边与他人互动，从而获得更多的旅游体验。对于上海而言，我认为大部分旅游产品都是为国内游客设计的，如何使这些产品对西方游客更有吸引力？这是个值得思考的问题。

我再谈谈旅游品牌的打造。过去我们在规划布里斯班的旅游品牌时，发现它并不被国际游客所看好。虽然布里斯班是一个很好的交通枢纽，但它在澳洲市场上并没有一个强有力的形象，于是我们在考虑怎么将自己推销出去。通过对酒店居住记录进行分析，我们发现周末的入住率最高，许多周边的游客都会来布里斯班过周末，这让我们发现了一个新的市场。不久，我们提出了一个全新的旅游品牌"周末之城——布里斯班"，它是个休闲旅游品牌。我们通过媒体对这个新品牌进行了大量报道，让游客知道布里斯班是一个充满阳光和温暖的地方，游客们能在那里寻找到许多乐趣。2014年，我们把布里斯班纯粹休闲的旅游形象逐渐转化成了以娱乐业为主的城市夜生活形象。尤其是越来越多地通过互联网进行旅游品牌的宣传。毫无疑问，这是当前旅游品牌宣传中最流行的方法。

我想强调的是，城市品牌打造是一个艰巨的任务，需要旅游组织、政府机构、高等学府之间的紧密合作。如果我们想打造一个文化多元、夜生活丰富的上海，就需要找到城市独特的吸引力所在，并充分考虑它带给游客的感受。我们需要充分认识品牌的重要性，通过创造性的思维来打造独特的旅游品牌。

上海：面向全球城市的思考

宁越敏

华东师范大学现代城市研究中心教授

今天我想谈谈上海最近二十多年的变化，以及未来 2050 年迈向全球城市发展目标的时候，它可能会是什么样子。首先要介绍一下世界城市或全球城市领域两个最著名的学者。我们知道，尽管英国学者皮特·霍尔在 1966 年就写了一本有关全球城市或者世界城市的书，但是把它进行理论化的是约翰·弗里德曼。约翰·弗里德曼和他的同事伍尔夫在 1982 年发表了一篇很重要的论文，1986 年弗里德曼又发表了一篇关于世界城市假说的论文。我想弗里德曼的理论框架是建立在沃勒斯坦的世界体系理论基础上的。沃勒斯坦的世界体系把世界分成三个部分，就是核心国家、半边缘国家和边缘国家。为什么分成这三个部分呢？因为他认为有一些国家居于半边缘的国家，进一步的发展才可能进入到核心国家行列中。那么反过来，核心国家如果衰落的话，它可能会降落到半边缘的国家，半边缘国家是不成熟的，处在世界体系的边缘。弗里德曼在借用这样一个假说的基础上，提出一个世界城市的理论，他特别强调世界城市对于国际或者是区域性资本的控制能力。因此他认为企业总部或者国际组织以及金融机构是判定世界城市的一个核心要素。由于在 20 世纪 80 年代的时候，整个中国的经济还没有和世界经济体系紧密地联系，所以在弗里德曼的世界城市体系中没有中国的城市。同时，弗里德曼还有一个很重要的观点，他认为除了资本，特别是金融资本的控制力以外，这个城市能不能为世界市场提供产品也是一个很重要的功能。

20 世纪 90 年代，萨森借鉴了世界城市的思想后，提出了全球城市的概念。我要特别强调，他提出的全球城市概念，他认为是生产服务业，今天我们又把它进一步说成是先进生产服务业也就是 APS，它才是全球城市最重要的功能。这是它主要的背景，是一个全球化的背景。特别是在 90

年代初，也就是所谓的华盛顿共识以后，整个国际社会弥漫了一种新自由主义思潮。这种所谓的新自由主义是什么呢？实际上就是要减少政府的干预，减少国家的干预，让资本在全球扩张。所以萨森这个全球城市概念的提出，配合了新自由主义的思潮，这个背景在座的很多中国学生可能并不熟悉。

那么在这样一个扩张当中，它的结构是什么呢？我们看到像纽约、伦敦、东京成为了一个顶级的城市。在这个概念的基础上，加上卡斯特尔提出的流动空间，这些概念被皮特·泰勒他们所接受，因此从 90 年代开始他们建立了一个全球化和世界城市的研究小组。前面比利时学者已经介绍了他们所使用的大量数据，这些数据建立在哪些基本点上呢？它的生产服务业 APS 只包括了五个部门，这五个部门包括金融、银行、保险、咨询和会计。我们看看这些公司是哪些国家所有的呢？基本上是美国所垄断的。所以在他们研究里面这个很有意思，他们采用了社会网络分析法，把世界看成是一个网络。在他们的研究中，上海的地位在不断地提升。但实际上，上海的地位是不是真的已经达到了这样一个等级呢？我们来看看弗里德曼的世界城市假说是否已经过时了。这是弗里德曼在 1986 年的一篇文章，他把世界分成核心国家和半边缘国家。在核心国家中，又把城市分成了第一级别的世界城市和第二级别的世界城市。同样，在半边缘国家也有第一级别和第二级别这样不同等级的世界城市。但是我们看到在萨森的全球化背景中，核心国家的概念没有了，半边缘国家的概念也没有了，好像世界是平的，因为它变成了一个网络，但是支配性完全被忽略了。实际上我们可以看到，在新自由主义的这种思潮影响下，跨国公司面向全球布局时，由于发达国家本身就拥有大量的跨国公司，它们在整个世界经济体系里仍然居于支配性地位。按照世界城市网络体系世界 WC2012 年的研究结果，伦敦和纽约是位于第一等级的，然后上海和北京分别位于第六和第八等级。但是，我想提醒的是，假如我增加一个新的 APS 的行业，比如说我们知道现在是互联网时代，而 APS 里面并没有包含互联网的公司，假如把互联网公司比方谷歌、Twitter、Facebook 也包括进去的话，中国在这个世界网络当中的链接会是什么样的？我们自己对上海和北京在世界城市体系中的地位要有一个清醒的认识。关于世界城市的这项研究中，2000 年的数据显示，上海排第 31 位，2010 年跃升到了第 6 位。但这仅仅是在五个行业里面上海的一个连接度，我要特别强调的是实际上这是跨国公司的全球连接，而在这五个行业的跨国公司里基本上是没有中国公司的。所以我们看世界城市体系其实我们还是要回归到弗里德曼的时代，这个世界仍然是个不平等的世界，仍然是核心国家支配的世界经济体系。如果我们运用其他的一些研究机构的研究成果，比如说像美国《外交政策》，这是一份非常权威的杂志，它有一个全球城市的排行榜，另外像日本东京有一个东京墨里基金会，他们也经常对全球城市进行排名，我们可以看到在他们的排名里上海的实力其实还是相当低的。比如说《外交政策》的排名中，上海从2008年到2012年的地位反而下降了一位，按照经济实力的话上海居第21位。在日本墨里基金会的全球城市实力指数排名里，总体来说上海得分稍微高一点，但排名也是在第20位。也就是说从目前的发展水平来看，上海也好，北京也好，和其他世界城市间的发展差距仍然是相当大的。

在这样的一个背景下，我们再来看上海到底如何定位自己的发展目标。我先举一下上海目前发展当中的三个问题：第一个问题就是上海的经济总量在全国的比例是逐渐下降的。在1978年的时候，上海的地区生产总值占全国GDP的比例是7.48%。当然我们可以说，在1978年中国大部分地区经济发展比较落后，所以使得上海的经济实力看上去特别强，那么随着中国其他地方经济的发展，上海的GDP占全国的比例逐渐下降，特别是80年代下降比较厉害。到90年代的时候，由于中国全面改革开放，大量的跨国公司到中国来投资，上海是一个优先的地方，因为它的区位条件特别好，所以在90年代的时候，上海的经济总量占全国的比重是提升的。但是2000年以后整个中国的经济向中西部地区发展，所以从2000年到2013年这个比例下降了一个百分点。最近几年，上海的经济增长速度低于全国的平均速度，这个趋势还将会持续。我们估计可能至少持续一年以上的时间。

第二个问题就是世界城市也好，全球城市也好，我们在研究这些概念的时候，总部和总部的数量可以看成很重要的指标，假如我们从这个指标来看上海和北京的话，两者的发展差距是越来越大的。这种发展的差距是从2004年以后出现的。我们可以看今年美国《财富杂志》公布的世界五百强数据，在世界五百强里面，中国内地拥有90多家，其中有52家总部位于北京，只有8家总部位于上海，这是第一个数据。我们再从营业额指标看，每家公司的平均营业额，北京是760亿美元，而上海只有470亿美元。这说明什么呢？说明上海的五百强规模比北京小很多。如果我们从先进服务业这个角度来看，金融是一个非常重要的部门。在这里面，北京拥有十家大机构，上海只拥有三家，而北京的金融机构规模平均营业额达到了790亿美元，而上海这三家金融机构的平均规模只有370亿美元。从中我们可以看到，在我们朝向全球城市这个发展目标的时候，其实上海和北京的差距已经扩大。特别是金融业，原先上海金融业在全国范围内的实力是最强的，但最近十年北京反而后来居上。比如，金融业就业人员北京有39.5万人，而上海只有30万人。再从金融业增加值看，北京达到了2 592亿元人民币，而上海是2 450亿元人民币，也低于北京。上海唯一比北京强的是国际化程度高一点。这里有一个指标，就是外资金融机构的存贷款余额，上海是9 400多亿元，而北京只有3 500多亿元。从金融业的发展我们可以看到，北京作为首都是中央银行所在地，全国最大的一些金融机构都集中在北京，因而导致北京的整体实力比上海更强一些，但国际化程度方面，上海的情况稍微好一点。

第三个问题，上海目前面临的问题是什么呢？就是它的国际化程度是比较低的，它的外资单向国际化的特点比较明显。伦敦也好，纽约也好，它们的国际化是双向的。这指的是什么呢？一方面，全球城市是本国资本对外输出的基地，同时也是吸收国际资本的一个城市。那么对中国的城市来说，上海也好，北京也好，从目前情况来看，它们主要还是吸收国际资本，而中国资本的对外输出才刚刚起步。2013年的时候，在上海的跨国公司地区总部是445家，投资性公司是283家，外资研发中心366家，这三个指标在最近十年里都是呈现迅速上升的趋势。但我们再看一下上海证券交易所，它的营业规模2011年排世界第四位，但是和纽约两家证券交易所的成交额差距还比较明显。更加重要的是在中国特有的体制下，一个公司如果要上市的话，它不是直接向上海证交所申请，而是要到北京的中央政府下面的证监会去申请。这是中国独特的一个背景。所以从这个角度来看，我们看到这个证券交易所它本身是一个市场经济的产物，但是在中国它的决策权和作为证券交易的地方是分离的。那么如果我们认为世界城市是对世界经济具有支配地位，国际经济中心对国际经济有支配地位的话，毫无疑问上海是没有这种支配地位的，有支配地位的是首都。这是因为我们目前的经济管理体制是一个集权的体制，仍然是逐步在走向市场经济。

第四个问题，上海目前的科技创新能力比较弱。刚才几位嘉宾都在谈科技创新，这里有一个非常有意思的数据。这是美国专利局公布的，如果我们检索发明人所在城市的专利数量，可以看到东京的专利数量遥遥领先于其他所有城市，其次就是硅谷，也就是位于硅谷的圣何塞。国内城市排在第一位的是深圳，第二位是北京，第三位才是上海。所以我们看到即便是专利登记方面，上海也仍然落后于深圳和北京。

最后来讲一下结论。第一个结论就是目前发达国家的世界城市或全球城市在世界城市网络当中，仍然占据一个主导的地位、支配的地位。这种支配地位主要是由发达国家特别是美国在资本和科技方面的实力所决定的。弗里德曼的世界城市体系划分为核心国家和半边缘国家，我认为仍然具有现实意义。

第二个结论就是，国家在世界城市的发展当中仍然起着重要的影响作用。特别是对中国来说，中央政府在决定资源配置的时候仍然起到重要作用。这就是为什么最近十年北京在世界城市发展的重要指标方面迅速超越上海的一个非常重要的原因。

第三个结论就是，随着中国经济实力的增加，中国的世界城市将开始一个双向的国际化进程，也就是说中国的世界城市将不仅成为国际资本集聚的场所，也将成为一个中国资本对外投资辐射的场所。有一个重要的数据，就是2013年中国对外直接投资已经达到了1 078亿美元，而中国吸收的外商直接投资是1 239亿美元。根据预测，中国今年（2014年）对外投资和吸收的外资两个数据会平衡。随着中国经济的发展，中国对外投资将会越来越多。不过，中国企业的国际化方面有一个非常重要的数据，显示的是中国最具国际化的企业，也就是说对外投资最多的企业，在Top 50里面有28家总部在北京，只有三家在上海。

本世纪以来，在中国国有企业的重组过程当中，已经出现了一批以北京作为总部的中央直属企业，北京拥有的世界500强企业数量已经超过了东京，而且中国最具国际化的企业也大多聚集在北京。最近十年北京服务业的发展很快，特别是所谓的先进服务业。所以，无论是在对中国经济的支配能力还是在对世界经济的影响能力上，北京远远超过了上海，因此北京是中国最具有发展潜力的一个全球城市。而且我个人认为，北京比较符合萨森概念上的全球城市，也就是以先进服务业为导向的全球城市。那么上海怎么办呢？上海和北京的发展路径可能是不一样的，上海仍然保持着比较强大的制造业，特别是上海所在的长江三角洲是世界上最重要的制造业基地之一。我们知道，中国的出口额已经超过德国成为世界第一位，而长江三角洲的出口额占整个中国的40%。也就是说，如果我们回顾弗里德曼对世界城市的一个界定，就是世界城市对世界市场具有影响作用，那么从这个角度来讲长江三角洲对世界制造品市场的影响力远远大于北京所在的地区。所以我个人认为在未来的发展当中，中国城市以北京和上海为代表，它们的发展路径可能是不一样的，北京可能是萨森意义上的一个全球城市，以先进服务业为主，但上海可能是弗里德曼意义上的一个世界城市，也就是说对上海来说，它的生产服务业、制造业将会有同等的地位。那么从这个角度来讲，我们可以看到，北京和上海之间将会有一个功能的分工。

全球城市面临的跨文化挑战：策略与方案

庄恩平

上海大学教授

　　刚才几位专家都从不同角度谈了上海如何建设全球城市。温登教授谈到了上海或中国的人口转移到城市问题，这种转移主要是讲中国的人口向城市流动，而我今天要讲的是国际人口流入到上海。陆教授谈到了城市的跨文化能力，我认为这是提出了一个新的视角来看待城市的软实力。只要各种人聚集在一起，最后要通过互动来解决可能会出现的问题，这个问题是什么呢，就是跨文化挑战。

　　上海 2050 年建设全球城市面临的问题将是跨文化挑战，这是我的一种预判，也是当今经济全球化背景之下，各国大城市将会面临的跨文化挑战。全球城市不仅是集聚全球的社会、经济、技术、旅游资源，而且还集聚全球的人力资源，不同文化背景的人在一起共事、学习与生活，所以文化多元化的社区环境必然成为全球城市的一个特征。同时，文化差异导致的文化冲突也随之会成为全球城市治理中一个不可忽视的社会问题。由于跨文化挑战已经成为现在欧洲一些城市社会治理当中的一个难题，欧盟委员会已经采取"跨文化城市"的战略，以应对跨文化的挑战。在这里我提出三个建议：

　　第一，以全球思维审视跨文化挑战。2050 年上海成为全球城市必然吸引更多国际人士，包括国际组织、跨国公司、跨国婚姻、留学生、海外游客以及海外移民，他们将会汇集上海。难以预料外籍人口将会达到多少比例，但是我们可以确信一点，那就是全球城市必然会以国际化、多元文化、全球人力资源作为显著特征。因而，由多元文化引发的文化冲突必将成为城市的主要问题，这也是全球城市发展的必然路径。这些外籍人士带给上海的是不同的价值观念、不同的思维方式、不同的信仰与宗教、不同的行为方式。这看似会导致文化冲突，但当我们以跨文化思维审视这一趋势的时候，就能在深层次上得到一个不同的解读与预判，即正视这些文化差异与文化碰撞给上海带来的机遇。我们要看到，不同文化碰撞、不同思维碰撞、不同观念碰撞，产生的结果不是相互排斥，不是相互冲突，不是孰是孰非，而是新思想、新视野、新观点，这就是上海所需的创新思维与创新思想，创新就是在不同文化碰撞中孕育出的，那时创新城市就会初现端倪。

从不同视角看同样一个问题的时候，也许各位看到的完全是不一样的。例如一张著名的图，有人一眼看出的是个少女，但也有人看到的是个老妇。谁对谁错呢？没有对错，只有差异。如果把文化比作冰川这个概念，我们要了解的不是冰川一角，而是冰川下面隐含的无形的障碍。我们准备好了吗？我们还没准备好。所以最后我们碰到了很多问题，我们不知道是什么原因导致，其实这就是根源。同样一件事情，以不同方式、不同思维来做的时候肯定不一样。我们要做的是什么？是提高这个城市的跨文化沟通能力。我这里提出一个"文化交际"的概念，这就是一个思维方式。

英语中有句话叫做："East is east, and West is West, and never the Twain shall meet!"也就是东方是东方，西方是西方，两者不能相遇，因为一相遇就要冲突。我把这句话改成："East is east, and West is West, and the Twain can meet!"两者为什么不能相遇呢，因为一相遇就会发生冲突。因为大家恐惧文化冲突，所以要回避文化冲突，为什么要回避呢，其实根源不在于东西方文化本身，而在于我们无法驾驭文化差异，因而也就无法应对文化差异。所以说，上海未来城市能否驾驭跨文化挑战，完全取决于城市治理者是否具有驾驭跨文化城市的能力，我认为这才是未来我们上海软实力的一个问题。

第二，学习与借鉴。1992年，联合国教科文组织召开的第四十三届国际教育大会提出的跨文化教育的目的是：尊重融合，尊重文化间的差异，减少各种形式的排斥，理解其他个体和其他国家，培养学生跨文化的适应能力，帮助学生在多元文化社会当中更好地生活。2008年，欧洲委员会和欧盟委员会联合发起了"跨文化城市战略"，旨在解决欧洲一些城市面临的跨文化挑战。跨文化城市不仅仅解决文化多样性问题，它更是一个保持活力、创新力、创造力和不断发展的城市。自2008年11个城市实施跨文化战略开始，到2014年已有41个城市，如英国伦敦、爱尔兰都柏林于2009年和2010年加盟。城市发展中的跨文化问题，不仅仅是欧洲城市所面临的问题，而且是全球化社会各国城市都将面临的共性问题，因此 2010 年 1 月日本基金会和欧洲委员会在东京联合举办了"亚欧跨文化城市论坛"，跨文化城市专家都参加讨论，之后发布了《东京宣言》，旨在加强跨文化城市之间的交流与合作，共同探讨全球面临的跨文化挑战。今天这个概念已经影响到了美国、加拿大、墨西哥、韩国等国家，许多国家的专家已经开始研究这个项目。

基于欧洲跨文化城市战略理念与发展路径，上海全球城市的发展内涵是什么，文化多样性在全球城市中如何相互适应，如何互动融合，如何让城市保持活力与创新力？为此我勾画出全球城市内涵的框架图。全球城市是个概念，是城市的模式，但城市的文化是动态的，是市民推进了城市文化的发展。同样，城市文化又影响市民的视野、思维与行动。跨文化不只是一个多元文化的概念，而是不同文化之间的沟通、互动、融合的动态过程。这种动态既可产生消极效应，就是文化冲突，又可以产生积极效应，就是文化间的互动与交融。关键在于人们是否能够驾驭文化差异，推动跨文化之间的沟通，提高互动与融合跨文化的能力。我们从现在起就应该重视跨文化能力人才培养，我们的教育就应该适应未来发展的需要，所以说我们要构建以跨文化思维、跨文化能力为全球城市提供活力与创新力的社会环境，展现上海市民作为全球公民的素养，体现上海城市软实力。多元文化人口将成为未来上海城市人口中的重要组成部分，他们会渗入企业、教育社区等领域。因此，我们要将他们生活的社区、工作或学习的学校或企业打造成跨文化社区、跨文化校园、跨文化企业，这是和谐城市的重要特征。

跨文化校园。如何利用多元文化资源弥补我国教育资源的不足，如何利用这些多元资源、多元文化，营造中国校区的跨文化氛围，营造跨文化课堂，形成中外学生互动的氛围，培养他们相互学习、相互适应、相互尊重、相互容忍、相互欣赏彼此文化的意识，从而拓展我国学生全球视野，提高跨文化能力？这些问题都是教育界应该要思考的问题。

跨文化社区。提高社区工作者的跨文化能力是关键。外籍居民来自不同国家，他们都有各自的价值观念、宗教信仰、民族习俗、思维方式，沟通方式，所以他们在文化认知、生活习惯、社区需求、邻里相处等方面难免会产生误解甚至冲突。面对这些由文化差异引发的误解或矛盾，我们应如何应对与消除呢？这些问题都是国际社区所要面临的问题。我们不仅需要改变社区管理模式，更要营造社区跨文化环境，而且还要拓展社区工作者的国家视野，增强跨文化意识，学习跨文化知识，提高跨文化沟通能力。只有这样，国际社区才能成为外籍居民的乐园。

跨文化企业。中国企业将融入全球市场，参与全球经营、全球并购、全球公司管理，整合全球人力资源，提高全球竞争力，然而我国企业跨国经营与管理的最大挑战也在于跨文化的障碍。其实，文化障碍是企业跨国经营管理失败的表象原因，而其深层原因在于企业经营者缺乏跨文化的意识与跨文化的管理、沟通能力，所以当企业面对文化差异或文化冲突时，他们无所适从，因而造成巨大损失。未来跨文化障碍必定是企业国际化道路当中的主要障碍。所以创建跨文化企业，提高企业经营者的跨文化管理能力，才能消除中国企业国际化道路当中的文化障碍，提高中国企业核心竞争力。因此，培养企业经营者的跨文化能力是我们的当务之急。

最后，跨文化能力人才培养迫在眉睫。无论是中国还是世界，今天还是未来，在全球化社会中跨文化问题将会成为永久的话题，这是由经济全球化背景所决定的。只有通过跨文化能力人才的培养，让这些人才在各行各业中发挥作用，跨文化问题才能得到缓解与解决。然而，跨文化学科还是一个新兴的未得到学界重视或认可的学科，跨文化能力人才培养还未引起教育界的重视。在这里，我郑重呼吁全社会高度重视跨文化能力人才培养，为不同文化人群的和谐相处，为上海2050全球城市的明天储备与输送更多的跨文化能力人才。

互动对话

提问者: 斯蒂芬教授,我想请问一下,全球城市的发展还需要一些怎样的新的创意产业的业态? 同时,这些新的创意产业的业态对全球城市的发展具体有哪些影响,对全球城市的品牌形象建设又有哪些影响?

斯蒂芬·科拉特克: 我想说的是,关注城市的经济基础是非常重要的。我们既有传统制造业也有各种新兴创意产业,而这些产业都是城市经济基础的重要组成部分。所以我的回答是,不要仅仅依赖于金融行业、房地产和商业服务。在德国,有一些城市会有规划或政策表明该城市的经济全靠服务业或金融行业,这就导致了这些城市失去了它的工业基础,所以它的经济基础也很薄弱。此外,新兴的创意产业也是全球城市的一个重要组成部分。所以,我们现在要做的是,了解全球经济,认识城市间的联系,而这些都将在传统产业和新兴产业的发展过程中起到重要作用。我希望我回答了您的问题。

提问者: 我有一个问题要问来自荷兰阿姆斯特丹的威廉先生。我们都知道荷兰有着许多创新型城市,像阿姆斯特丹和鹿特丹等。那么您能不能跟我们分享一下,根据荷兰的城市发展经验,上海如何能够从传统的经济增长模式转变为创新型经济模式?

威廉·凡温登: 我认为这是个较难回答的问题。我想你一定也看到了上海发展得非常快,日新月异。我们也越来越多地看到,中国各方面做得有多出色,因此我们也有许多要向中国学习的地方。那么我觉得荷兰城市规划得好这一传统值得借鉴,我们不仅仅关注每个建筑,我们更关心的是将这些建筑联系在一起的公共空间。在建设一个城市之前,我们并不是随便在这里建一栋楼在那里建一栋楼,而是在最开始就有一个将城市看成一个整体的观念引导,我觉得这是非常好的一点。例如在阿姆斯特丹,有一条非常著名的运河，我们早在 16、17 世纪时就在像这样规划了。这是荷兰的一个非常悠久的传统，因为我们是一个非常小的国家，没有太多的空间，我们能做的就是把有限的空间最大限度地利用起来。我想这是你们可以借鉴的一点。另外一点就是荷兰一直以来就非常开放，也因为我们是一个贸易性的国家，自古以来就有外面的人来来往往，因此我们吸收借鉴世界各国最好的东西来为我们所用。那么在这方面我觉得中国跟荷兰是非常相似的。这个回答可能比较简短，但是我觉得学习的最好方式是去别的国家实地参观感受。你可以来阿姆斯特丹，我们可以带你看看它各方面的状况，那么你就可以决定哪些方面是对你们发展有益的。眼下这对我来说太难回答了。

提问者：宁教授，我想请问您一个关于世界城市的小问题。刚才您说，对于上海来说，如果要发展成一个全球城市这个未来目标，还是要基于先进制造业的创新和发展。但是，我们有的研究也会发现就是长三角包括上海，现在很多制造业在往外转移，中心城区可能因为生活成本比较高，所以更多地会发展一些生活性或者生产性服务业。制造业这个比例，您觉得未来应该怎么样保持平衡呢？或者在借鉴像东京这样发展比较成熟的全球城市时，上海到这样一个阶段有没有什么规律可以借鉴，去平衡这个比例呢？是保留制造业，让上海有这个创新空间？

宁越敏：我简单地回答一下，我记得多伦多大学有位教授是做城市数据库的，他在做城市数据库的时候，就面临着一个问题也就是城市的尺度问题。其实这个问题非常重要，因为上海的面积是 6 000 多平方公里，而纽约只有 800 平方公里，所以我们不能够简单地把纽约的产业结构和上海相比，因为在 800 平方公里的纽约，或者像大伦敦也就有 1 500 多平方公里，它们是不可能做什么制造业的。这是它们的服务业占比重非常高的根本原因。而中国的城市都是区域，北京也好，上海也好，全都是区域，面积都非常大，所以中心城区是以服务业为主，但是还有非常广大的郊区，这是一个根本性的区别。

总结辞

陆建非
上海师范大学校务委员会主任、教授

　　刚才大家围绕城市发展谈了许多很好的看法。上海当初能够成功申办世博会的原因有很多，其中一个就是上海提出的主题"城市，让生活更美好"，反映了人们的愿景和理想。从城市到大城市，大城市到大都市，大都市到大都市圈，这是一个现代化的标志，尤其对发展中国家来讲，城镇化越发达，现代化标志越凸显。但高度集中的城市也带来城市病的问题，例如贫民窟问题、流行病问题、拥堵、暴力、雾霾污染、贫困、车祸、抢劫、卖淫等，所以，一方面是现代化的表征，一方面又是一个悖论，是人类的万恶之源。因此在这样的背景下，上海想出了一个非常巧妙的题目，"Better City, Better Life"，在好多国家竞标的时候，这样一个宏大的命题吸引了很多投票者，因此获得了世博会的主办权。当然我并不是说获得高票数完全是这个原因引起的，但至少是有利于得分的。还有联合国宣布了51%的人口居住在城市，这也是现代化的重要进展。因此，思考大家所讲的这些问题，我们应该不仅仅把城市日作为一个纪念日，更重要的要把城市日看作一个反思日、展望日，反思我们在城镇化过程中所犯下的错误。

　　在今天的发言中，不少都涉及对全球城市和世界城市的展望。怎样才称得上是一个全球城市？如何构建一个真正的全球城市？很多专家从各个角度，试图在指标、参数、标准、要素、体系方面来论证，我想这样的论证还会持续下去，只是角度不一样。有的从产业角度，有的从旅游角度，有的从文化角度，还有的从人口角度，角度各不相同，但条条大道通罗马，这个罗马就是我们所讲的全球城市。因此，我觉得非常有趣，也非常多样，这给城市学这个领域增添了很多光彩，提供了很多新鲜的调料，也增加了很多不同的视角。

　　我印象很深刻的是，大家更聚焦的是全球城市的辐射力、全球城市的支配力、全球城市的创意、全球城市的活力、全球城市的多样性，以及全球城市的宜居性。大家的发言不太关注 GDP 了，更关注文化软实力。有专家讲到全球城市的品牌如何塑成、如何构建，讲到人口不仅仅是人口的多少，还讲到人口的多样性、人口的素养、人口的跨文化交际能力，也有一些专家讲到人口的年轻化、人口的老年化，这也为全球城市人口构造、人口分布提供了一些视角，这也是非常有意义的。另外，大家在发言中不约而同地讲到全球城市不一定在首都，全球城市不一定是沿海，全球城市不一定是大，全球城市也不一定是历史悠久，这些观点也给我们带来了很多有益的启示。

总结今天的会议，我想提供三点建议。第一，明确我们所处的时代是一个城市时代，是人类发展的新的里程碑。联合国讲到 51% 的人居住在城市，难道不就是城市时代吗？因此围绕城市理论、城市视野、城市治理、城市历史、城市基因以及城市精神的讨论，为我们以后的探索提供了更多话题。第二，我觉得今天的研讨会完全符合联合国提出的人类要实现可持续发展的目标。联合国提到的可持续发展是三个要素的协调，一是经济，二是社会，三是环境，这是一个比较大的维度。第三，无论是上世纪80 年代费尔德曼提出的理论，还是上世纪 90 年代萨森提出的理论，或是1996 年卡斯特尔提出的理论，都提出了一个难题，就是我们如何去破解全球化城市构建的难题。今天的专家来自世界各地，以后我们的研讨会还要进一步扩大范围，要用一种更宏观的眼界来看待我们面临的挑战，以集体智慧和共同行动破解难题、规划未来、分享经验、共谋发展。城市发展是各方利益博弈的结果，这个结果应该是向善、向美、向真，唯有这样，和平和发展的主题才能成为人类发展的共同主题。

Shanghai in 2050— A Megacity in Motion, But in which Direction?

Peter Karl Kresl

Prof. of Bucknell University USA

I'm going to begin by talking about something somehow speculative—the moving direction of Shanghai. For example, in 2050 will Shanghai be too large and populous to be competitive as it is today? Will our megacity going the way of dinosaurs, or will they retain our agility, vitality and creativity that will allow them to continue in their current position of command in the global hierarchy? What will social conditions be like in a city with a population of 40 million or more, most of whom were streamed in from rural areas, unable to bring with them adequate education skills and all capital. In 2050, Shanghai will certainly be a megacity, but this is all that we can without any confidence to say at this time. With a population today of 23 million inhabitants, several important uncertainties will have powerful effects on the city's future course of development. In this presentation, I propose to identify the more readily apparent of these elements of uncertainty, and to suggest how they might affect the wellbeing of the city's residents in the competitiveness of its economic sectors.

First, what does it take to be a world city? In 2011, Beijing raised this issue with regards to its own future in a conference. Huang Yan, director of Beijing municipal commission on urban planning asserted there were three elements in a world city: 1. Per capita income in excess of $15 000. 2. Global influence in politics, economy and culture. 3. Status as a center of headquarters for international organizations. In China two cities have a per capita income of roughly $15 000—Beijing and Shanghai. Beijing has global influence on politics, as does Shanghai on economics. Chinese cultural figures Lang Lang as well as many other musicians and artists and dancers have global significance. Shanghai has certainly achieved a status of site for corporate and organizational headquarters. So using Huang Yan's criteria, Shanghai qualifies as a world city.

According to Saskia Sassen, a global city had to have a decision-making and command function. John Friedmann wrote of the spatial organization of the new international division of labor but noted increased social class, migrants, and polarization. Peter Taylor focused on world cities as places that provided stimulating menu variously conceptualized for information knowledge and creativity to intersect in the production of new service commodities. Beyond this, what can one say? I'm sure there were anxieties a couple of decades ago attaching to the characteristics of a city of 20 million inhabitants. Perhaps we should now have concerns about the viability of the city with 40 or 50 million inhabitants. Tokyo has over 37 million inhabitants today and for this and other reasons, firms and international agents feel it is necessary to have a Tokyo address. But what if Shanghai is with twice its current population? We may not see a straight line expansion of more population, higher per capita income, viable income distribution, increased global economic and cultural significance, and sustainability in its various manifestations: environmental, demographic, amenity, mobility and so forth.

There are two cautionary notes here. First is the experience of cities in the industrial countries that were dominant cities until the crisis of the 1970s when the US industrial heart land became the rust belt, principally because of the change in the price of the crucial industrial import petroleum. Cities in the German Ruhr and British Midlands mirrored this collapse. Second is the change for positive, as well as negative, in the situation of many cities doing due to changes in the technologies of transportation, communication and production. Some cities did enter model logistics wrong, others right. Others lost or gained airport hub status. Manufacturing had shifted from the United States to China and now it's moving back to the United States to Mexico as production technology and labor cost had changed, and small cities can participate the extensive larger cities in global activities due to changes in communications technology. Joseph Schumpeter wrote about creative gales of destruction, where technology, price changes (the change in the price of oil, change in technology of communication and transportation) totally transformed the world economy. These creative gales of destruction destroy old economies, but new economies (if creativity is present in the situation) arrive to take their place.

So one can intelligently ask a question: what will Shanghai's competitive position be in 2050? Will some crucial elements in Shanghai's success change for the worse (price of input, change in technology)? The point of this is to argue that while Shanghai's future may be more brilliant than its recent past, there's possibility also it may be considerably less brilliant. How important is science? (The famous question in dating, hah) Will Shanghai be too large to be competitive? What is the optimal science for a city? How negatively will a few extra million residents be for Shanghai? Is Tokyo, with its 37 million, a good model for other cities? B. Begović suggested that optimal city size would probably be below 500 000, while a recent OECD study suggested that optimal city size for short term productivity effects should be about 6 million residents. No one has found 30 million residents to be the best size for a city. The conclusion offered in a report *Hot Spots 2025* issued by the magazine *the Economist* was that the top ten most competitive cities will range from the world's biggest, Tokyo (current population 37 million, who knows in 20 years), to some of the smallest, Zurich, Switzerland with an estimated population of 1.4 million. Indeed, there is no major correlation between a city's size and its competitiveness ranking in any index, no significant relationship between city size and urban competitiveness. I have found it to be the case in the studies of US cities and Li Pingfei has found this to be true also for Chinese cities.

I think following policies that will make Shanghai a rival to Tokyo as a large city would not be a sensible strategy. Planners should keep their focus on enhancing the city's competitive core, essential economic activities that make it a competitive city. The new Shanghai Free Trade Zone, China's first, is a step on the right direction. Many sectors remain restricted to foreign investment and firms and much effort need to be paid to its system innovation to make more progress. Finding Shanghai's absolute and comparative strengths and weaknesses and its role in the global economy would require an empirical study and more time than to be devoted to this task here.

Shanghai's City Attractiveness as a Global City and the Role of Leader Firms

Leo van den Berg

Prof. of Erasmus University Rotterdam

It's almost 10 years ago when I first came to Shanghai. In the last decade, Shanghai has become a global metropolis, scoring high in the ranking of the 500 most competitive cities of the world. Shanghai is currently the largest port and industrial base of China. The city scores well in technological innovation, global linkages and cultural diversity. Shanghai is the engine for the economic development of several cities in a wide metropolitan region, like Nanjing, Nanchang, and Yangzhou. In 2010, Shanghai organized the World Expo with the slogan "Better City, Better Life". I think it's clearly the ambition of the city to make Shanghai one of the most attractive cities in the world to live, to work, to visit and to invest.

After the successful industrialization period, the city has moved to a new stage with new challenge. In order to make the ambition to create a better city and a better life come true, the city has to be active in many fields. In the first place, it is essential to strengthen the knowledge base of the city. In the future, the quality of the labor force of Shanghai has to be substantially higher in order to meet the increasing demands for high-educated workers. Secondly, it is equally important to realize a related mix of economic clusters and activities. Thirdly, to achieve a better city and better life, Shanghai should be a safe city, and a city that offers adequate access to social services like housing, health, education and so on. In order to keep and attract the necessary high educated people, the attractiveness of Shanghai as residence becomes one of the most important location factors of the city. A clear and safe environment, high level facilities, for instance, housing, cultural educational and recreational, and an attractive and not polluted natural environment are fundamental elements in this respect. A substantial improvement of Shanghai in this way can be regarded as one of the biggest policy challenges in the years to come. Lastly, Shanghai must enhance its infrastructure construction. In the future, Shanghai will more and more function as the spider in regional, national and international network of cities. To play this role well, the regional, national, international accessibility of Shanghai needs continuous improvement, also an increase in the quality of the infrastructure like (for instance) communication.

In order to strengthen the sustainable attractiveness of Shanghai, the creation of partnerships with stakeholders is crucial. This requires vision, leadership, communication strategies and social and political support on all levels. In order to make this work, continued improvement in the quality of urban management is indispensible. In the creation of partnerships for achieving sustainable competitiveness, leader firms in Shanghai should play a key role. International operating firms, more and more, have self interest, to act sustainable both globally and locally. Indeed, many international operating firms are locally dependent because of their investments in debut environments, because of the existence of a local supplier base and customer, contract, or simply because of geographical features of the location where they are present. At the same time, local communities, labor markets and government agencies are dependent on the sustainable development of the local but internationally operating business community for job and employment, for tax revenues, for added value, for then transfer of knowledge, and for capital investment opportunities. Both international businesses and local stakeholders are confronted with new rules of the games. On the global level, with regards to sustainable development, they both need to secure their local dependencies.

In fact we are experiencing a convergence of public and private interests. The urban welfare is dependent on the thriving private sector and the private sector needs well organized and sustainable cities to survive. A win-win situation can be created by bringing together the interests of the city's business community, local governments and other urban stakeholders. Firms can play an important role in promoting sustainable development of the cities in which they are active. Firms typically engage in philanthropic action through sponsorships of the local zoo, the theater of orchestra, however, most importantly, firms should take cooperative responsibility through strategic engagement and partnerships with other urban stakeholders, both at the urban regional level and longer global business networks, and global supply chain. In doing so, leader firms effectively linked sustainable development of cities across the world.

The empirical question remains: how and why do leader firms contribute to sustainable development in different settings? In a recent EURICUR study that we have done, we have researched the role of firms in sustainable development of the city of Shanghai and its sister city Rotterdam, two port cities. The drive to sustainable development offers new opportunities for port cities to break out their lock-in situation. Port cities have to potential to become leaders in new clusters, such as environmental technology, just as other old industrial regions. A major example of the latter is the Ruhrarea in Germany that has transformed from the core of Europe's heavy industries to the leading center in Germany of environmental technologies. It is important to note that the change of new future branches in the Ruhr area, such as environmental technology, came from firms themselves. Firms were forced by the market to diversify and to invest in new branches. In addition, local governments and the State of Nordrhein-Westfalen changed strategies from the support of industries to the support of new industries. Also firms in port cities are forced by strict government regulations and changing market demands to invest in new branches and cleaner technologies. Port cities can gain competitive advantages to other regions due to the already existing knowledge of new technologies regarding clean technologies. Moreover, this annually created knowledge can be applied because of the presence of the most polluting activities of the playground with many stakeholders with different interests.

To analyze the strategic actions of leader firms, we have set up a theoretical frame that set up four settings in which leader firms in Shanghai and Rotterdam may contribute to sustainability, and the four are region, supply chain, cluster and network. Our research shows that the two cases have similarities as well as differences which can be explained by the large contextual differences of the two cities.

In terms of the regional setting, in both cases, leader firms invest in community and environmental projects, with an exception of some cases of strategic investment to improve the labor pool and attract possible clients. The sustainable investments in the regional setting have mainly been done by philanthropic investments. The drives and incentives for investments differ in the two cases. In Shanghai, with a lower starting point, the investment in the region are needed to get political and societal support, whereas in Rotterdam, basic conditions, such as clean water, have already been fulfilled and investments are mainly done to keep societal support and indirectly to promote business.

In the supply chain setting, the strategic actions of leader firms are more or less similar. In both cases, chain leaders aim to realize sustainability from cradle to grave and include all dimensions of sustainability. Leader firms use both pressure and offer support to their clients and suppliers to increase sustainable behavior. Many initiatives related to sustainable prediction are started by the chain leaders with the aim to develop new products that will result in a large market share and the creation of new growth of markets.

In the cluster setting, the two cases differ widely. In Rotterdam leader firms mobilize other firms and policymakers to invest in CCS, that is carbon capture and storage, and in order to fulfill requirements from the Kyoto protocol in the short run. In the longer time frame, they hope to develop new technologies and techniques and create new businesses, and in Shanghai SCIP is an illustrative case: a new chemical park with strict environmental and safety standards that has been created. The municipality of Shanghai is an initiating party, a leader of the development. It uses a leader firm to create best practice and links leader firms to each other and with local firms to find solutions and to share experiences. Well obviously I have to shorten my presentation. Well, let me see. Shanghai and Rotterdam are both in a different phase of their development which has consequences for the leader firm behavior of the companies located in both areas, in both cities. The sustainability policy of most companies has worldwide scope, but the context in which its policy must be executed is different in every location. That leads to a global policy that is adapted to numerical local situations.

That brings me to the conclusions. In our research, we have studied the behavior of leader firms in Rotterdam and Shanghai. It appears most companies are primarily focused on reducing their pollution and improving safety for their workers. Next through that, currently many companies are working on improving their performance on CO_2 emissions. Both in Rotterdam and in Shanghai, the companies also recognized their role in improving the sustainability of the region, albeit the secondary goal of their policies. Invest in sustainability of the region is understood as taking initiatives to improve living conditions, quality of life and education. There is little difference in the way the management of Shanghai and Rotterdam think about sustainability. It's clearly the context again that causes the variation in actions taken by firms in both cities. In this discussion about reactive against proactive behavior of firms, there is a great variation in the way that firms act.

A real proactive strategy towards sustainability is not common. Many companies have an active approach towards the sustainability issue and act according to the demands from the community. A proactive strategy where the company itself in setting the standard, and develops new ways and new partnerships to improve the sustainability of a region is still rare. Nevertheless, there is a trend towards more proactive behavior. The lessons that companies learned in Europe and the United States about sustainability are put into practice in then Shanghai context which leads to a situation where leader firms are co-shaping the sustainability policy and practices in the whole Shanghai region. This is a hopeful observation in a process that aims to improve the livability and attractiveness of Shanghai in the years to come.

The World Council on City Data: A Global Platform for Standardized City Data

Patricia McCarney

University of Toronto, Canada

President & CEO of the World Council on City Data

I was invited to discuss a couple of things with you today. One is its evolution of this new World Council on City Data. And the other one is the building of a new ISO standard-international organization for standardization on city data, which we call ISO37120. It is the first standard for cities, which is coming out of ISO. I'm very proud to have worked with the China National Standards Body, the ISO and 20 countries to move the standard forward. This year (2014), we have published it.

I think it's important to talk about why cities should have metrics. Of course, a city's economic strength is one essential factor. When you couple the economic strength of cities with demographic strength of cities, you do get a coupling of both demographic and economic presence on the World Stage for cities, which would be occurrent over the last few decades. So with this, we have this incredible need for city data. For example, we could get the demand scale and the investment scale of a city's infrastructure merely according to scientific calculation on the basis of city data. We need to be smart about our investment in these new infrastructure, because what we build today will still be with us for 50 years from now. If you think back to the history of North American cities, most of which were built in post-war stage. The majority of these investments are highways, roads and expressways and these infrastructure is still in use, which leaves a footprint on the city. So if we have the good data today, we can invest the infrastructure that is really needed for the cities of the future.

So let me just now move to the second part of my presentation, which is around how we start to build the global standard for city data and then lead to the ISO standard that was published in May. There are challenges in the field of city data. We list four here, but of course there are more. One of the key challenges is about city boundary. When you start to compare cities, if you think about putting together a table in one of your papers, if you have more than one city down the left and you have more than one indicator across the top, you can always bet that you will have at least 15 to 20 footnotes on the exceptions to the data that is in that small table. The exceptions to the data have to do with these four factors. Usually it's around the city boundaries themselves. In the path, there are no standardized definitions on what to measure, no standardized methodologies on how to measure, and no mechanism for data sharing across global cities. Of course, there are other challenges around city data. When we move to certain cities in Africa, Asia and North America, the informality of those cities is also a very big challenge and that's the work program right now going on with Ben from our colleagues here to work on building up data on what we called "informal areas" of the city.

So we started to standardize data, build the standardized definition and methodology, and we build it from 9cities that we piloted in the very beginning of 2008, working with World Bank. In those days, we started with a small group of 9 cities and then we rewrote the methodologies, definitions and established boundaries, etc. And we built that network of 255 cities and 82 countries. The reason why it grew so rapidly from just 9 pilots to 255 cities was that there is a huge need for data by cities, city managers and city mayors. City mayors are increasingly asking the question: how are we doing relative to our peer cities globally. So our study is quite necessary and urgent.

We then went to Geneva and cooperated with the International Organization for Standardization(ISO) in order to build up an ISO standard system. ISO is a standardization body, which normally standardizes things like bulbs. It standardizes parts of your computers, everything in your cell phone, tractors, automobile parts, but not cities, not city indicators by the long stretch. So we went to Geneva and asked the question about getting the standard for the works we've been doing for 6 years. And there was really very little interest at that time. We Canadians went home and said OK, we could work to get standard at the ISO. Well then, the Japanese government stepped up, and said they would like to talk to ISO about infrastructure metrics and technical metrics for infrastructure. And then French government also went to Geneva and said they would like to talk about city standards on management system. So as a result, we put together this ISO TC268 and so ISO TC268 was created. I chaired that working group 2. We convened with 20 countries, a number of partners and international agencies. We've been building this standard now for the last two years. We started in 2012. As you can see, China is one of the members of this technical committee. We have 20 participating countries to vote and 17 observing countries. This is our working group. We meet every 3 or 4 months and we talked a lot about indicators and we worked through the definitions and methodologies. We have this working group and there's been a lot of efforts, compromises and agreements we had to come together to reach in building this standard. So it went through 6 international meetings and then 5 drafts with 200 comments, coming out from the international global ballot. And the end of the story is, we did it, we got ISO37120 published and that's the first standard on city indicators.

So what is 37120? There are a group of 100 indicators and 46 core indicators, which means that cities who want to be in conformity with ISO37120 will report at least 46 of these core indicators. And these indicators are all around city services and quality of life, so the 100 indicators are across these various themes. The usual items that the city wants to measure are the typical performance measurements on quality life indicators, and most cities are gathering some data somehow. Therefore, it's not that hard to start, when we work with cities to get them to the capacity to report because many of them are already reporting these data. The 46 core indicators are the first step in bring conformity of cities. So the users are any city, any municipal or local government and the standard is meanwhile a tool for city managers, planners, business leaders, designers, citizens, researchers, professors and another professionals. And I want to mention in the process of building this standard that, many cities and many countries in voting continuously asked us to keep adding more indicators. So although we tried to limit it to 75 but then it grew to 100. We felt that, if there were more than 100, ISO standard would not be adopted, because it's too difficult for cities to report too many indicators. But what happened is that every time a country voted, they came forward to say why don't you add biodiversity, why don't you add tree planting, why don't you add a set of particular matter PM10, as for air quality, one also asked why don't you add PM2.5, the fined grain, emergency response, what about flooding in cities hurricanes. So we started to look at this other body of indicators that were demanded through the voting process. And we came up with a proposal to develop a new TR, which is a technical report on resilience in cities. We are actually building now ISO 37121 on resilience in cities. And the themes that we are looking at include all kinds of themes around emergency preparedness and risk.

So I'd like to move now to the building of the World Council on City Data. This WCCD has come about because of the ISO standard. As a result of ISO 37120 which has been passed, we built the World Council on City Data. The council is the global harbor now for the learning partnerships and for the data collection and reporting on ISO 37120 for standardizing metrics. As we built it, it will be open data platform on standardized data. So for all of us researchers, it would be a fantastic tool for comparing data on cities. It's coming, and I'll tell you where we are. We started by creating a group of foundation cities in the World Council on City Data. We invited 20 cities to be a part of the WCCD. Shanghai is one of our foundation cities of the World Council on City Data and the Development Research Center here is the focal point for this work. Besides, we've tried to have geographic representation in some size distributions as well. We have cities like London, Amsterdam and in western Asia; in Middle East region, we have Dubai, the holy city of Makkah, Amman of Jordan; in Latin America, Buenos Aires, Bogota and Sao Paulo. So there's a number of cities in Europe, like Barcelona and Rotterdam. We also have Melbourne, Boston and Toronto. We have a pretty good mixture geographically and also in terms of size. So in Africa, for example, we have the larger city of Johannesburg and smaller city of Minna, Nigeria. With this standard now approved, we are able to move to 255 cities, with all of our partners, because we can build this platform on global city metrics, which allows cities to showcase the progress on the world stage. So we are moving forward with our cities and our partners that we've been building for the last 6 years to have a very strong new World Council on City Data as we speak.

I just want to mention that a lot of people asked why cities need a set of globally standardized data. There's many answers and we still add to the list as cities tell us these when we ask them these questions. One is to make sensible decisions through data analysis, to benchmark and target, to plan and establish new frameworks for sustainable planning, and to leverage funding with senior levels of government. This is something that actually has been brought to our attention in the case of many North American colleague cities. We evaluate the "impacts" of infrastructure projects on the overall performance of a city. Also cities are very interested in building creditworthiness and insurance security. So, insurance companies are important, especially for cities at risk of hurricanes and tsunamis, etc. Besides, to build smart and sustainable cities and to learn and share lessons across other cities globally are also in the following list. This exchange of knowledge city to city on the standardized set of metrics is probably the most important contribution. For global cities stakeholders, there're also a number of reasons that the need for standardized data is being considered. One is to determine entry points for investment, to benchmark investments, to build smart and sustainable cities, to evaluate the investment over time and to strengthen the effectiveness of city governors.

I also want to mention that we moved into the post-development period with the UN Sustainable Development Goals now, evolving from millennium development goals, and this set of standardized data for cities can also start to build a basis for the SDGs, which could not only better target what the SDG should be, what's in the past we didn't have when the MDG was being set up, but also help to benchmark and to monitor progress in order to achieve those targets. We're also using the data to build institutes at the University of Toronto. So we are putting some data together. From our path, they are cities and prosperity, cities and aging, cities and sustainable infrastructure. They are all on our website.

Just say a few words about cities and aging. We tracked at a global level how aging is a phenomenon starting to affect cities all through the world. This is particularly vivid in sub-Saharan Africa and North Africa. You can see 366% increase in aging population. It's a phenomenal number. We looked at age cohorts, as we are collecting data on age cohorts for cities through the world. Shanghai and Beijing, their agings aren't too bad this point in time, with only 9% and 10% in the age group for age 65 and up.

We also work with UNISON on the child friendly city index and we are developing a number of new indices over the next 6 months. We work on some comparative graphics, some visualization on how to work through this. For example, you can also look at health indicators or different themes, such as regional concentrations of the data. You can actually see how health indicators play out. You can choose another theme, such as education, and start to track cities with different educational capacities in their cities. This is the first time we have city data that we can actually do this.

Besides, I want to finally mention there's one more important aspect of all these, which is the cities' inner boundary issue. We piloted a way to aggregate from the boundaries of cities up to the region, the economic functional areas of cities, whether we called them the metro, the agglomeration or the greater urban area. It's one of the biggest challenges in comparing data across cities, because everyone draws the boundaries differently. We piloted an aggregation tool, looking at Toronto as a case study. This is one of the ways that we have been suggested by our senior level of government to draw the boundary.The built-up area is really the urban area. So we started to track the different ways the Toronto region is being bounded. And we looked at the built-up area, and then we tracked how municipal boundaries lay over that. There're all separate cities around the Toronto urban region, all of which reported on this data individually, so the question was how do we aggregate that up. We started to draw the boundary and then we looked at the night patterns of light to see if we had it right. If this built-up Toronto urban region was really as we mapped it, which it turned out that it was quite close. And then we started to compare that to different aggregation around the world, including Greater Chicago, the San Francisco bay area and the Shanghai-Nanjing corridor to see how you can aggregate data up on the standardized basis to the broader urban region.

What we found at the end of that study was that when we get started to aggregate up, we can actually see the Toronto urban region in terms of higher education degrees, for example, it's really competitive with San Francisco bay area, which sits Silicon Valley, but nobody knows this in Toronto, until we have good data to aggregate. And then we look at median income, foreign-born population, commuters using other than a personal vehicle to work and we aggregate all the data up. I just want to mention that this issue of boundaries is so difficult, because if you look at the city mayor's website in 2010, where Shanghai is ranked second. The city population is 14 900 000; the metro is 19 200 000, so Karachi in this ranking is the first, because it's the largest city when you look at the city proper. You can see it for other cities, and Karachi is the first when you look at the city, but NO.9 when you look at metro, and so on. There's a very big discrepancy on how you think about boundaries. And then if you look at Shanghai again, and look at the title, this is urban agglomeration, which isn't the city or the metro. So this boundary issue, when you start to try to compare cities worldwide, it's a part of the biggest problems on getting comparative data.

And then I really want to let you know that some of the cities like Buenos Aires using ISO 37120 to benchmark its development goals and national planning strategy. In the case of Toronto, we're using it more for competitive location for investment arguments. We're working now with Shanghai on how to formulate the 2050 development strategies.

In order to become standardized cities, the first step is to sign up expressions of interest. The second step in the process is to be certified and then they should file 46 indicators and their register. We have application form for cities now that the cities could fill out. So we're working with our foundation cities and our cooperative international agency partners to build this forward over the next 5 to 10 years. I hope we will have 100 to more cities in China by then to celebrate this movement towards standardized data.

Industrial Clusters, Innovation and Global Urban Network Formation

Stefan Kratke

Prof.of European University Viadrina Frankfurt (Oder)

Shanghai represents an outstanding regional motor of the Chinese economy and an up-and-coming urban center in the world city network. My contribution to the global city forum will concentrate on the innovative capacity of large cities' industrial clusters and their relation to the global urban network formation of manufacturing industries. This particular perspective is shaped by my country of residence, Germany, which represents an economy that rests on a large extent of manufacturing industries. It has highly-developed technological competence and strong innovative capacity, but in contrast to any country, German economy has been primarily concentrated on the financial sector and business services. Today, all across the world, the economic development of cities are increasingly affected by globalization process. We are facing a continued extension of strengthened national economy networks that include more and more cities, local and global, north and south, and the complex fabric of world city network. That's why I prefer to speak of globalizing cities whose economic development prospects are shaped by their specific positions within global network relations.

Innovative capacity of urban economies is of strategic importance for economic success and meanwhile, urban agglomerations are centers of innovation. In geographical terms, centers of innovation activities are for the most part encoded in metropolitan agglomeration. As we got, the special dimension of economic development and the most important feature is the formation of the local clusters. Talking about regional or local clustering, we relate it to the special concentration of distinct developing chains, elements, such as the leading firms and the supply firms. The cluster results from their transaction and cooperation. Particularly, the metropolitan regions might be regarded as super clusters, which comprise, for example, a cluster of finance and business services, media industry cluster and several different manufacturing industry clusters. These different clusters are not necessarily interlinked but the interaction of different cluster actors mainly goes towards the formation of new industries, such as in the case of multimedia industry and the Los Angles urban region.

In recent years, the debate on regional and urban innovation capacities has focused on the topic of knowledge networking, since innovation relies on the creation and new combination of technological and organizational knowledge. In contrast to what we mentioned above, the regionally network is based on specialized firms and research institutions, which are the important driving forces of cluster dynamics. In short, the greatest stimulus to innovation arises from the networking of knowledge resources. However, this networking takes place on various special scales and this knowledge networking can become a key factor in the region's economic development. Based on these, a regional or an urban innovation system might be conceptualized as a construct with 3 aspects: first, the regional firms' internal innovation capacity, which has to do with the individual firms in research of development; second, the region's innovation infrastructure, which consists of public and private research establishments, universities, technology transfer agencies and so on; third, regional knowledge networking, that interlinks actors on the regional or local levels with formal or informal relations that channel inter-organizational knowledge flows. With 3 guides to the innovative capacities of clusters, knowledge networks are of particularly importance in the innovation process, and they are more interactive and durable than market links. The innovation relates inter-firms cooperation and exchange of knowledge and ideas, which in turn generates new knowledge.

At this point, I would like to proceed the relationship between industry clusters and global urban network formation. From my point of view, the particular string of large urban agglomerations was regarded as innovative capacities in the coupling of global and local interlinks within the background of cross-international transfer of industries. Global firms are settling up a trans-national network of subsidiary firms in which distinct urban regions are choosing as notes of foreign business activity in service provision as well as in manufactory. At the local level, these global firms' establishments form part of respective urban regions' industry cluster, which contains for the most part local firms. The development of network relations between global firms establishments and local firms within the respective cities' industrial clusters is a very important source of knowledge exchange and strengthened innovative capabilities of the whole ensemble of cluster firms.

Within the Shanghai automotive cluster, for example, the Germany-based global manufacturer VW has set up a large firm establishment in form of joint venture, whose manufacturing activities are resting on a network of more than 500 Chinese supply firms from the Shanghai urban region.The global firm establishment integrates into a geographic urban industrial cluster functioning as a pipelines for knowledge flows, and innovation impulses within local industrial cluster. This might be regarded as most important economic impact of global urban network formation.

On this background, I would like to proceed to my last point—the role of manufactory industry in global urban network formation. In the contemporary world city network, inter-urban linkages encompass a multitude of cities, both local and global, north and south. For many years, research on the formation of global cities and global urban network has concentrated on global service providers. Yet globally-operating manufacturing firms as well choose distinct urban regions all across the world as locational anchoring points. For example, the global production network of German car manufacturing VW includes the global city regions of Sao Paulo, Mexico City and Shanghai. As a consequence, I've performed a global scale analysis of how manufacturing industries connect cities across the world. The analyses cover 120 top global firms from 3 manufacturing sub-sectors—automotive industry, information technology sector and pharmaceutical and biotechnology industry.

The ranking of globally-connected urban centers of manufacturing differs considerably from the well-known ranking of global service centers. That's why we have to be aware of multipleglobalization in the world city network. Urban regions included in the world city network are characterized by specific profiles of globally-connected economic functions. The world city network includes global cities focusing on advance producer services and financial sector in particular as well as many other cities with different sectors profiles of their globally-connected activities.

My research detects the positioning of particular cities within the global production network of distinct manufacturing industries. The analysis distinguishes a city's incoming links which demonstrate an urban region through destination of capital flows and the urban region's outgoing links that reveal this urban region through source and outflow of capital flows. The incoming links can also be interpreted as a measure of urban region's attractive power in terms of always platform function, which refers to the penetration of foreign markets to the utilization of production capacity, or to access to specific knowledge resources. The outgoing links of a city, on the other hand, can be interpreted as a measure of urban region's control capacity.

Let me show you and present some selective findings that refer to the automotive industry, a very traditional industry. The ranking of cities with regard to the node centrality in automotive industry selectively demonstrates the top ranks of the total 340 cities included in this sub-sectors global networks. Urban regions with strong supply of outgoing links, such as Tokyo, are primarily functioning as command and control centers in automotive industry. Of course, there are also urban regions which show a rather balanced relationship of outgoing and incoming links, that no definite functional destination can be assigned to these cases. According to the outgoing links of cities in the automotive industry, Tokyo and Detroit take on the first and second rank.

On the subsequent ranks, we find out, for example, the urban regions of Stuttgart, Milwaukee, Nagoya, Wolfsburg and Munich. The overall picture indicates the dominance of global firms from some European countries, the United States, and Japan in this particular industry. However, it is very remarkable that today several urban regions of global source appear on comparatively high rank positions. Two of these are cities of India, in particular, Mumbai and Pune. In China, the urban region of Shanghai has achieved a high rank and in Brazil, the urban region of Sao Paulo has joined the top 50 list. This clearly indicates the increasing integration of China, India and Brazil in global production networks.

Furthermore, a ranking of cities in Asia, with regard to their nodes centrality in global production network within 3 manufacturing sub-sectors, detect the significant number of Chinese cities which are involved in global firms production networks. In particular, the large number of incoming links underscores a strong attractive power of Chinese urban regions in globally network of manufacturing.

As a last point, I proceed to a comparative ranking of the outstanding network of nodes, global services and global manufacturing. I compare the ranking of global service centers offered first by Peter Tyler and the globalization city study group, with the ranking of globally-connected manufacturing centers presented before. As a result, we can distinguish 3 groups of cities. First, we find cities that process a surplus rank in manufacturing. These cities are characterized by strong global connectivity in manufacturing sector, which considerably exceeds their rank position in the field of global services. Examples are the urban regions of Hanover, Nagoya, Milwaukee and Stuttgart. Second, there are cities with other balance relation of global connectivity in both the service and manufacturing sector, such as Toronto, Bangkok and Sao Paulo. Third, the rank comparison detects cities that process a surplus rank in the finance and service sector. Cities that are born in this section are characterized by strong global connectivity in service sector activities, which exceed the degree of global connectivity they have achieved in this field of manufacturing. Here we find well-known examples of the established global cities, such as New York and London, as well as a number of cities in Asia, such as Hong Kong, Beijing and Shanghai. Altogether, the comparison confirms that globalized cities are characterized by different profiles of globally-connected economic activities.

Let me now come to some concluding remarks. First, I have been emphasizing the continued relevance of urban region for industrial innovation processes. Second, I've emphasized that the most important stimulus to innovation arises from the networking of knowledge resources within regional or local clusters of economic activity. Third, we can describe innovation related to knowledge generation as resulting from the interplay between local networks and global knowledge transfer. As a consequence, the particular strings of metropolitan regions and large cities, with regard to innovativecapacities, are largely active in the coupling of global and local interlinks within regional clusters often industrial activity. The development of network relations between local firms and global firms' establishments within a city's industrial cluster, can function as an important source of knowledge exchange and strength in the innovative capacities of cluster as a whole. Furthermore, my presentation emphasized the role of manufacturing industry in global manufacturing network formation. A large number of cities are functioning as locational nodes in the global value chains of manufacturing industries. This should be considered as a relevant aspect of globalizing cities. The inclusion of many cities in global value chains of manufacturing sector presents a perspective on the variable position of cities in the globalizing economy. In conclusion, there are different pathways and several trajectories of cities in globalization, which might have significant implications for urban economic development strategies.

Chinese Cities in the World City Network

Ben Derudder

Prof. of Ghent University

There are different approaches to this topic of world city network. And what I would like to do is to present what might be called GaWc. It is probably most well-known research, which focuses on the relations between cities and the office networks of business and producer services firms. What I will do is, as I choose the result of related data gathering, to focus on the position of Chinese cities as a sample.

So let me very briefly introduce you our approach. GaWc actually starts where Saskia Sassen has stopped. In some of our books, she emphasizes that what drives city economies is their role in the production of knowledge, knowledge to be able to manage this global production networks. So you got the global production network, what we have seen in the presentation of professor Kratke, but what you also need is the creation of knowledge to be able to command and control this global production networks. Companies are very big and large, and they would have a lot of different types of locations. You need knowledge to be able to somehow organize this. Saskia Sassen basically claims the global city photo. It includes the economic rise of cities such as London and New York, but we see more and more cities in terms of globalizing cities, so you can find this in many cities across the world. It's because the size of production, not industrial production, but the production of knowledge through services. This has been facilitated by the rise of ICT, of course, deregulation, economic globalization and so forth. We could also see the rise of specific type of services, which we would like to call, advanced producer services (APS), that are needed and used by organizations and firms to organize the global production network.

Just one example, big companies advertise in all different kinds of context, but obviously, what they do not do is to have a different advertising firm in every and each country. They tend to have one advertising firm that has global presence, and they use it to somehow mitigate the global and local tensions by adapting global products to local original standards. So you could get the global network of advertising firms that comprises global presence and local knowledge. These firms' centers tend to be located in limited or rather limited number of cities, which are turned out to be world or global cities.

What this GaWc do is that we take this as a starting point to make assessment and examine the position of cities in global networks to do a systematic analysis of the office networks of APS firms. So although complicated the mathematical model becomes at some point, we will not burden you with that model today. But there's some mathematical models in our research, but no matter how complicated it is, the starting point is actually quite simple. We're going to start from a systematic analysis of global service firms, observe where they are located in cities, and look at the interaction patterns between cities that emerge from this kind of analysis.

I think it is a good starting point. There are two pictures I took at Schiphol Airport in the Amsterdam about 10 years ago. It's an advertisement of Deloitte, a typical service producer. The message expressed is very clear. They say to potential clients: do you want to know where you are? You know where you are. You don't have to look it up on the website, because you know it well in Amsterdam, in New York, that anyone knows Deloitte has a presence and also in Shanghai, in Sao Paulo and so on. The most interesting part from the research perspective is once you go down the list, to some smaller cities, what about Nanjing, what about Wuhan, and if you look at the global presence of this kind of firms, you get a picture of how these service firms use cities in the global networking strategies.

This is one example, Amrop Hever, which is a human resources firm. In China, Amrop Hever have 3 offices, they have one in Beijing, one in Shanghai and one in Guangzhou. In Australia, they have one in Melbourne and one in Sydney. How many offices a firm has would depend on the sector and the firm, so the accountancy firms sometimes have offices in thousands of cities. Law firms tend to have offices in perhaps more than 20 cities. So it depends on the sector and the sector will somehow produce geographical bias. But the idea is that if you make it openly, and the agglomeration of a lot of these firms and agglomerated pattern emerge, it will deal with this agglomerated pattern. So the interesting thing here is, if you look at Chinese cities and the Amrop Hever will open its fourth office, where would that be? It would be Chengdu, Wuhan, Nanjing and there are other options as well. So it's only through systematic analysis that you can see what kind of pattern that emerges.

So some details about how we go about this. First thing I need to mention is that there has been an underestimation of the model. We do something extra. We also look at how important the dots are for the city, because not all offices are equally important. There're some headquarters that make the city more important to that firm. You have normal or typical offices, but you have headquarters specific for Asia too. So first of all, we take an extra step to measure the importance of a firm to a city and we do that in a standardized way so that we can compare firms. And we do that through a 6-point scale, which we call it a service value, judging how importance of a firm to a certain city. It goes from 0 to 5 and it's quite too extensive. 0 simply means that the firm is not in the city and 5 means a firm has a global headquarter in this city. So 4 means it has a regional headquarter and 3 means multiple offices or a national headquarter and so on. So when you move to the data, what you will see is a lot of cities, a lot of firms and for each of the city and the firm, it would have a service value ranging between 0 and 5.

So now how do we use these data? What we're not going to do is to simply add up the dots or the values, which shows you how importance of the city on its own terms and what actually we're going to do is to apply network methodology presented by professor Kratke, which shows you the interaction within the firms networks. Quite simply put, I will give you an example later. We've got value here, CDC, which means simply city-dyad connectivity, the relation between any pairs of cities by simply multiplying the service value. So the idea is that if a firm has a global headquarter in New York and a regional quarter in London, there's a lot of potential interaction between both. If a city has no presence, that is a 0 and another city has a normal presence, that's a 2, 0 times 2 and you get 0, which means there's no potential for interaction because the firm has not presence in this city.

So city-dyad connectivities are the relations between cities and if you add these all up, you can get a GNC, the global network connectivity of a city. It basically means that if you aggregate the relations of a city with other cities, you can get an idea about how well-connected that city is. These would be the 2 major values we would be working with—city-dyad connectivity, relation between cities and GNC by adding up all these relations. So this is basically how it works. What you simply can do is that you can for instance, look at the connectivity between any pairs of cities, the first one is New York and Shanghai, simply for firm A. It has connectivity with another. It means something in comparative terms with the other cities-dyad connectivity. You can do so across all firms. So if you do 5 times 2, 4 times 2, 5 times 0, 3 times 5, that gives you all the intercity connectivity between that pair of cities. So the city-dyad connectivity of New York-Shanghai is 33. If you do that for all cities, because there are only 3 cities, you can plus 33 and 15, and New York City has a global network connectivity of 48. Once again, 48 does not mean something on its own right, but when you start to compare across cities, you can have a ranking of how well-connected these cities are and how different service firms connect cities.

We have been doing this since 2000 and today we will mainly focus on the latest data gathering which was carried out in 2013. Obviously, we have done this for 4 firms and 3cities, but rather, we have selected all cities with more than 2 million inhabitants depending on the boundaries, plus all cities with a key economic importance, so we've got 526 cities. We've got 175 service firms in different sectors, including 75 financial service firms, 25 management consulting firms, 25 advertisement firms, 25 law firms and 25 accountancy firms. So there are the biggest firms we selected from different rankings, so not just 75 banks, but 75 biggest banks.

Table 1

$CDC_{\text{New York-Shanghai, Firm A}}$
$=5 \times 2=10$
$CDC_{\text{New York-Shanghai}}$
$=10+8+0+15=33$
$CDC_{\text{New York}}$
$=33+15=48$

	Firm A	Firm B	Firm C	Firm D
New York	5	4	5	3
Shanghai	2	2	0	5
Johannesburg	2	0	1	0

And then, finally, I will explain how we could get the cities and how we get the firms. What we do is to scan the websites of different firms, because service firms are quite clear where they are located. It is a part of their advertisement strategy. So if you look at the website of Deloitte, you will get something called offices location, and you can see where Deloitte is located. Sometimes, if you are given extra information, you can use it to get their service value. What you can see in the case of law is that there's a kind of expertise which has presented. So in the case of Brussels and Beijing, you can see there's a lot of extra parts located in those cities, because everything related to EU is located in Brussels. That office would be an important one for law firms. Therefore, we have 526 cities and 175 firms which also lead to 90000 pieces of information, and then we could obtain service values what I've shown here. This is the kinds of results you can use.

So what I would like to do now is to explain a couple of these results specifically for Chinese cities. This ranking just focuses on Chinese cities here. But this ranking is available on the website of GaWc, so if you simply put it into Google, you go to the website and you will see the rankings for all cities across the world. If you look at the numbers what is basically shown here, you would find out that GNC is the percentage by the comparison of this target city and the most connected city of the world, London. So London is the most connected city and the center of office networks of major service firms. It's closely followed by New York, and the leading ranks of London and New York are closely followed by Hong Kong and Singapore. There're more Chinese cities in our data, but these are the only cities that have a connectivity which is at least 10 percent of London's. So Hong Kong is the most connected Chinese city, the third in the world, and it's by now closely followed by Shanghai and Beijing. So these are 3 cities standing out in China in terms of their global connectivity and their office network of service firms. Although Shanghai and Beijing are not necessarily much bigger than some other major city in China, they are standing out which really means that if there's a service firm coming to China, it tends to locate in these cities. Then Taipei has a specific place that is rank 4 and then you get Pearl River Delta cities of Guangzhou and Shenzhen.

Obviously, global network connectivity of individual cities is the most visible outcome of this kind of research, but once you've got the city-dyad connectivity, you can do a lot of different things. You can start looking for instance at spatial pattern, because 2 cities with similar connectivity can be connected with very different cities. City like Toronto may have a similar connectivity with cities in Europe, but the relations of spatiality may be quite different. There's different ways in which you can cover the city-dyad connectivities. You can look at the city relations with all 525 other cities. But the interesting thing is, there's one more thing that you can do is to aggregate these city-dyad connectivity, and specific patterns would emerge. So you might look at the strength of connections of Chinese cities with other Chinese cities and Chinese cities with all European cities.

These are the kinds of things that you can do, but the other thing that we do is to look at what we call the globalism of cities. And what this basically means is that you look at how well a city is connected with 10 most connected cities in the world. Since not all connections are equally important, you can see it's quite important for a city like Shanghai to be well-connected with New York, London, Chicago and so on. So this table really shows this. It shows the average strength of connectivity with major cities. When you need to understand the different values here, 0 means there's no specific pattern. It's not really strong or weak connection, but it's random like. If it is really weak, it means the city has connectivity, but with the other cities, not with Chicago, not with New York, and so on. That means if you have a large positive value, you are really strongly connected with each of these cities. Although the same pattern reemerges, if you go into the details, you can see a number of different patterns. For instance, Shenzhen, it's above all a well-connected Chinese city, which makes a trend much localism than globalism. Here once again it shows you that Hong Kong, Shanghai and Beijing stand out. They are not just well-connected. They are also above all well connected with the world's most connected cities. There's 3 cities in China which really have well-developed connections with London, New York and their office network of service firms. They are once again Hong Kong, Shanghai and Beijing. So there're different things you can do, but within the same pattern, you can see how well Chinese cities connected to the European Union, to Africa, to specific cities, if you like.

Table 2

Rank	City	Globalism	Rank	City	Globalism
1	Hong Kong	3.2	10	Shenzhen	0.2
2	Shanghai	2.9	11	Dalian	0.2
3	Beijing	2.9	12	Qingdao	0.2
4	Taipei	1.3	13	Hangzhou	0.1
5	Tianjin	1.3	14	Xi'an	−0.3
6	Chongqing	0.8	15	Xiamen	−0.4
7	Guangzhou	0.8	16	Nanjing	−0.5
8	Wuhan	0.7	17	Macao	−1.1
9	Chengdu	0.3	18	Kaohsiung	−1.4

And then, what you can do also is to look at the reverse, what you would call localism. How well a city is connected to the cities within the same region (with different definitions of regions, the most obvious one being your own country). So if there emerges a large value, it means the city is well connected with other Chinese cities. So what you say here is an almost reverse pattern. If you look at the city Wuhan, it has really provincial nationalized connections. It has some global network connectivity. But that global network connectivity is in practice, above all, connectivity with other Chinese cities, so what basically show here is that a couple of Chinese firms in the data. The biggest Chinese banks are by now, part of the 75 biggest financial institutions. So there are networks in the data, but you see cities here like Wuhan, connect with Chinese firms, not all global firms. All Chinese cities have local tendency, that's quite normal. It shows you the effect of Chinese banks here. But you see quite a logical pattern emerges here, it may attract major global cities. Deriving connectivity from these connections with Chinese cities, cities in Taiwan, of course, are less connected with Mainland Chinese cities.

Since we did this gathering from 2000, it's possible to do a lot of logical analyses. You can look at how cities do in the global ranking. For example, Shanghai by now is a top 10 city, but it wasn't in 2000. So you can look at the trajectories of different cities. And again what it turns out is that I think it will not come as a surprise, for in our research, it shows that every single Chinese city has become more connected between 2000 and now. That is not a surprise, but what may perhaps be a surprise is that the 3 cities that really emerge here have been big winners. Both Nanjing and Shanghai have become more global connected, but in the end, above all, Shanghai, as a leading city, has been gaining more than other Chinese cities. The same is true for Beijing and Dalian, but Beijing has been gaining more than others. At the same time, one other thing that has predicted by some analysts is that Hong Kong will at some point, suffer from the transition. But this has not been the case, because even Hong Kong has been one of the biggest winners since 2000, if you compare to its position now, it keeps on gaining global connectivity.

So it has simply been a snapshot of the kinds of things we can do. I focus on Chinese cities here and a couple of their connections. But most of things we do are in this general spirit. So if you look at transnational connectivity of cities, you could choose one specific producer service firm and do the research.

The Intercultural Communication Competence of a City: An Important Benchmark for Global City

Lu Jianfei

Chairman of the Council of Shanghai Normal University

We're talking about "Global City" or "World City" as we call it. So this is actually changing the original description of Shanghai, a "Metropolitan City", because we are trying to build Shanghai from an international city to a global city. So I will discuss with you how to build a global city from the perspective of intercultural communication.

In 1950s, the American anthropologist Edward Hall used the word "intercultural communication" for the first time in his book *The Silent Language* which is regarded as a milestone in human history. Intercultural communication refers to the communication between individuals or groups from different cultural backgrounds. But he didn't mention cities as the communicators. So I think this kind of intercultural communication competence between cities should be proposed under current globalization background. The city intercultural communication competence, I think, includes two layers: one is intercultural communication competence of citizens, which consists of verbal communication competence, non-verbal communication competence and cultural competence, and the other one is the intercultural competence in terms of city environment which consists of hard environment power, like the geographical location and the natural environment as well as soft environment power like the external publicity and public services.

The verbal communication competence of the citizen is very important, and I believe it's the footstone of intercultural communication competence. According to the latest data, foreign population in Shanghai come from 214 different countries and areas, and there're more than 1 000 population as permanent residents from 20 countries in Shanghai. Different measure indexes for global city indicate that a global city not only needs the high quality interdisciplinary talents who must master foreign languages, but also requires common citizens to be able to communicate in foreign languages, especially in English. English, as a lingua franca, plays a significant role in the international exchanges. So in order to create a convenient communication environment for foreigner friends who study, work and live in Shanghai, it is necessary to improve the English level of common citizens. And for professionals, who master English well, it is also an opportunity to understand all the latest information in their professional fields, because it relates to the terminology and information that common people do not know.

Last but not least, global city requires multilingual environment. Only three languages are used most frequently in Shanghai: Shanghai dialect, English and Mandarin. Obviously, it's not enough. We also need people who speak French, Spanish, Portuguese and Japanese and so on. And to popularize English among Shanghai citizens, I think the foundation should be laid in schools. There was an argument lasting for a year whether English should be eliminated from the college entrance examination. But in the end, in Shanghai, English closely bonded with Chinese and Mathematics, will continued to be tested in June. In addition, the English listening test and spoken test will be added into the college entrance examination in 2017, which is a great leap forward and conducive to the elimination of "dumb English". In addition to that, I think in communication we always say "to understand and to be understood". For "Chinese Wisdom", how can we express our wisdom to the world, and how can we share our national stories with the world. This is not only about language, it's more about the degree of what we understand the foreign language and culture and what foreigners understand our language and culture.

Non-verbal communication competence is also important, which includes all the communication without using words. It tends to be neglected in our daily life and work. To be specific, non-verbal communication can include gestures, body language, facial expressions as well as the use of space and esthetic orientation etc. If we couldn't handle it well, there could be some misunderstandings, cultural conflicts, and even cultural shocks. In daily communication, actually more than 50% of the information is conveyed through body language, 38% is through voice, and 8% is through verbal form. Therefore, I think the public space is like a window showing to the world, and the behaviors Shanghai citizens presents in this window determines city's image of Shanghai. In many occasions, our manners are presented by the non-verbal communications, and inappropriate non-verbal behavior would shadow the city image and bring discomfort to foreign tourists and residents as well. They feel uncomfortable. I think this is quite common in our daily. I have to mention that especially some inappropriate non-verbal behaviors actually have decreased attractiveness of a city, for example, being aloud, inappropriate space between people, smoking in the public space, littering, taking photos without permission, unnecessary honking. So I think in the process of building Shanghai into a global city, we should strengthen citizens' legal awareness and social morality consciousness, and should cultivate their intercultural communication capability, so that they could play a dominant role and be initiative in the city development, which requires the government to put emphasis on the very specific details, for instance, to enhance the public space awareness. I think this is a key part for the construction of global city.

If the cultural competence is well used, it actually can show the flexibility and adaptabilities of the communicators. As I have mentioned, the intercultural communication competence refers to a communicator's ability to interact efficiently with people from different cultural, and social economic background. Actually cultural competence also involves one's conception of one's own cultural identity, native cultures and foreign cultures, one's knowledge about different culture practices and world views, and one's attitude towards cultural differences and their intercultural communication skills. When people come across cultural conflict or cultural shock, how to deal with it? How to understand other's culture and to adjust oneself? All of those embody one's cultural ability. So I think in the process of building Shanghai into a global city, we need to promote its affinity, so that people coming to Shanghai feel like they are at home. So in the exchanges with the foreigners, we should caution against being self-centered which would cause the cultural conflicts even cultural shock. And in this process, we should establish the intercultural identity. In Shanghai we need to take the initiative to create and spread the distinctive city brand in this intercultural communication of cities. We know that Shanghai have advantages in many aspects including local features, cultural heritage and a good city development planning. But I believe that if we highlight the special features of Shanghai, we would impress the foreigner friends much deeper. We should not only care about the commonalities of human being and the commonalities of cities, but also we should make some surprising points to increase the affinity of this city.

The livability and affinity of Shanghai, I believe is part of the hard power of Shanghai's city environment. Shanghai is a city located near the sea and it has four distinctive seasons, but now the environmental pollution problem makes it far from satisfactory. We have to get a standardized indicators system as well as an advanced planning for pollution control. I don't think we should use the midwestern China as our benchmark, because we are moving toward the global city. For weather forecast, we can do much better to perfect its system and relative indexes, for example, the UV index which is very important for the tourists in summer time, travel index, laundry index hydrology index, and pollution index. This would be very useful.

Standardization and internalization are obviously the soft power of city's public service. The standardization and internalization of public services determine the sense of identity and happiness of every cultural group. Surely we should have our own characteristics, but when the local feature violates the general international conventions, people especially the foreigners may feel uncomfortable. We have many examples in this aspect, among which the translation of public sign is a big problem. Many public signs especially like the guideboard, road sign, door plate, and guide map are too old to identify and some of them are even damaged. The translation problems of them are the most serious problem. We can see some examples of that. For the toilet, we often use the word "WC" to represent, but actually many foreigners don't understand at all. Because in English, "WC" means "water closet"," 抽水马桶 " in Chinese. So according to the international convention, I think "man's room", "lady's room" or the more euphemistic word "restroom" are more proper. Another point I want to mention is that many Chinese sign says " 禁止什么 "" 严禁什么 "" 不

许什么""违者罚款"(... is forbidden, you cannot do ..., people who violates will be fined) which conforms to Chinese culture. But I think we can design it more gently, like we can use "Staff Only" to represent "顾客止步". Besides the improperness in translation, we even have many mistakes in the translation of public signs especially in many tourist attractions, which looks ridiculous. I think we need to accord to the customs of foreigners in translation, being proper and standard. In the public signs, another typical example is "Special seats for the old, the weak, the sick, the disabled and the pregnant", which is few to see in foreign countries, because they deem it an impolite practice to "labeling" on people. So we shouldn't restrict to our traditional expression when design public signs, changing our concept a little bit may be better like "Offer seats for those who need help". The sign on the metro in Shanghai has been done well, but in many buses and other cities, the sign of "the old, the weak, the sick, the disabled and the pregnant" is still very common to see.

I think to express the cities information to the outer world is very important. We use the word "express" is because we need to be fast when passing our information to the world, for which translation is too slow. Now there are only two English newspapers (*Shanghai Star* and *Shanghai Daily*) and one foreign language TV channel (ICS), which is far from enough. I think we should catch up with Hong Kong in this regard. Therefore, it's urgent to create more English media and website, keeping them up-to-date. Bilingual electronic screens are also needed in office building concerning foreign affairs, international hotels as well as the public transport means. In addition to that, I think we also have to organize specialists to make bilingual maps, culture-maps, and have them managed, checked and verified by special organizations, thus improving the coherence of its international language environment. The use of foreign languages like French, Spanish, as I said, should be greatly encouraged in Shanghai.

Shanghai is doing well in theaspect of public service facilities, but it still has a lot to improve in the barrier-free service for the handicapped. For example, in the parking, the walking and the reserved seat for the handicapped, we have to make more effort to catch up with many of the global cities. Compared with Tokyo, Shanghai still has a large room to improve in the rubbish classification.

We know that recently Shanghai Qiangsheng Holding limited company released a new type of taxi—luxury British style TX4 taxi which is very popular in Shanghai and has been reported for several times. Why is it so popular? First I think is it has a larger room than the ordinary one. Second is that it can serve people timely. Third, the driver wears suit, tie and even white gloves, with very gentlemanly service like British taxi service. So, it's a surprise for Shanghai local people. Besides, people prefer to pay more to enjoy this so called international standard service which makes people feel more comfortable.

For city intercultural communication competence, I think there are four benchmarks: smoothness, appropriateness, enjoyableness, and effectiveness. The smoothness means that when you arrive at this place, there is no unnecessary barrier for you to deal with affairs. It is not only about the smoothness of procedures, but also the smoothness of emotion as well as language. Appropriate refers to the behavior manner of the citizens in this city. People need to be neither cringing nor arrogant and make the foreign friends feel at home, which I think should be promoted in the education of citizens in the whole enhancement process of city intercultural competence. Enjoyableness means the city can leave a pleasant impression for visitors, which will give them a beautiful memory and make them want to revisit the city for the days to come. The last one, effectiveness is not hard to understand. I believe we have a lot of services and facilities not efficient enough. For example, the planning of the toilet in Shanghai is a big problem. The allocation of the toilets is improper: some places have too many while some other places have too few.

In conclusion, I think in city intercultural communication, it's necessary to enhance both cultural competitiveness as well as cultural affinity of the city, which is a matter of duality. Those two issues are interrelated and interdependent. On one hand, we have to stress the cultural competitiveness, competing with Europe, America and other foreign countries. On the other hand, we need to enhance the affinity of Chinese culture to free foreigners of the aggressive impression of China, so that they can accept Chinese culture and have the longing for a revisit to China. Therefore we should study deeper in this regard, which is significant for the enhancement of the city's brand and image and also conducive to the creation and increase of city's affinity.

Planning Urban Innovation Ecosystems

Willem Van Winden

Amsterdam Government Chief Adviser, the Netherlands

Urbanization actually is an engine for economic development. We know that well-planned cities like Shanghai are great engines for the growth and for innovation, but there's more to weight. It's not only about size and density; it's not only about growing bigger, but also about growing smarter. And I think new approaches are needed not just in that building and rebuilding urban area and make new transit system and so on. And this is really a big urban management challenge: how to better connect people, companies and universities? How to boost urban performance in that way? We've done a lot of studies and researches about these questions. How can cities become smarter? By this "smarter" we don't mean persuing more technology, we think more about it in terms of how to better connect the asset that you have in your city.

First, I want to go back to the very basic thing. It's economies of scale. The well-known advantages of urban scale, "agglomeration economies" as it's called, are the benefits that come from being in a large agglomeration rather than in a small village. If you are in a big city, as a company or a person, you are much closer to the action, and you are closer to the new things, to what's really happening. And that helps you as a company or a person also to be more innovative yourself. Also in big cities, knowledge information and innovations spread fast from one company to the other, because people change jobs and take their knowledge and experience with them. So skill and density in cities offer opportunities for new connections. And as Joseph A. Schumpeter, a famous economist said, it offers code for new combinations and innovations.

But then, of course the question is how big should it be? How big is big

250 | 上海2050 SHANGHAI 2050

enough? If you look at a city like Shanghai, this is a key question. Some people would stress the negative side of the ongoing urbanization process and might say that a further and ongoing migration to the cities could cause the creation of slums, like we see in some Latin American cities. But you may also stress the positive side and say that: Okay, entrepreneurial people are moving into the cities, and they do so because they see opportunities there. They see there is much to do. And more urban migration also will boost land prices so that factories that use a lot of land would be pushed out of the city, and they could be replaced by more service-oriented and less polluting activity, and this is like what you see happening in many cities, in Manhattan, in Tokyo, in Seoul and many other places. So also these cities like Shanghai and Tokyo attract people with fresh ideas. So that can be an argument for trying to restrict migration, but also you restrict the input of all these new kind of impetus.

Another reason is that a well-organized process of urbanization allows for a better allocation of resources. Big urban labor market will result in a better match between supply and demand. More dense cities tend to be less polluting than those with big urban sprawl. Travel by car becomes impractical in those cities and it's replaced by public transportation. In denser cities, industries are moved out because of the rising price and are replaced by service industries as I said. So big cities can be more specialized and can provide an energy boost for new business and new investment.

Having said that, of course, the key question is, for any country, how to manage urban growth? Is it wise to develop many smaller cities and to keep the very big ones a little bit smaller as well? Or should you focus on the top 3 like Hong Kong, Beijing and Shanghai? We've heard that these topics are wildly debated now in China, and not only in China but I think also in many other countries. We've seen since the opening of the economy such a big growth in the Chinese cities especially the big ones. And even that growth was restrained because you had your restrictions on immigration. Many people don't get resident permits that they need, so they cannot collect social benefits and so on. At the same time, there is this evidence of positive effect of agglomeration and density. A recent OECD study, for example, shows very convincingly that densely populated cities like Shanghai and Wuhan in China are considerably less polluting than other cities. In addition, actually we see that the denser the cities are, the higher the wage levels could be. And many big Chinese cities are actually not yet at the density levels of places like Tokyo or Seoul.

So this is where a lot of people talk about now. They talk about the skill agglomerations, small cities, and big cities. Actually the point I want to make here is that yes density makes sense, it's important, but there is more. To understand the economic performance of cities, we must also look a little bit closer at the source of the growth: entrepreneurship and innovation. How do these things evolve in cites and in big cities? How does knowledge spread from one company to the other? How does innovation process happen in different types of industries because one industry is very different to the other? Importantly, how can we organize and build our cities in such a way that innovation is going faster and better? That's not just a matter of having more people and more companies per square meter. That is about developing the city as an open innovation platform, as I call it. And, this platform metaphor has become more relevant because innovation processes in companies have changed. We see that the stereotype of Steve Jobs, as a lonely guy, developing in his own garage a new computer or the stereotype of a single researcher in his lab developing something. This is not really how innovation works. Actually, innovation is very much an open process where people and companies work together, where there are a lot of networks as so it is a networking activity where you combine pieces of knowledge, you combine people, you combine different skills in companies. Development in technology had become so fast that you cannot but work together to create innovation in a company. The work of Henry Chesbrough on open innovation has become very influential, and he shows how high-tech companies are increasingly engaging in open innovation networks and co-create new products and services rather than do it within the walls of their own company. So this open innovation model is not just relevant for big companies, it's now also spreading to other smaller companies and to other industries including the service industry.

So you might raise the question: what does this open innovation mode imply for cities and for the way you develop and plan cities? I would say that one implication that we are already seeing is that innovators people or companies prefer environments, where they can easily find partners. Of course, globalization is there and we have global networks, but local partnerships, as already explained, are very very important. So what do we need for that? We need to create in our cities environments that facilitate networking, that facilitate face-to-face exchange and communication. So in many cities now we see the emerging of new types of innovation districts, where this is really happening, or you have a mix of companies, people, bars, housing, residential, leisure, everything mixed. Because these are what the new knowledge worker wants, and these are the environments where the innovations are emerging. So this type of environments, you have to plan them. It's not just about putting office blocks or office tower here and there. It asks a very careful approach to the public places that connect the buildings and the mix of functions that you have in those areas. And probably this type of urban innovation districts are becoming the new hotspots for the urban knowledge economy, and they are much better equipped for the new innovation paradigms than the old science parks that we used to construct which are mono-functional and a little bit boring with only universities and buildings and so on. One great example of such new innovation district you can find in Stockholm in Sweden, it's in the Söderhamn district, south of the city center. It was not planned as a science park at all, but now it becomes the main technology hub of Sweden where all the new startups are coming, and companies like Minecraft, maybe you know it, or Spotyfy, all of them coming from there actually, because it's such a nice mixed environment with all the amenities, all the assets and the very good quality public space.

So a key question for cities is how can you facilitate or create the type of dense and diverse environment that cater for innovation? And also what can I ask, how can you increase the synergies in this city between the different partners and again, this is not a matter of building, this is a matter of organizing, this is a matter of bring people together in new smart ways. And I will show you some cases from cities that I studied where this is done in a good way, I think. The first example is Germany Aachen. It's a small town actually in the west of Germany with a very famous and good technical university, and this university is building a new campus. And the old ways of building a campus is just opening up a lot of buildings and put all your faculties and staff and all your students there, but not in Aachen, they do it in a different way. They create a concept where the university is much more connected with the business from scratch. So what do they do? They define a number of research topics where they think well, this is what we are very good, for example, automotive. And then they invite companies to locate on that automotive campus. So actually the big campus is a collection of smaller mini campuses that each has their specialization. So each mini campus will be a collection of companies, SMEs, research institutes altogether in one building and all of them will use the same research facilities and the same labs. The companies cannot come all of them, they have to sign an agreement with the university to engage and contract research for the next 10 years, so they really must commit themselves to work with the university. They must promise to send their boss to the university to do guest lectures. The stuffs of the company can follow master courses in the university at a reduced rate. So this is really from the beginning building in your own new campus a structural collaboration between business and research. And results are already very good. They attracted already one hundred companies to this campus. A lot of them come from Munich, from Stuggart and also from abroad. And these companies are very interested because they know if we settle here, we are very close to the best talent to the best students, and maybe we can pick them first. They are very interested in this collaborative research. So I would say this is a matter of having a good concept rather than a good building per se.

The second example is from Tempere, Finland. Tempere is a small town again with three universities. What they did is trying to connect the students' work in the university much better to what the city needs. So they create a structure called DEMOLA. Here it is, DEMOLA HOWITWORKS. Actually DEMOLA is an intermediary organization between the university on the one hand and the companies and the city in Tempere on the other hand. How it works is that companies from the city can ask a question, they can put formulate or problem statement or something they want to do. For example, Intel, the chip maker, they wanted to have a system that they can measure how the buses are moving around. So they put this question, and say: okay we would like to have some research on this. And then students can apply to solve that problem. They can make a team for mixed students from different disciplines and the students will work for the thesis on this very practical and concrete problem. The students learn a lot in practice, Intel company gains from the students' work, and the city of Tempere also benefits because it creates a lot of energy. So actually what they do here is make much better use of the university as a resource. I think that is smart. In Tempere, they don't just see the university as an education center. they also see the university as a connector to companies and to solve urban problems. Interestingly, the students who do the work they own the intellectual property, so if it is successful, they can become very rich, and some of them actually did.

A third example of what I called smart city thing is maker spaces. This is what you see in more and more cities, it is a place where you have some machinery, where you have some equipment, and anyone who likes can go there and make something, can produce something. So here you see a couple of people who want to do something, and this is a way of involving ordinary citizens in the knowledge economy. And there is one example from Barcelona for instance, where there was a child who always had to water the plants because his mother told him: "you have to water the plants everyday." And he was a little bit sick of it, so he wanted to make a machine to water the plants. So he went to the maker space and he said to the leader there: "I want to make a machine to atomize the watering system." And then they linked him with a retired professor from university and some other experts, and they could use the equipment in the maker space. In the end they designed a small water system so that the guy can water his plants automatically from now on. This is a very simple thing, and an increasing number of people now go there. You can take also courses, and you can do a lot of things. This is a way it doesn't cause very much and it's very attractive and interesting.

I want to come to a sort of conclusion. I started my talk about this agglomeration and density, and that more agglomeration more density in the agglomeration theory can produce good effect, and maybe it generates less congestion because you derive out many the manufacturing and so on. But city managers that want sustainable growth and prosperity are wise to do more than just do those like growing the city, building the transit systems. The current trend of open innovation asks for cities to be platforms of innovation. And the cases I mentioned provide some examples of that. I would say the dean of that

Aachen University understands that a good campus is more than a collection of university departments. He designed his campus as a platform for a fruitful exchange between business and science. And in Tempere we see how a simple and cheap intervention on leashes a lot of creative and entrepreneurial energy in the university is, and also helps organizations to innovate. The example of the maker spaces shows that the innovation is not confined to academics and high-tech companies, everybody can be an innovator. Everybody can be involved, from young to old. And it's very exciting to see what is happening there. So I think that urban prosperity and innovation will depend on this type of new concept. And cities that foster this types of organizational innovations, or soft innovation if you like, have a bright future ahead.

The Brand Image Construction of Global Tourism City

Zhang Hui

Prof. of Beijing Jiaotong University

I have to say that the topic "Shanghai 2050" seems quite intriguing. For people at my age, it remains unknown that if could live to that time. Nevertheless, we are at least capable of making a prediction on those days in the near future.

The World Tourism Organization gathered great numbers of experts from various fields that include tourism, marketing, economy and social study. When predicting the developmental trend of world tourism, they have taken it for granted that by the year of 2020, China would be the 4th largest country with oversea travelers, which follows the U.S.A, Germany and Japan. But it has turned out that China's oversea travelers had exceeded Japan in 2002, and exceeded Germany in 2005, and exceeded the US in 2008 and became the world's largest outbound tourism market. In this context, it is not easy for those experts to predict what Shanghai will be like in 2050, because a city's development depends on various factors.

Let's think about a profound question, what is the future development of cities? Just now, some experts have already made a description about cities. The economists, sociologists, urban planner, they have been contemplating on this question for long. In my view, the answer is to develop urban tourism. You may be surprised because industrialization has always been the main theme of urban development. How did come up with the idea that the future development of the cities will be on tourism. In order to explain this, I would like talk about the origin of city.

In Chinese, the word "city" has two meanings. One is the "castle", and the other is "market". The first city in the history of mankind largely has defense function. And the concept of city did not come into being before nomadic society. In the early stage of nomadic society, people constantly move from place to place. The famous emperor Genghis Khan had governed almost 2/3 of the world's territory, but we could not even find his tomb, because of the nomadic culture of his empire. The notion of city had come into being only by the age of agriculture. Back into that time, the city only had political symbol as its main function was to control the towns and villages around it. All the resources of the towns and villages were under direct control of city. Therefore, whoever governs the city has the power of controlling major resource of the region around the city. In this context, the city mainly serves as a military defense which is designated to protect and serve the region around. Thus, there were not many dwellers in the city.

Now let's come to the other function of city as "market" in history. Under this function, the city is a place where people can exchange commodities. Consequently, a new concept of city was gradually formed. From this perspective, city has become an important part of human civilization. And with the development of cities, human beings marched into the new era of agriculture society. Cities at that time played its function in military defense and religious ceremony. It became a place for consumption, and cities and the region it controlled developed into an interdependent and self-sufficient society.

From the perspective above, the early stage of cities is the combination of military defense and market which major function was to provide protection and market place for the people.

The industrialization brought the greatest change to the cities. With the process of industrialization fostered rapid urbanization. Enormous peasants flowed into the city where has been established as a manufacturing base. Thus, cities embrace their golden age of development. On the eve of WWI, most people in countries like Britain, France, Germany and US dwelt in cities. By now, almost 2/3 of the world population has become city dwellers. The cities is now not only become home for millions, but also become the most remarkable symbol of human civilization.

Two major changes has taken place in cities after industrialization. The first change is that the original function of cities as a political center has transformed into economic one. The second change is that the cities' function of serving its surrounding countryside has changed into serving its dwellers. Undoubtedly, these two changes can clearly indicate the future developmental trend of cities. However, what would be the negative consequence of such a trend? Due to rampant industrialization, there was a formidable growth of industrial wealth which created favorable conditions for us to shorten labor time. Along with the development of industrial cities, the time of labor for city dwellers has gradually reduced. Meanwhile the division of labor has also reduced the labor time of family production. This has caused a peculiar phenomenon, that peoples' working time and free time has been separated. Thus, city dwellers began to have to free time.

Adding this to the fact that the industrial labor has deprived people of their happiness, a special industry which focuses on entertaining and amusement has been generated. But current urban construction of our nation does not consider people's needs in entertainment. Previously, our secretary has mentioned the problem of public transportation at the Peoples' Square. In fact, it is a problem caused by lacking of urban recreational facilities. This is what we really need to contemplate on.

We can say that people's leisure is squeezed in the industrial production of a settler lifestyle. It is based on the industrialization of production corresponding to a way of life. So when industrialization promote urbanization in the future, people are tired of the usual environment produced, so it would have on the consumer space, making a tour of the city into the era. Human beings have three forms of society: nomadic society, agriculture society and industrial society. These three societies are different from each other mainly because of their difference in wealth producing. Nomadic society always moves around to produce what they need for their society. The farming communities settle in one place to produce their social wealth. As for the industrial society, they way of producing wealth is through settling in different places. Especially with the rapid development of the Internet and mobile office, city dwellers begin to move among different cities to produce their own social wealth. In this context, we entered an era of urban tourism. In this new era, urban service industry will focus not only the demands of local residents but also concern the needs of travelers. Take Beijing as example, infrastructure like lawn, public toilets and squares can only meet the demands of permanent residents. However, challenges are tough, because Beijing only has two million permanent residents, and Beijing receives 260 million tourists each year. If we distribute the current infrastructure for 260 million people. Then we will find that the toilet is not enough, the square is not enough, parking lot not enough, and everything is in short of supply. In other words, the city was originally developed to serve its own residents. Cities in of future should move concern the needs of both the local residents and the travelers. I think this indicates the conspicuous trend of tourism.

Let's briefly summarize what we are discussing. Industrialization created a casual entertainment, and urbanization has created tourism. Leisure entertainment is a product of industrial development, while tourism is the result of the development of urbanization. Both are subject to the characteristic of industrialized urban lifestyle. The more the industry developed, the higher the degree of urbanization will be, and more people will emphasize the importance of entertaining and traveling. That is why in mid-90s of last century, tourism became the world's largest industry. As a general conclusion, the functions of the cities evolves with the development of cities the urban functions has constantly evolved from military content to commercialization and travel. In agriculture society, cities have shown its feature of militarization and commercialization. While in industrial society, they have presented the feature of entertaining and traveling. The post-industrial society has indicated the trend of tourism. Therefore, cities in agriculture society serve for the region around, while cities in post-industrial cities serve mainly for travelers and local residents.

From the current development trend in the world, we have a lot of data to prove that the proportion of the service economy in overall economy has grown enormously. Moreover, the output value of the service sector's share in total GDP is growing rapidly, and service industries have providing vast chances of employment. For example, the proportion of urban service industry in the economy of developed countries is more than 85%. Almost 80% of the workers are employed in the third industries. There is a gap between our nation and those developed nations. Therefore, we shall make strenuous efforts to adjust and optimize the functions of our cities so as to fulfill our ultimate goal in this regard.

Image Construction of Global Destinations

Noel Scott

Prof. of Griffith University

I would like to talk a little bit about the work in Australia and some examples in Australia about tourism and tourism cities. I think for example that Shanghai is or could be a great example of a tourist city. But a tourist city or a city with a very good reputation and image as a place to visit is really built upon the city itself. So you need to distinguish between the things that make a city, its landscape, especially the experiences that it produces, how its organized and of course, the people.

The secondary part is finding a brand and doing advertising to attract people. So, what I am going to talk about today is some examples in each one of those areas, of how my city or the cities in Australia have done that. So the first thing I want to talk about is the organization of tourism within the city. There are a couple of key things about tourism that you need to realize: it is a fragmented industry; there are not many big organizations involved. And many government organizations are involved in this. There is tourist administration which is in China is CNTA, state tourism, regional tourism organizations, local tourism organizations.

So, one way of organizing these people and asking them to work together is through developing a brand. It is a great statement of how the city or the region or the nation will be promoted. That means you need to talk it the various organizations and ask them and get them involved. So in Australia we have a tourism organization call Tourism Australia which is equivalent to CNTA. They organize or coordinate each of the states to do branding, and the different brands for the nation, state and region fit together, that's called brand architecture. So there are these brand values for Australia which talk about what Australia is about. It's about mateship, it's about being grounded, being ordinary people, pretty optimistic and sometimes a little bit funny.

Let's straight forward, so those brand values of Australia should be seen in any advertising marketing that is for Queensland or for example, for the Brisbane Gold Coast. So you need a vertical coordination, but of course you also need horizontal co-ordination. That is getting the different organization within the state or the region work together.

Recently, *Tourism Queensland,* which is a state organization expanding its role to taking events. So there used to be a *Tourism Queensland* and *Events Queensland*, and those two organizations have now been put together into one organization in order to encourage synergy between them.

A second example, this often happens in governments in many countries around the world is that the various ministries that the government organizations that involved in tourism in some ways. For example, the agriculture departments, or the transport department or the tourism area do not talk to one another. So therefore, if you want to try to develop new products or services, they do not work. So in Queensland, the government has developed what they call a tourism cabinet. It is a group that meets several times a year, involves all the different ministries who have an involvement in tourism, and they do about their planning and talk about tourism. That's horizontal collaboration or horizontal co-ordination at the state level.

So, very important area for tourism in a city is its organization, and second is its infrastructure. And there is a lot of different infrastructures that goes into making an attractive city, and we heard some of these things from Professor Zhang and others.

Every major city seems to have some sort of attraction, the Eiffel Tower, the Golden Gate Bridge. Do you need one of those things? I do not know, but many major cities have one.

What does Brisbane have? Has anyone been to Brisbane? Put your hands up. So Brisbane wanted to be seen as a relaxed, sunshine location. So they looked and they said how can we communicate that to our customers? What infrastructure do we need to make ourselves create the image? So they built some, they built a beach in the center of the city and its free. So you can go there and you can play on the beach and in the background you see the city center. As for me, that infrastructure adds to the destination image that is being designed. It does not just happen. It is a conscious decision that about what infrastructure you put in place.

Of course, this often happens along with major events. So in Brisbane, we have had a Commonwealth Games, then like Shanghai, we had an EXPO in 2010. They were good because they were creating images as sports or perhaps as an entertainment city. But more recently, we have got the G20, that's a significant event perhaps moving the image of the city more towards finance and serious activities.

So, you can change your image perhaps by using events somehow. But of course, the thing is what the visitors feel. And Dr. Ma and I have been doing some work with Professor Gao on Emotions and The Brand Promise—What do you feel when you go to a city? What's the feeling of the city? I will talk about this a little bit, you know, Brisbane has chosen to use the same ideas as New York. I love Brisbane, I love New York. But the idea is that your brand should express an emotion that is realistic. So this is about residents loving the city and visitors loving the city.

What is the emotional feeling that you want from Shanghai? How can you delight the visitor? And we are doing some research looking at what type of experiences produce delight. I was lucky enough with Dr Ma to get an experience in Shanghai. It was a restaurant, and it was not about making food, but it was fun. In order to get inside the restaurant you have to put your hand in one of these holes. And if you put your hand in one hole, then a door opened and you saw a mirror. And you got a fright because that mirror is showing you. But if you put your hand into a right one, then you can go into the restaurant. That's what some of the previous speakers talking about in terms of co-creating an experience with visitors. Creating and emotion in a tourism or a product like a restaurant.

I think, we need to think about trying to produce which create that sense of feeling. Here is an example, in Brisbane, we have a bridge, but a very smart entrepreneur decided to think it's not a bridge, it's an adventure. So now you can walk across the bridge right up high, seeing the city because you got a great view, and you are having a very exciting experience. And if you look here, that's what you trying to produce for visitors; you are trying to produce smiles. Let's think about Shanghai as a tourism city; think it as a city that might produce a smile. How do you do then? It is very interesting.

We have been talking to businesses trying to understand how to create experiences, improve the experiences that the tourism offers. In example, can you get Chinese people to learn surfing? That's tricky! A lot of Chinese people don't like to swim in the ocean. So how do you change and adopt your product to a different culture? But at the same time, when I live on the gold coast, I see tourist wanting to visit the beach. Every Chinese person who comes to the gold coast, the first thing they do is to walk on the beach. So it's interesting, how can we turn it into a tourism product?

What we did is "let's make a beach culture experience". People do not have to go and be active in the ocean. But people from China want to learn about this beach. They want to talk to people about what it is like—The Beach Culture.

So, we moved this product from being an adventurous western product to a beach cultural experience. For Shanghai, I think, many of your products are designed for Chinese people. But how can you adapt those to a western perspective?

Finally, the branding Brisbane. So, there are lots of reasons to visit a city for leisure travelers and for business travelers. We looked at how we promote the Brisbane; Brisbane is the capital city of the Queensland. When we did our research, we found that many international visitors did not really think much about Brisbane. It's a place to visit, it's a good transit link, but it has not got a very strong image in Australian market. So we thought how we started to promote ourselves There was a market. The market was people who want to stay in hotel for short term over the weekend because that was when the occupancy rate was lowest. We looked at the resources of the city and said this is a place for entertainment. Not for the global visitors, because global visitors would not find the entertainment in Australia so attractive, this was in 1997. But we said we could offer exciting entertainment for people who live close to Brisbane. So we came up with the idea Brisbane City of Sundays. It was the first brand for

Brisbane, it was a leisure brand. We came up with advertising, we wanted to say Brisbane is funny, sunny relaxing place, and we had the weather man telling you that there is a lots to do in Brisbane and it's going to be warm and sunny.

Later, in 2004 we moved the image further away from just pure leisure into a more sophisticated night-life image still based around entertainment. And of course, along with the brand, there goes a lots of other collateral materials like advertising, providing ways for individual businesses to linking to the brand and do advertising connectivity. And of course there we got internet advertising brand now which is a major form of people use to do destination branding.

I think there is many lessons that cities around the world can provide for Shanghai and cities around the world can learn from Shanghai. I think city branding is a big thing. What you need is a good organization that means organizations in different business working together—government, industries and universities. And you need to think about your attractions or your emotional outcomes from visiting the city, the feeling you want Shanghai to produce. Cities tend to be exciting, have a lot of night-life, have a lot of entertainment and culture and lots of different things. And thirdly, you need to think about branding and developing experiences.

Shanghai: Reflection on Global Cities

Ning Yuemin

Prof. of the Center for Modern Chinese City Studies,

East China Normal University

Today, I would like to give a talk on the development of Shanghai over the past 20 years as well as its goal to be a global city around 2050, like what kind of city Shanghai will develop into.

First of all, I would like to introduce you two famous scholars in this research field of world cities or global cities. As we all know, although the British scholar Peter Hall wrote a book on world cities in 1966, it was John Friedmann who theorized it. John Friedmann, with his colleague Woolf, published a paper of much significance in 1982, and he published another paper on hypothesis about world cities in 1986.

I think Friedmann's theoretical framework is based on Wallerstein's world system theory which divided the world into three parts: core countries, semi-peripheral countries and peripheral countries. Why is the world system divided into such three parts? Because he reckoned that progress would upgrade those semi-peripheral countries to core ones, vice versa, regress would degrade core countries to semi-peripheral ones which are immature and positioned at the periphery of the world system. On the basis of this hypothesis, Friedmann proposed a theory on the world cities. What he stressed much was the capability of world cities to control global capital or regional capital. That's why he believed company headquarters, international organizations and international financial institutes are core judging factors of world cities. In 1980s, the whole Chinese economy was not related with the world economical system that closely, therefore there were no Chinese cities in Friedmannn's world cities system.

At the same time, Friedmann held another important viewpoint—apart from the control-force of capital especially the financial capital, the capability of supplying products to global market is another important function. In 1990, on the basis of world cities, Sassen proposed the concept of global cities. Here I would like to point out that what Sassen focused on the global cities was the producer service, while today we further it into advanced producer service or APS, which holds the most important function of global cities. The above is the background of global cities, and actually a background of globalization.

Especially in the early 1990s, that is, after the so called Washington Consensus established, a trend of thought of new liberalism was prevailing throughout the whole international society. What is the so called new liberalism? Actually it means the reduction of government interference, namely the reduction of state interference, so that capital can expand globally. So, Sassen proposed the concept of global cities under the trend of thought of new liberalism. I think maybe such a background is unfamiliar to many of Chinese students present here today. Then what is its structure during such an expansion? As we can see, cities like New York, London, and Tokyo have become core world cities. Peter Taylor et al. accepted this concept as well as the concept of flowing space proposed by Castel and they established a research group on world cities and global cities in the early 1990s.

Just now, this Belgian scholar introduced a large amount of data they used in their research. But which basic points was the data built upon? Its APS includes five sectors: Finance, Banking, Insurance, Consulting and Accounting. Do you know in which countries do this five sectors distribute? Actually, they are almost monopolized by the USA. So, it is very interesting that those Belgian scholars adopted the social net analytical method viewing the world as a net.

We can see the result of their research: Shanghai has been upgrading. While, is it true that Shanghai has reached such a level already? Let's take a look at Friedmann's hypothesis about world cities, is it outdated already? Here is a paper published by Friedmann in 1986 in which the world was divided into core countries and semi-peripheral ones. As for those core countries, their cities were divided into first class world cities and second class ones; the same case was with those semi-peripheral countries. But as we can see there was no concept of core countries or semi-peripheral ones under Sassen's globalization background.

It seems that the world is flat in our mind because of its becoming a net, but those dominate countries are neglected completely.

In fact, under the trend of thought of new liberalism, when multinational companies expand globally, those developed countries still play the dominant roles in the world economic system because of their large amount of multinational companies. According to the research result of 2012 World Cities Net System, London and New York are already the first class world cities, and Shanghai and Beijing are the sixth class and the eighth class respectively.

But what I want to remind you is, suppose we add a new APS, as we all know, it is internet times nowadays, but no internet industry is counted in as the APS, if we also take those internet industries such as Google, Twitter, Facebook into account, what a kind of role will China plays in the world then? We ourselves should hold a sober knowledge of the roles Shanghai and Beijing play in the world cities system.

This is a research on WC (world cities), the data in 2000 showed that Shanghai ranked the 31st, while it jumped to the 6th in 2010. But Shanghai was judged only by those five sectors, here what I want to reiterate is that this was actually judged by the global expansion of multinational companies, while there was almost no Chinese company in such five sectors, therefore when we talk about the world cities system, it is still the one of Friedmann's times. In fact, the world is still unequal and dominated by those core countries. If we refer to research results from other research institutes, take the American Foreign Policy a very authentic magazine as an example, we will find that there is a world cities list in it.

There is a Tokyo Morry Fund Association in Japan, which always ranks world cities, and we can see Shanghai ranks rather low on their list. For example, on this list from the magazine *Foreign Policy* in 2012, Shanghai ranked the 21st according to its economy, down one spot from 2008 to 2012. While on the list of world cities potential index from Tokyo Morry Fund Association, Shanghai got a bit better grade on the whole while still ranked the 20th. Which means from the perspective of the current development level, both Shanghai and Beijing still have a large gap to bridge between them and other world cities.

Under such a background, let's seehow will Shanghai set its development goal. First, I would like to show you three challenges during the development of Shanghai.

The first one: the ratio of Shanghai's economy in national GDP keeps declining. In 1978, Shanghai's regional GDP accounted for 7.84%. Of course, we may say the reason is most areas in China in 1978 suffered from slow development so that Shanghai seemed to enjoy a powerful economy comparatively. As other areas developed rapidly, the ratio of Shanghai's economy started gradually declining especially in 1980s. While in 1990s, thanks to those multinational companies coming to China to invest, the ratio of Shanghai's economy stayed climbing up because Shanghai was their first choice to invest on account of its location advantage. Since 2000, as we can see, the economy of the central and western regions of China has been growing rapidly, the ratio of Shanghai's economy dropped by one percentage point. While over recent years, because Shanghai's economy shows a slower growth than the average growth of China, this downward trend will maybe sustains for one year plus according to our estimation.

The second one: when we make judge on world cities or global cities, what kind of company headquarters and how many company headquarters they possess will be important indicators. We find that the development gap between Beijing and Shanghai is growing when we judge them by these indicators, which began from 2004. Then let's make a reference to the data of Fortune 500 companies published by the American *Fortune* Magazine, there are more than 90 Fortune 500 companies in the mainland China among which 52 companies are located in Beijing only 8 in Shanghai. This is the first data. Then let's take a look at the average annual turnover of those companies in Beijing and Shanghai, Beijing 76 billion USD each, while Shanghai only 47 billion. What does that mean? It means the scale of Fortune 500 companies in Shanghai is much smaller than that in Beijing. If we see it from the perspective of APS, Finance is a very important sector. There are 10 major financial institutes in Beijing, while only 3 in Shanghai. The average annual turnover of those 10 institutes in Beijing is 79 billion USD, while only 37 billion in Shanghai. From the above data, we can see that the gap between Beijing and Shanghai is actually growing on their road to achieve their goals to be global cities.

Especially the finance, at first the finances in Shanghai were the most competitive ones in China, while they were surpassed by those in Beijing over a decade recently. For example, there are 395 thousand workers in financial services in Beijing, while only 300 thousand in Shanghai. Then, the finances value added reaches up to 259.2 billion RMB in Beijing, while Shanghai 245 billion, lower than Beijing even in this competition. Shanghai is better than Beijing only in one aspect: its deeper internationalization. According to their deposit and loan balances of foreign financial institutes, it is 940 plus billion in Shanghai, while only 350 plus billion in Beijing. From the perspective of finances, we can see that Beijing is stronger than Shanghai because the majority of the biggest finances are located in Beijing in that it is the location of the Chinese capital and the Chinese central bank. While on the other side, Shanghai is a bit deeper international than Beijing.

The third one: what challenge is Shanghai facing now? That is its international level is comparatively low because of its one-way flow of foreign investment. In London or New York, the flow of foreign investment is two-way. What does that mean? On one hand, global cities are bases of output of domestic capital; on the other hand, they are cities of input of foreign capital. Then, for Chinese cities, no matter Beijing or Shanghai,according to their current situation, they are cities mainly of input of foreign capital rather than output of domestic capital which is just starting out. We can see here in 2013, in Shanghai there were 445 regional headquarters of multinational companies, 283 investment companies, 366 foreign research and development centers. All these three indicators have shown a rapidly upward trend over the past decade. However, what I stress is the output of our domestic capital is just starting out.

Then let's have a look at the business scale of Shanghai stock exchange which ranked the 4th in the world in 2011. But we can see that the turnover gap is very large comparing it with other two stock exchanges in New York. What's more, under the unique system of Chinese market, if a company wants to go public, it cannot apply to Shanghai stock exchange directly but have to apply to CSRC (China Securities Regulatory Commission), a subordinate department of the central government in Beijing. This is the unique background of Chinese market. From this perspective, even though the stock exchange is the product of market economy, in China, it doesn't have the decision right. If we say world cities dominate the world economy and a international economic center dominates global economy, then it is Beijing rather than Shanghai that plays this role of domination, because our current economic management system is centralized, anyway, we are on the road to the market economy.

The fourth one: the ability of science and technology innovation in Shanghai is comparatively weak. Just now our guests talked about the science and technology innovation, here is a very interesting data which was published by the US patent office. If we want to retrieve the patent quantity of cities where inventors reside, we will find that Tokyo is far ahead before any other cities in the world, and Silicon Valley ranks the second place, actually the San Jose in Silicon Valley. As for Chinese cities, Shenzhen ranks the first place in China, Beijing the second, Shanghai the third. So, we can see, even though in the patent registration, Shanghai lags behind Shenzhen and Beijing.

Finally, the conclusions are as follows. The first one: world cities of developed countries are still playing the dominant roles in the world, which is determined by their capital and technology, especially in America. Friedmannn divided the world cities system into core countries and semi-peripheral ones. I believe his truth still endures today. The second one: state is still playing important roles during the development of world cities. Especially for China, the central government still plays an important role in the decision of resource allocation, and that is one very important reason why Beijing surpassed Shanghai so soon in recent decade, as far as those five important indicators of their development into world cities are concerned. The third one: as the Chinese economy grows, world cities in China will start a process of two-way internationalization, that is, they will be not only places where foreign capital gather but also places of output of domestic capital. Here is a very important data, in 2013 the Chinese direct foreign investment reached up to $107.8 billion, while the input of foreign direct investment was $123.9 billion. According to the predication, the output of Chinese direct foreign investment and the input of foreign direct investment will strike a balance this year. As the Chinese economy grows, the output of Chinese direct investment will increase. While, here is another data about the internationalization of Chinese companies. It is about the most international Chinese companies, namely the companies with the largest output of domestic capital. In these top 50 companies, there are 28 companies located in Beijing, while only 3 in Shanghai.

Since the beginning of this century, amounts of companies directly under the central government have emerged from the reorganizations of state-owned companies in China. The number of Fortune 500 companies in Beijing has surpassed that in Tokyo. Besides, the majority of the most international companies in China are located in Beijing. In the past decade, the producer services in Beijing, especially those APS, enjoyed a considerable growth. Therefore, Beijing is a global city with the most potential, because Beijing plays a much more important role of dominating the Chinese economy or influencing the global economy than Shanghai. And I personally reckon Beijing comparatively accord with Sassen's concept of global cities, that is, Beijing is an APS-oriented global city. Then what about Shanghai? Maybe Shanghai is on a different development road from Beijing, because it remains those comparatively strong manufacturing industries, especially the Yangtze Delta area where Shanghai is located is one of the most important manufacturing bases in the world. As we all know, China has surpassed German as the biggest export country in the world, while export of the Yangtze Delta area occupies 40% of all, which means, if we go back to Friedmann's definition of world cities, that is, world cities exert influence on the global market, then, from this perspective, the Yangtze Delta area exerts much more influence on the world manufacturing market than the area where Beijing belongs. Here I personally believe that in the future Beijing and Shanghai, the two representative Chinese cities, maybe choose different development roads: Beijing accords with Sassen's definition of global cities because of its APS as its main industry, while Shanghai accords with Friedmann's definition of world cities because of its producer services and manufacturing which will share equally importance. Therefore, from this perspective, we can see that Beijing and Shanghai will meet different function divisions.

International Challenges in Global Cities: Strategy and Solution

Zhuang Enping

Prof. of Shanghai University

Just now, some other Chinese scholars and experts shared their opinions on Shanghai's becoming of global city from different perspectives, from which I discovered that we all look at the same problem from different angles. Professor Winden had talked about China as well as Shanghai's migration to cities, and here this kind of population flow mostly includes migration from countryside to urban areas, especially the population flow into Shanghai. Today, I want to focus on international migration, which means international population will flow into Shanghai. Professor Lu also mentioned the intercultural competence of the city, as far as I am concerned, which's a new perspective on city's soft power. As long as all kinds of people gather together, solutions for the potential problems will emerge from their interactions. The question is-what is this potential problem? My answer would be intercultural challenge.

Shanghai's challenge in becoming Global City is intercultural challenge, which is also my anticipation for potential problems facing the global city of Shanghai in 2050. Under the background of the economic globalization, metropolises all over the world will also confront with intercultural challenges. So, globalized society has destined the development of Shanghai reflecting multicultural city. Global cities not only agglomerate social, economic, technological and tourism resources, but also agglomerate international talents, for they are more livable places for international talents to live in and study. Thus, people from different cultural backgrounds will cooperate, work, learn and live together, and multicultural community will become a feature of the global city. Meanwhile, cultural conflicts, caused by cultural diversity, will become a considerable social problem in social management. Therefore, the anticipation of intercultural challenge faced by the global city has its reasons. Today, intercultural challenges have become a conundrum in the social management of European cities, so for this reason the European Commission has taken measures—intercultural city strategy to meet with the challenges brought by intercultural conflicts. I want to offer three suggestions from my point of view:

First, scan the intercultural challenges from global concept. In 2050, the global city of Shanghai will inevitably attract more international talents, including international organizations, transnational corporations, transnational campuses, international students, foreign tourists and immigrants, and they all will gather in Shanghai. We cannot predict the population of those international talents, but it will be sure that global city will mark globalization, multi-culture as well as international human resource as its marked features. Therefore, cultural conflicts caused by multi-culture will also become a major problem in the development of the city, which's also an inevitable path in the process of becoming a global city. From the appearances of the analysis, those international talents will bring different values, different thinking patterns, different beliefs and religions, different manners to Shanghai, which on the surface would cause cultural conflicts, however, when we look at this development trend from intercultural perspective, we will get a different interpretation and anticipation in an in-depth level, that is, facing up to those opportunities for development brought by cultural differences and cultural conflicts. Because, what emerges from the collision of different cultures, thinking patterns and ideas is not mutually exclusive, not conflicts, not rights and wrongs, but new ideas, new vision, new perspectives, which is what Shanghai needed for innovative thinking and innovative ideas. Innovation is bred out of the collusion of different cultures. By then, Shanghai will embrace the new horizon of being an innovative city.

When we look at same problem from different perspective. For example, there's a famous picture, when we look at the picture, everyone present will see a completely different picture. It is a girl. But some of you maybe see something else—an old woman. Who's right and who's wrong? When we look at the same thing from different perspective, at the end, you will see different things. There's no right or wrong, there's only differences. This also can be used in this aspect.

If we compare culture to iceberg, what we want to study is not the tip of the iceberg, but the obstacle hidden under the tip. Have we made the preparations? Not yet. So in the end, we came across lots of questions, and we don't know the reasons for these problems. As a matter of fact, this is the source of these problems.

When we do the same thing in different ways and in different ways of thinking, it generates different effects. What should we do? I want to mention "cultural communication". This is a kind of thinking pattern.

There's one sentence which reads: "East is east, and West is west, and never the Twain shall meet!" Never the Twain shall meet, because where the Twain meet, there generates conflicts. And I changed this sentence into: "East is east, and West is west, and the Twain can meet!" Why Twain can't meet? Because once they meet, they generate conflicts. Why do they generate problems? And what's the origin of these problems? Because everyone considers once they meet, they will generate conflicts, and everyone fears of cultural conflicts, thus everyone should avoid conflicts. Why should we avoid conflicts? Actually the primary cause lies not in the eastern or western culture itself, but in our capability of managing cultural differences. So whether Shanghai has the capability of managing intercultural challenges entirely depends on whether the city managers have the capability of managing intercultural city. As far as I am concerned, this is the very problem that matters to Shanghai's soft power.

Second, study from successful examples. In 1992, the United Nations Educational Scientific and Cultural Organization held the 43rd International Education Conference and proposed the purpose of intercultural education: respect integration and cultural differences, reduce all forms of exclusions, understand other individuals as well as other countries, cultivate students' intercultural acclimatization, help students to lead a better life in an intercultural society. In 2008, the European Commission and European Union jointly launched "the Intercultural City Strategy", aimed at addressing the intercultural challenges faced by a number of European cities. Intercultural city is not only to solve problems of cultural diversity, but also it is a city of vitality, innovation, creativity and a source of continuous development. Since 2008, eleven cities have launched intercultural city strategy. Up to 2014, there have been 41 cities, such cities as London, Dublin Ireland, attended in 2009 and 2010 respectively. Intercultural issues in city development are not only the problems of European cities but common problems of all the countries around the world. So in January, 2010 the Japan Foundation in Tokyo and the European commission jointly organized "the Euro-Asian Intercultural Forum", in which officials of European Commission as well as experts in intercultural city participated in the discussion and released "Tokyo Declaration", aimed at strengthening the cooperation with European Commission and promoting communication and cooperation between cities to discuss the intercultural challenges facing with the world. So the concept today has already affected America, Canada, Mexico, Korea and other countries and cities. Besides, experts in many countries have begun studies on this aspect. Based on the concept of European intercultural cities strategy and development path, what's the connotation of Shanghai's development of global city, how cultural diversity among global cities adapt to each other, how they interact, how they integrate, how to make the city maintain its vitality and innovation? For all these questions, I sketched out the framework for the connotation of the global city.

Being a city model, global city is a concept, however, the culture of a city is dynamic and the development of urban cultural is promoted by its citizens. Similarly, the cultural of a city can also make a great influence on its citizens' vision, thinking and action. Intercultural is not only multicultural concept, but a dynamic progress where different cultures communicate, interact and integrate with each other. This kind of dynamic progress not only can make positive influence, like interaction and integration between cultures, but also can make a passive influence, like cultural conflicts. The key lies whether people have the capability of managing cultural differences to promote intercultural communication and improve the ability of intercultural interaction and integration. From now on, we should pay much attention to intercultural education, which should meet the needs of social development. So we should build a social environment with intercultural thinking and capability, which provides vitality and innovation for the global city, showing citizens' global citizen literacy and reflecting soft power of Shanghai city. Multicultural citizens will become an important part of Shanghai's urban population in the future, flowing into enterprises, education community and other fields. Therefore, we should build the community they live in, the school or enterprises they work or study at, into intercultural communities, campuses, and enterprises and that is the important feature of a harmonious city.

Intercultural Campus: there are some problems that education fields should take into consideration, like: how to take advantage of multiculturalism to enrich education resources; how to compensate for the lack of educational resources; how to make full use of these multi-resources, multi-cultures to create China's intercultural campus atmosphere and intercultural classroom atmosphere, where domestic and overseas students interact with each other to develop mutual learning, mutual adaptation, mutual respect, mutual tolerance, mutual appreciation consciousness for each other's cultures, through which expand their global vision, improve their intercultural communication capability.

Intercultural community: improving the intercultural capability of the community workers is the key. Foreign residents come from different nations and they all have their own values, religious beliefs, ethnic customs, thinking and communication patterns, so these will inevitably lead to misunderstandings and even conflicts in cultural awareness, habits, needs of community, neighborhood harmony, etc. Facing with these misunderstandings or conflicts generated from cultural differences, what should we do to deal with it and eliminate it? These issues are the problems faced by the international community. We should not only change the community management models and build intercultural community environment, but also expand the horizon of the communityworkers, by enhancing their intercultural awareness, teaching intercultural knowledge and improving intercultural communication skills. Only in this way will the international community become the paradise for foreign residents.

Intercultural enterprises: China's enterprises will be integrated into the global market, participating in the global businesses, global mergers and acquisitions as well as global management, integrating global human resources and enhancing global competitiveness. Yet, the biggest challenge of China's multinational enterprises is intercultural barriers in management and administration. In fact, intercultural barrier is apparent reason for the management failures of multinational enterprises. The underlying reason lies in lack of intercultural awareness, intercultural management and communication capability of business managers. So when enterprises face with cultural differences or conflicts, not knowing how to manage them results in huge loses. In the future, intercultural barrier must be the main obstacle on multinational enterprises' way of becoming internationalization. Therefore, it will surely be able to eliminate the cultural obstacle and promote effective cultural management capability to create intercultural enterprises and improve the management capability of the enterprise managers. Only in this way will improve the core competitiveness of Chinese enterprises and create harmonious social environment. Therefore, cultivating business operators' intercultural competence is our current priority.

Finally, cultivating intercultural talents with intercultural competence is current priority. No matter China or the world, today or tomorrow, with the background of globalization, intercultural issue will become a permanent topic, which is determined by the background of economic globalization. Therefore, only by cultivating intercultural talents and making them play an important role in all professions and trades in the society, can mitigate and solve the intercultural problems. However, intercultural study is a newly emerging field, which has not received much academic attention and approval. So, I appeal to all related departments and education field to attach great importance to cultivating of intercultural talents for people of different cultures to live and work in harmony and for tomorrow's dynamic and innovative global city of Shanghai 2050 to reserve and deliver intercultural talents.

Dialogue

Audience: Professor Stefan, I have a question, for the development of global city, which kind of innovative industry is needed? What kind of effects these new innovative industries might have on the global cities' development as well as on the branding of these global cities?

Stefan Kratke: My answer is, it's very important to take care of the economic base of cities. There're traditional manufacturing industries as well as new innovative industries of all kinds, and they both must be seen as an important part of the economic base of cities. So my answer is, not rely solely on financial sector and real estate, and business services. In Germany, we have some cities with plans or policies which let people totally rely on the services or financial sector, and lost interest in their industrial base, so they are very weak in their economic base. Besides, new innovative industry is a very important part of global cities. Therefore, nowadays, we have to study the globalizing economy and the inter-urban connections, which are important in the development of these industries. I hope I could answer your question!

Audience: I have a question for Mr. Willem from Amsterdam, the Netherlands. As we know that Netherlands has many innovative cities such as Amsterdam and Rotterdam. Would you like to tell us what can we learn from Dutch experiences, and how could Shanghai transform its local fashion from production to innovation?

Willen Van Winden: I think that's difficult. Shanghai is growing and changing very fast, as we see. We have to learn also a lot from China, and we are increasingly seeing that for example, how you are doing things very well.

In Netherlands what you could learn is that we have a good tradition of urban planning where a lot of attention is put not only on the individual buildings but on the public spaces that connects the buildings, so that when you build a city, you don't just put buildings here and there, but from the beginning you create a more unified concept, and then it's good. For example in Amsterdam, it has a canal, a very famous canal. We planned like that in the 16th or 17th century. So it's a very long tradition of the Netherlands, because we are a small country we don't have much space, so the space that we have, we must use it very wisely. And I think that's a lesson that you could take. And the other thing is that maybe in the Netherlands we are traditionally very open, so lots of people come and go because we are a trading nation, so we pick the best things from all over the world and try to use that. I think in this way the Chinese people are much similar to Netherlands also. That's a very short answer, the best way of learning, I would say, is to visit each other. You can visit Amsterdam, and we show you around. You must make a conclusion what is good for you or not. It's difficult for me to do right now

Audience: I have a question for Professor Ning. about world cities. You said that, for Shanghai, if it wants to develop into a global city, whose goal is still built on the innovation and progress of its advanced manufacturing. But sometimes in our research, we can find that nowadays many manufacturing industries in the Yangtze River Delta (Shanghai included) are moving out to other areas, and because of the high life expenses in the central area, there is more possibility for the development of services for life or product. I wonder how to balance the percentage of the manufacturing in the future, or what lessons can we learn from those mature global cities like Tokyo if Shanghai wants to achieve such a level, or by innovation, we remain the manufacturing in Shanghai and balance its proportion?

Ning Yuemin: I would like to answer your question briefly. I remember there is a professor in Toronto University who does the research on the database of cities, and in his work, he met a problem of urban scale. Actually, it is very important. Because Shanghai is 6 000 plus square kilometers, while New York only 800km^2, so we can't simply compare the industrial structure of New York with that of Shanghai, because there is no possibility of development of manufacturing on the 800-square-kilometer land of New York or the 1 500-square-kilometer land of big London. This is the root cause why their services take up a huge proportion. But in China, all cities like Beijing and Shanghai are very large areas, so, services are main industries in city centers, but they still possess large suburbs, which is the basic distinct.

Remark

Lu Jianfei

Chairman of the Council of Shanghai Normal University

Many inspiring viewpoints about city development have been offered just now. Shanghai has hosted the World Expo for various reasons, one of which is to achieve its theme "Better City, Better Life" that describes the city vision. To develop from city to metropolis is the mark of modernization. The higher the level of urbanization is, the more highlighted the modernization mark, especially for developing countries. However, the highly centered city also causes "City Disease", such as urban slum, epidemic disease, traffic congestion, violence, haze, poverty, robbery and prostitution. So, under this background, Shanghai proposed the smart theme "Better City, Better Life", which attracted many voters, earned higher marks, and gained the opportunity to host the World Expo. What's more, the United Nations declared that 51 percent of population lives in cities and it is an important development of modernization. Realizing this, we should regard the world cities day as a day of commemoration, and more importantly, a day of reflection and expectation, to reflect and repent the mistakes that we have made in the course of urbanization.

The expectation of global city is talked a lot today. But what is a global city, and how to construct it? Many experts have given their viewpoints from various aspects like index, parameter, criterion, element and system. I believe the discussion will continue whether it is from the perspective of industry, tourism, culture or population. As to build global city, all roads lead to Rome. It is very interesting and adds various perspectives and glory to urbanology.

What impresses me most is that we focus on the urban radiation, domination, innovation, vitality, diversity and livability. More attention is paid to cultural soft power rather than GDP. Some experts talked about how to shape the brand of global city, some about population, the number as well as its diversity, literacy and cross-cultural communication, some about rejuvenation and aging of the population. All provide new perspective for population structure and distribution of the global city, which is very significant. Besides, the views that global city is not always the capital city, is not always along the coast, is not always big, and is not always with long history also bring us benefits.

I will offer three points to today's meeting minutes. First, we should make clear that we are in the era of city, a new milestone in the development of human beings. Doesn't it mean the era of city when the United Nations pointed that 51 percent of the population lives in cities? So, today's discussion about urban theories, city vision, governance, history, gene and urban spirit provides more topics for city exploration. Second, this forum fits the aim of sustainable development of human beings proposed by the United Nations, that is, the coordination of economy, society and environment. Third, the theories put forward by Feldman, Sassen and Castells from 1980s to 1996 all proposed the challenge of how to solve the problems in the course of global city construction. Today we have experts from worldwide, and our forum will enlarge its range so that we can face the challenges, plan the future, share ideas and achieve development with broader horizons, collective intelligence and concerted efforts. City development is the game of the interests of all parties. I believe it is towards the virtue, the beauty and the truth. Only in this way can peace and development be the theme of human development.

CLOSING
SPEECH

闭幕演讲

中国城市经济学会副会长、上海社会科学院院长王战
在全球城市论坛闭幕式上作闭幕演讲

Wang Zhan, Vice Chairman of China Society of Urban Economy,
President of Shanghai Academy of Social Sciences, delivers a closing
speech at the Closing Plenary Session of the Global City Forum

从"城市，让生活更美好"
到全球文明城市

王 战

中国城市经济学会副会长

上海社会科学院院长

数年前，随着中国（上海）2010 年世博会的举办，"城市，让生活更美好"的主题得到了充分的演绎，这一主题也已深入人心。作为上海世博会的重要成果，世界城市日正是"城市，让生活更美好"精神遗产的延续与传播。进入 21 世纪的第二个十年，世界格局、科技发展、人类认知都有了很大的变化和推进。今天重温"城市，让生活更美好"的内涵，就会形成更多的新知，尤其是对"城市，让生活更美好"的界定。著名城市学者科特金在《全球城市史》中把城市的终极愿景归纳为"安全，繁荣，神圣"，这三个词显然是有递进意义的。当今，尽管还有最不发达国家的人民在争取安全或繁荣，但的确有更多的世界人口可以为神圣的城市愿景而努力。当然，在今天的语境之下，神圣的含义就是文明。纵观世界城市的建设历程，实际上也是暗合了"安全，繁荣，神圣"这三个阶段。

现代意义上城市总体规划的全球实践始于 20 世纪 50 年代。50 年代，无论是西方阵营基于凯恩斯主义的思维，还是东方阵营基于计划经济的思维，都执行了技术主义的城市规划路线，提出了次序性、控制性的城市功能与空间部署，但部署执行缺乏弹性的缺陷也逐渐暴露。

20 世纪 80 年代末，当代意义上的全球化启动，新自由主义思潮席卷世界，发端于企业战略规划的城市战略规划思潮与实践开始兴起。把城市思维、经济中心强调为自由市场力量，而非约束性规划力量对城市的塑造，指导了一批城市的更新和复兴，但也导致了城市阶层对立、社群隔离等深层次的矛盾。

2008 年，美国次贷危机的爆发以及持续多年的全球蔓延，使人们试着重新审视自身的诉求与城市的愿景，关于对理想生活、理想城市的认识与评价标准正发生着重大的变迁。幸福、和谐、低碳成为新的主流诉求，以人为本的城市规划设计恰恰与“文明”的终极追求相吻合。为此，世界一大批城市，从纽约到伦敦，从多伦多到约翰内斯堡，纷纷启动了2030、2040、2050的新一代城市发展战略规划。

上海作为第一个以城市为主题的综合性世博会举办城市，自然有责任为世界范围的新一轮城市发展战略阐述作出贡献，也为中国的新型城镇化伟大实践作出贡献。上海新一轮的发展愿景应当是具备重大文明特征的，应把2050年的上海愿景目标称为全球文明城市。21世纪是一个多元化、多级化发展的世纪。多元文明的交流、交融将替代西方文明单一主导的局面，未来具有全球性影响力的文明城市将更有可能在文明交汇点上崛起。上海170年的历史表明，上海正是这样一个文明交汇点城市。

未来具有全球性影响力的文明城市更有可能在文明交汇点上崛起，不同于文明渊源型城市强调的文明传承性和正统性，文明交汇点上的城市更强调文明的传播与交流，关注本土文明对世界的贡献，因此更可能获得世界性的认可和接受。上海全球文明城市应当至少融汇全球各种文明，承载生态文明、信息文明的内涵，并且，随着人类认知的拓展，还应该展现更大的内涵，但不变的一点是，上海要强调中华文明意义上的全球性贡献。

当然，全球文明城市是一个理想状态的描述，当代人以及后代人需要竭力去做的是，在实践中接近这一目标。为此，就涉及路线图的设计，可分为10年一段。到2020年，上海应该基本完成“四个中心”建设，那就是经济中心、金融中心、贸易中心和航运中心。但它的内涵发生了很大的变化，因为在提出“四个中心”的20年中，一个非常伟大的事件改变了它，那就是信息技术革命。所以，在“四个中心”建设中，必须考虑三个问题：一是上海必须建成一个智慧城市，上海在全国是最早提出建设智慧城市的。二是必须以上海都市圈的空间为依托。三是上海的经济中心建设必须以建成具有全球影响力的科技创新中心作为内涵。上海之所以成为上海，因为它后面有长江，有一个城市非常密集的长三角城市群。根据六大世界城市群目前的年均增长率测算，到2030年，长三角这个城市群很可能成为世界上最大的城市群。上海就是这样一个世界最大城市群的首位城市。但有一个很重要的制约条件，就是上海能不能跨过生态文明这一道槛。因为，在这么大的区域中，如果不是绿色发展，那么将丧失道德标准。

到2050年，上海应该成为一个“全球文明城市”，从确切意义上讲，上海应该成为具有信息文明、生态文明以及东方文明影响力的全球城市。

上海的全球城市建设，一是要强调信息文明。今天，我们还沉浸在工业文明中，实际上信息文明已经悄悄到来，上海在这方面应该走在前面。二是要强调生态文明。在今后 30 年，西方文明和东方文明将互动、融合，当然也会产生很多碰撞，在这方面，上海由于其历史的独特性，应该会在这些文明中发挥出影响力。中国上海世博会主题馆所演绎的"人—城市—地球"，恰恰体现了世界各种文明关于人类发展、城市建设的交流和沟通。

过去 30 年间，中国有 26 000 多万农民进入城市，这是古今中外所没有的，其间中国并没有发生重大的社会动荡，而且中国城市依托人口红利取得了长足发展。其中，具有价值的中国经验可为世界的城市化推进所分享。当前，中国正进入新一轮的城市化，即新型城镇化，在推进城镇化的同时，应主动反思中外城市化正反两方面的经验教训，其终极追求的就是上海世博会主题："城市，让生活更美好"。

From "Better City, Better Life" to Global Civilized City

Wang Zhan

Vice Chairman of China Society of Urban Economy

President of Shanghai Academy of Social Sciences

Several years ago, with the host of Shanghai World Expo in 2020, "Better City, Better Life" has been fully interpreted and firmly established. As an important achievement of World Expo, World Cities Day is precisely the continuation and spread of the spiritual heritage delivered by "Better City, Better Life". In the second decade of 21st century, the world pattern, science and technology, as well as human cognition have achieved great change and progression. Today, let us review the connotation of "Better City, Better Life" to form more new understanding, especially on the definition of how to be "Better" in city life. Famous urban scholar Joal Kotkin concluded the ultimate vision of city in three words—"security, prosperity and sacred" in his masterpiece *The City: A Global History*. Apparently, these three words have progressive significance. In today's world, even though people in the least developed countries are still fighting for "security" or "prosperity", indeed, more population can strive for the city vision of "scaredness". Of course, in today's context, the true meaning of "sacred" is civilization. The construction course of the world city, as a matter of fact, coincides with three stages of city vision— "security, prosperity, sacred".

Worldwide urban overall planning practice in modern sense started in 1950s. The Western camp based on Keynesianism and the Eastern-bloc based on planning all have performed a technical doctrine of urban planning, proposing the ordered and controlled city function and space deployment with gradual exposure of unpractical and inelastic defect.

In the late 1980s, since the launch of globalization in contemporary sense, the new liberalism has swept the world, with the thoughts and practice of urban strategic planning originated in corporate strategic planning rising. City mind and economic center were considered as the free market rather than a binding planning power for shaping the city, which led the revival and renewal of a batch of cities. But it also led to the deep contradictions, such as urban class antagonism and social isolation.

In 2008, with the outbreak of subprime crisis in the US and its global spread lasting so many years, people began to reexamine their appeal and the vision of the city. Meanwhile, the evaluation standard of ideal life and city also changed greatly. Happiness, harmony, and low carbon become popular. Since people-oriented city planning is consistent with the ultimate pursuit of "civilization", many cities like New York, London, Toronto and Johannesburg are launching new strategic planning facing the year 2030, 2040 and 2050.

As the host city of the comprehensive World Expo that first proposed the theme of "city", Shanghai should resume the responsibility to make contribution to the new round probe into worldwide city development strategy and new-type urbanization in China.The vision of Shanghai new round development should have obvious characteristics of "civilization" and its ultimate pursuit is "global civilized city". The 21st century witnesses the development of diversification and multi-polarity. The communication and integration of multi-cultures will replace the pattern that is dominated by western culture. It is in higher possibility for cities with global influence to rise on the intersection of civilization. Shanghai is a city like this with her 170-year-old history.

Cities with different cultural origins stress the inheritance and legitimacy of civilization, while cities on the intersection of civilization pay more attention to the spread and communication of civilization and the global contribution of native civilization, and it is easier for them to be recognized by the world. Therefore, the "global civilized city" of Shanghai should integrate civilizations in the world and cover the connotation of ecological civilization and information civilization. Its connotation will be continually extended with the development of cognition. But one thing will never change, that is, Shanghai should stress her global contribution in the sense of Chinese civilization.

Of course, the "global civilized city" is an ideal description. Its achievement needs our practice and our descendants' endeavor. And here comes theroutes of development. By 2020, Shanghai should have been constructed into one of the international centers of economy, finance, trade and shipping. And its connotation also changes a lot due to the information technology revolution. Therefore, three points have to be considered in the course of 4-center construction. First, the aim is to be a wisdom city that is first proposed by Shanghai. Second, Shanghai metropolitan area serves as a support. Third, to be a globally influential center of science and technology innovation should be part of its economic center construction. Yangtze River and Yangtze River Delta urban agglomeration promote the development of Shanghai. It is predicted that Yangtze River Delta urban agglomeration will top other five and be the largest one in the world in 2030 if calculated according to current average annual growth rate. Shanghai is the primate city of this urban agglomeration. However, the crucial premise is that Shanghai achieves ecological civilization and green development, or else the ethnic standard will lost.

As to be a "global civilized city" in 2050, I mean, Shanghai will be an influential city with information civilization, ecological civilization and oriental civilization, with the former two stressed. Now we are immersed in the industrial civilization, but information civilization is approaching and I believe Shanghai should be ahead. In the following 30 years, western civilization will interact and integrate with the east, and collisions cannot be avoided. Owing to the historical specialties, Shanghai should be influential in those civilizations. "People, City, Earth" displayed in the theme pavilion of Shanghai World Expo is just the reflection of the communication of human development and urban construction in the world.

In the past 30 years, 260 million rural population has poured into cities and no major social unrest happens, which is rarely seen in the world. What's more, thanks to the migration dividend, the cities have made substantial progress, the valuable Chinese experience during which can be shared to promote global urbanization. At present, China is approaching a new round of urbanization, which is called "New Urbanization". We are not only promoting urbanization, but also reflecting on the experience and lessons at home and abroad to ultimately pursue "Better City, Better Life".

CLOSING
ADDRESS

闭幕致辞

上海市常务副市长屠光绍
在全球城市论坛闭幕式上作闭幕致辞

Tu Guangshao, Executive Vice Mayor of
Shanghai, delivers closing remarks at the Closing
Plenary Session of the Global City Forum

致 辞

屠光绍

上海市常务副市长

今天是首个世界城市日，这是第一个由中国在联合国推动设立的国际日。当今人类社会已经进入以城市为主的时代，城市已经成为人类文明进步的重要载体，同时当今世界又进入了一个转型的时代，城市成为这个转型时代的核心。因而，加快城市发展，提升城市品质，实现资源可持续利用，实现经济社会全方位转型，已经成为许多城市共同面对的课题。当前上海正处于转型发展的关键时期，这些话题显得更为紧迫和现实，亟须通过开展全方位的战略研究、启迪思路和探索路径。

在上海创新转型过程中，战略规划研究一直发挥着重要作用，它不仅可以广泛吸取社会各界智慧，形成共识，促进民主决策，而且能够发挥思想的指引作用。改革开放以来，上海已经开展了数次对城市发展具有重大影响的战略研究，其中提出的很多思路和建议已经转化为上海城市的发展战略，体现在城市总体规划之中，也反映在上海历次经济社会发展五年规划之中。这些发展战略对推进浦东开发开放，对上海国际经济、金融、贸易、航运中心和社会主义现代化国际大都市建设发挥了重要的指导和引领作用，推动了上海经济发展方式和产业结构实现战略性转变。同时，上海城市发展战略研究还反映了决策民主化、科学化的特色，历次战略研究都汇聚了上海以及全国乃至全球不少地方共同研究的智慧，因此也是集体智慧的结晶。上海市政府对于城市发展的决策，就是建立在充分论证、民主讨论的基础上，决策以战略研究为基础，凝聚集体智慧，发扬民主作风，尊重不同意见，并通过反复讨论，探寻解决问题的路径，才保证了决策的科学性。

目前，上海正在按照国家"两个一百年"，也就是中国共产党建党100年和中华人民共和国成立100年的目标要求，面向新的发展阶段，积极开展"面向未来30年的上海"发展战略研究。我们将按照国家对上海继续当好改革开放排头兵和创新发展先行者的要求，充分反映未来世界形势发展变化及主流趋势、全球政治经济格局变化态势，顺应未来全球城市体系的演进趋势，从国家战略高度以及全球大的格局当中谋划上海中长期发展，勾勒上海城市发展愿景，明确发展理念和发展方向，推动城市创新驱动发展。

此次全球城市论坛作为世界城市日系列论坛之一，在主、分会场上，各位嘉宾和专家学者围绕"面向未来30年的上海"发展战略、全球城市建设等主题，进行了深入的交流探讨。这次论坛不仅对"面向未来30年的上海"发展战略研究的前期成果进行了充分交流，实现了思想的碰撞，而且为这项发展战略研究的进一步深入打开了国际视野。与会嘉宾和专家学者给上海未来发展战略提出了很多颇有建设性的思路和意见，使我们收获颇丰，也深受启发。与此同时，大家围绕全球城市创新与竞争力提升、全球城市发展困境的突破、城市发展环境转变等内容展开了深入的交流，为全球城市发展也提供了大量的思想财富。我们相信，此次全球城市论坛中提出的城市发展的一些建议，必将对上海城市未来发展提供有益的帮助和借鉴。

上海有幸成为首个世界城市日活动的举办地，这是对中国为世界城市日设立所作努力和贡献的肯定，也是对今后上海全面提升国际影响力的巨大鞭策和鼓舞。全球城市论坛的举办，开启了世界城市交流合作的新平台，必将促进世界城市交流合作步入新的阶段，在推动世界城市发展中发挥积极作用。从这个意义上来讲，全球城市论坛马上要闭幕了，但它更意味着一个新的开始。

Address

Tu Guangshao

Executive Vice Mayor of Shanghai

This is the first World Cities Day, the first international day promoted by China and set by the United Nations. Since human society has approached the age of city and the era of transformation, with city as the carrier of human civilization and the core of transformation, the issues of improving urban value, realizing sustainable resource utilization and achieving all round transformation of economy and society have become the common issue in city development. Shanghai is in the critical period of transformation and in great need to conduct strategic research and find way out, so these issues seem more urgent and realistic.

In the course of Shanghai innovation transformation, the research of strategic planning, which widely draws wisdom and promotes democratic decision-making, is exerting important function. Since the reform and opening up, Shanghai has carried out several researches, many of which has transformed to development strategy and become part of the city overall planning and Shanghai Five-Year-Plan for economic and social development. Those researches and strategies play a key role in Pudong opening-up strategy and lead the construction of this modern socialist metropolis to be the international center of economy, finance, trade and shipping, promoting the strategic change of economic development pattern and industrial structure. Shanghai city development strategic research bears the characteristics of democratic and scientific decision-making and is the collective intelligence of the city, other places in China and in the world. We can see that as to the scientific decision of city development, Shanghai Municipal Government puts emphasis on convincing argument, democratic discussion, strategic study and collective intelligence and revises the decision again and again to explore the way out.

Currently Shanghai is launching the planning research of "Facing Shanghai in 30 Years" development strategy according to the overall demand of 100-year anniversary of the foundation of the CPC and PRC. Facing the new development stage, in accordance with the country's requirements of being the forerunner of reform and opening-up and innovative development, Shanghai will explore the trend of world situation and the change of global political and economic structure, complying with the evolution trend of global city system in the future, planning for the medium and long-term development from the height of national strategy and global pattern to draw the vision of city development, making clear the development ideas and direction, and promoting the innovation-driven development.

As one of the series forums of World Cities Day, the global city forum has attracted experts to further discuss about "Facing Shanghai in 30 Years" development strategy and global city construction, to exchange ideas and to provide international vision. We benefit a lot from your advice. Other themes like global city innovation and the promotion of competition, the breakthrough of global city development dilemma and the change of city development environment also give us fresh ideas about global city development, which I believe can supply helpful and constructive reference to Shanghai development.

It is a great honor for Shanghai to be the first host of World Cities Day, which is the affirmation of Shanghai in promoting the set of World Cities Day and greatly inspires Shanghai to enhance its international influence. The hold of global city forum opens new platform for global city communication and cooperation, and will promote it further in global city development. The global city forum is about to close, but it also means a brand new start.

APPENDIX

附 录

首届世界城市日
介绍

"世界城市日"（World Cities Day）是联合国认可的国际日，它来源于上海世博会的精神遗产，以上海世博会"城市，让生活更美好"（Better City，Better Life）作为总主题。"世界城市日"具有鲜明的时代特色，对人类社会的可持续发展具有重大意义。

1. "世界城市日"的源起

举世瞩目的中国 2010 年上海世界博览会于 2010 年 4 月 30 日在美丽的黄浦江畔隆重开幕。在中国 2010 年上海世博会 184 个难忘的日子里，246 个国家（地区）和国际组织紧紧围绕上海世博会主题，完美地演绎了世界各国人民对未来城市生活的美好愿景。2010 年 10 月 31 日，在上海世博会闭幕当天举办的高峰论坛上，对整个上海世博会进行总结的《上海宣言》正式发布，并成为全球城市可持续发展进程中的一份重要文献。宣言在结尾处发出倡议，建议将 10 月 31 日上海世博会闭幕之日定为"世界城市日"，让上海世博会的理念与实践得以永续，激励人类为城市创新与和谐发展而不懈追求与奋斗。

2012 年 4 月，中国政府正式启动"世界城市日"的申设工作，并成立了一个跨部门联合团队来共同推动申设工作。在中国政府和有关各方的共同努力与推动下，国际展览局全体大会、联合国人居署理事会和联合国经社理事会先后通过决议，建议设立"世界城市日"，联合国各主要成员国均对设立"世界城市日"表示了支持。2013年12月28日，第68届联合国大会最终通过决议，决定自2014年起，将每年的10月31日设立为"世界城市日"。

2. 设立"世界城市日"的时代背景与重大意义

设立"世界城市日"，汲取全球智慧，聚焦城市发展，有利于城市时代人类社会的共同进步与可持续发展，有利于提高各国城市建设和管理水平，有利于稳步推进健康可持续的城市化进程。每年一度的"世界城市日"将呼唤各国城市关注城市化进程中的重大挑战，在全球范围内探讨和实践解决方案。这将为处于不同发展阶段的全球城市提供一个交流城市发展经验、共同解决城市问题的良机。

2.1 设立"世界城市日"是城市时代人类发展的需要

今天，全球50%以上的人口已经居住在城市，到2030年，近60%的世界人口约50亿人将聚居在城镇地区。作为商业、文化、科技、生产力、社会发展的枢纽，城市在带给人们空前丰富的物质和精神财富的同时，也产生了前所未有的挑战。全球的城市面积仅占地球陆地面积的2%，能源消耗却达到了60%—80%，并产生了高达75%的二氧化碳排放。快速的城市化还导致了人口膨胀、交通拥挤、环境污染、资源紧缺、贫富差距、文化冲突等日益严峻的城市问题。可持续的城市发展也因此成为21世纪全球社会面临的最紧迫挑战。"世界城市日"的设立，将聚焦城市发展问题，关注全球城市化进程中的效率提高和技术创新，促进在人口高度集聚的城市实施行之有效的管理，减少资源和能源消耗，实现城市健康有序的增长。

在经济全球化的大趋势下，各国相互依存、相互影响，共同面对气候变化、能源安全、粮食安全、公共卫生安全等全球性问题。随着城市时代的来临，许多重要经济、社会和文化事务的协调与解决已从国家和区域层面深入到城市层面。与此同时，城市居民身份日益多元，利益格局日趋复杂，导致传统的城市解决方法已经难以为继，"世界城市日"的设立将探索建立新的以城市为主体的联合协商和协调机制。

2.2 设立"世界城市日"将有效促进全球城市尤其是发展中国家城市的可持续发展

今天，世界上10个城市居民中有7个生活在发展中国家。今后几十年，约 95% 的城市扩张将发生在发展中世界，亚洲、非洲和拉丁美洲的主要发展中国家正在从具有几千年农耕文明历史的农业大国，转变为以城市社会为主的工业化国家。城市的飞速发展与扩大，不可避免地带来负面的影响。除了全球城市发展过程中产生的普遍性问题外，广大发展中国家还面临着城乡融合、经济转型、资源约束等特有问题。这些问题的解决，有赖于各国政府的政治智慧、各国人民的共同参与，也需要借鉴世界各国尤其是发达国家在城市建设和管理方面的经验和教训。

在信息化时代，资本和人才等市场要素正突破原有的地区性约束，以城市为节点在全球范围内自由流动；与此同时，金融危机、气候变化和文化冲突等挑战在国际与国内层面共同演进，对发达国家原有的城市管理机制提出了挑战。实践证明，现代城市可持续发展问题呼唤全球性的解决方案。在全球化时代，没有一个城市可以独善其身。因此，"世界城市日"的产生恰逢其时。

2.3 设立"世界城市日"符合联合国追求的可持续发展目标

联合国自成立以来一直倡导的目标是："为全人类创造更美好的世界"，而创设"世界城市日"，关注城市可持续发展问题，一方面与全球的发展与奋斗目标吻合，另一方面也体现了人类与城市发展的具体需要。

1992 年的里约环境与发展大会达成了"共同但有区别的责任"原则，以及有关气候变化、生物多样化和环境保护的一系列公约。近 20 年来，全球在可持续发展上虽然取得一定进步，但是进展缓慢，由于资金、技术和人才的缺乏，公约的一些内容没有得到有效执行。在全球化的世界，人类面临的各种危机相互关联，只有加强全球合作才能应对这些危机。

联合国倡导的可持续发展三大支柱——经济、社会发展和环境保护——相互紧密依存，都是城市可持续发展所涵盖的重要领域，并关系到人类未来的福祉。全球可持续发展的成败从未像今天一样与城市的发展紧密相连，正因如此，全球快速城市化被列为里约 +20 会议议程的优先重点。将于 2016 年召开的第三届联合国住房和可持续城市发展大会的主题也已确定为探讨可持续的城市化和城市的未来。

迄今为止，联合国认可的国际日已有 106 个，其中涉及城市发展问题的有国际电信日、世界文化多样性促进对话和发展日、世界环境日、世界人居日、消除贫穷国际日、争取和平与发展世界科学日等，它们均从不同角度关注城市面临的困难与挑战，但直接以城市为综合关注对象的国际日还亟待产生。因此，设立"世界城市日"有望成为联合国国际日大家庭的重要补充。通过设立"世界城市日"，联合国可以在全球范围内建立城市可持续发展问题的高级协商机制，加强各国政府关注城镇化进程中重大城市问题与挑战的政治意愿，进一步发挥个人、民间团体与组织在解决城市问题中的作用，并可以对各个领域涉及城市问题的资源进行综合、整合与提升。

城市的可持续发展是全球无论发达国家、发展中国家还是欠发达国家共同关注的主题。设立"世界城市日"，可以最大限度地吸引和动员世界上大多数国家参与共同探讨城市发展过程中面临的各种问题，更好地发挥联合国在城市可持续发展领域的影响力。

2.4 设立"世界城市日"将有力推动中国的新型城镇化进程

过去30多年来，中国的城市发展取得了令世人瞩目的成就，其发展模式、经验教训为其他发展中国家提供了宝贵的借鉴及参考价值。当前中国正在推进的新型城镇化，坚持走以人为本、四化同步、优化布局、生态文明、文化传承的中国特色新型城镇化道路，推动大中小城市和小城镇协调发展，这正是对"可持续城市化"内涵的诠释。

推动设立"世界城市日"，体现了中国政府对于本国和全球范围内可持续城镇化问题的关注，将有利于展示中国在城市建设与治理方面的成就和理念，也将有利于中国学习各国在城市化和可持续发展方面的成功经验。中国政府还将通过经验分享和在资金、人力、物力等方面的大力协助，搭建发展中国家同发达国家深入探讨城市快速发展过程中的挑战和经验的平台，促进全球城市乃至全人类的可持续发展。

"世界城市日"的筹办及其与联合国人居署、联合国经济社会事务部等国际组织的深度合作，将有效拓展上海的地方外交和城市公共外交，提升上海的国际化程度和国际影响力，促进"四个中心"和现代化国际大都市建设，将有利于上海继续当好改革开放的排头兵与科学发展的先行者。

3. "世界城市日"主旨与年度主题

各方一致同意，"世界城市日"应包含一个永恒的主旨，每年在此主旨下更换不同的年度主题。主旨体现"世界城市日"的目标、愿景与实现路径，通过与标识（logo）重复不断地出现加强受众对"世界城市日"这一品牌的深入认识。而年度主题则可结合当年的热点城市问题和国际社会关注焦点，在符合总主题演绎方向的前提下不断变化，以体现时效性与国际性。

经过协商，明确了以上海世博会主题"城市，让生活更美好"（Better City，Better Life）为主旨，这一方案既揭示了"世界城市日"与上海世博会的紧密联系，同时也与联合国人居署历年所关注的城市可持续发展方向保持一致，更体现了设立"世界城市日"的终极目标和愿景。通过讨论，首个"世界城市日"的主题确定为"城市转型与发展"（Leading Urban Transformation）。各国发展的实践表明，只有通过经济和社会转型，摆脱高能耗、高污染、粗放式的传统城市发展模式，才能实现城市的可持续发展。如何处理转型与发展两者之间的关系，是当前和今后一段时间各国城市普遍面临的热点和难点问题，值得在全球范围内进行研究与探讨。

4. "世界城市日"中方协调机构设置及主要职责

经联合国人居署同意，上海成为首个"世界城市日"的主场活动城市。为了更好地推动筹办工作，2014年9月2日，"世界城市日"事务协调中心在上海成立。作为"世界城市日"中方主要执行和协调机构，上海世界城市日事务协调中心承担了首个"世界城市日"的各项宣传、组织与筹备工作。在活动仪式结束后，协调中心还将与联合国人居署等国际机构和国内外智库充分合作，通过组织论坛、展览展示、案例遴选、宣传推广、知识分享与培训等活动，协助各级政府和社会团体、企业、个人应对城市化进程的挑战，共同解决国内外各类型城市的可持续发展问题。

5. 首届"世界城市日"主要论坛活动

5.1 上海 2040 高峰论坛
主办单位：上海市城市总体规划编制工作领导小组办公室

承办单位：上海市城市规划设计研究院

论坛简介：按照上海市委、市政府工作部署，上海新一轮城市总体规划编制工作已全面展开。为进一步体现"开门办规划"，作为首届"世界城市日"系列论坛活动之一，上海市城市总体规划编制工作领导小组办公室（主办方）于 2014 年 10 月 31 日举办上海 2040 高峰论坛。本次论坛特邀联合国人居署官员，首尔、芝加哥、米兰等国外城市市长代表，美国、比利时等国专家出席并做主题发言。与会嘉宾就面向未来 30 年的上海空间发展战略进行研讨，为上海新一轮城市总体规划编制提供经验借鉴。

5.2 全球城市论坛

主办单位：上海市人民政府发展研究中心

世界银行（World Bank）

承办单位：上海师范大学

支持单位：世界城市数据联盟（World Council on City Data）

上海市城乡建设和管理委员会科学技术委员会

上海城建（集团）公司

论坛简介：2014 年，上海启动了面向未来 30 年的发展战略研究课题，广泛动员国内外专家和社会力量积极参与。论坛邀请包括世界银行和国务院发展研究中心在内的 70 多个研究团队，分别从全球视野、国家战略、专业领域等不同角度对上海 2050 年的目标任务进行系统研究和专题研究。经与世界银行协商，将首届全球城市论坛的主题确定为"上海 2050：崛起中的全球城市"。论坛邀请联合国经社部官员、世界银行专家、城市市长和国内外知名专家学者汇聚美丽的黄浦江畔，探讨全球城市发展趋势，研判 2050 年上海的发展战略，把脉城市发展重大议题，共同谋划上海未来美好蓝图。

5.3 2014 国际健康城市论坛

主办单位：中国市长协会

上海市健康产业发展促进协会

承办单位：上海瑞茵健康产业有限公司

支持单位：中国浦东干部学院

论坛简介：随着历史的发展、社会的进步，健康城市的设计、规划、建设和发展，也将与时俱进地进入一个全新的历史时期。新理念的推广、新机制的论证、新标准的制定、新模式的运行，将引导出一个持续影响城市转型与可持续发展的新话语体系。秉承开门办论坛、持续搭平台、精心树品牌的宗旨，2014 国际健康城市论坛借助高新科学技术和广泛社会力量来共同构建包容度大、参与度深、体验度强的开放式框架来共求发展。

2014 国际健康城市论坛于 2014 年 10 月 31 日举行，宗旨是研讨、弘扬视野更广阔、格局更宏大的健康城市建设理念。

5.4 中国新型城镇化发展论坛

主办单位：中国建筑学会

支持单位：上海市城乡建设和管理委员会

上海市交通委员会

上海市宝山区人民政府

上海市规划和国土资源管理局

协办单位：上海市建筑学会

上海现代建筑设计（集团）有限公司

同济大学建筑设计研究院（集团）有限公司

CCDI 悉地国际

论坛简介：为回顾和总结我国城乡建设经验，通过繁荣建筑创作和促进科技创新，探索集约高效、生态环保的新型城镇化发展道路，在《建筑学报》创刊 60 年和 2014 年全球首个世界城市日之际，经研究决定在上海召开中国新型城镇化发展论坛暨《建筑学报》创刊 60 周年纪念活动。本次论坛邀请多位院士大师、中国建筑学会领导、长三角地区有关部门领导、国内知名建筑师代表、著名专家学者、企业家代表、高等院校代表等参会，是 2014 年建筑界一场高端行业盛会。

5.5 第三届公共外交国际论坛：城市外交的实践与探索——中欧对话

主办单位：中国察哈尔学会

荷兰国际关系研究所

德国对外文化关系协会

承办单位：上海公共外交协会

支持单位：中国公共外交协会

论坛简介：中国的城市外交实践一直走在理论研究的前面，城市外交工作既推动了地方经济、社会和文化的发展，也为国家总体外交做出了重要贡献。改革开放以来，随着我国城镇化和城市国际化速度日益加快，城市在国家发展战略和国外交往中的作用越来越突出，而如何通过城市外交，推进国际化战略，实现城市发展战略目标，也已成为许多城市关心的重要课题。第三届公共外交国际论坛将实践案例与学术探讨结合起来，搭建中外专家学者、政府官员之间的交流互动平台，在多个方面扎实地推进中国的城市外交工作。

5.6 地下管线与城市安全学术论坛

主办单位：上海市公路学会

协办单位：阪申土木技术咨询（上海）有限公司

论坛简介：城市地下管线是城市基础设施的重要组成部分，是城市的"生命"，地下管线的泄漏、火灾、爆炸、坍塌、内涝、断气、断水、断电将威胁整个城市运行和严重影响市民的生活质量和生命安全。至 2013 年底，上海各类公路总里程已达 12 300 多公里，城市道路总里程为 4 860 多公里。目前各类地下管线（包括水、电、燃气、电信及其他）的总长度已达 10 多万公里，多埋在道路下面，为城市输送着物质、能量与信息。地下管线与城市安全学术论坛从国内外、境内外地下管线的规划、设计、建设和运营管理的现状、技术措施等各个方面进行讨论和交流，旨在为上海的城市可持续发展和"四个中心"的建设、建成较为完善的城市地下管线体系、大幅提升上海应急防灾能力提供一个科技合作交流的平台。

Background

As an international day recognized by the United Nations, the World Cities Day is derived from the spiritual heritage of Expo 2010 Shanghai China and takes "Better City, Better Life", the theme of Shanghai World Expo, as its general theme. The World Cities Day bears distinct characteristics of the times and plays a significant role in the sustainable development of the human society.

1. Origin of "World Cities Day"

The remarkable Expo 2010 Shanghai China was grandly opened on the bank of Huangpu River on April 30, 2010. In the l84 unforgettable days during the Shanghai World Expo, 246 states and international organizations perfectly displayed the fine vision of the people around the world for the future urban life by closely centering on the theme of the Expo. On October 31, 2010, at the summit forum held on the closing day of Shanghai World Expo, the Shanghai

Declaration which summarizes the whole Shanghai World Expo was formally released and became an important literature in the process of sustainable development of world cities. The ending of the Declaration proposed designating October 31 of every year when the curtain of Shanghai World Expo fell as the "World Cities Day", so as to permanently extend the ideas and practices of Shanghai World Expo and encourage human beings to make unremitting efforts for city innovation and harmonious development.

In April 2012, Chinese government officially started the work related to the application for the designation of the "World Cities Day", and set up a cross-departmental united team to jointly push forward the work. Under the joint efforts and driving of the Chinese Government and parties concerned, the Bureau of International Exhibitions (BIE) General Assembly, the United Nations Human Settlements Programme (UN-HABITAT) Governing Council, and the Economic and Social Council (ECOSOC) have successively approved related resolutions on designating the "World Cities Day". In addition, major member states of UN supported the designation of the "World Cities Day". On December 28, 2013, the 68th Session of the United Nations General Assembly finally passed a resolution on designating the October 31 of every year, beginning from 2014, as the "World Cities Day".

2. Background and Significance of the Designation of the "World Cities Day"

Designating the "World Cities Day", drawing the wisdom of the world, and focusing on urban development are beneficial to the common progress and sustainable development of the human society in the urban age, the improvement in the urban construction and management level of all countries, and the steady advancement of the health and sustainable urbanization process. The annual World Cities Day will appeal to all countries to focus on major challenges in the urbanization process and discuss and practice related solutions around the globe. The World Cities Day will provide global cities which are in different development stages with a golden opportunity to exchange urban development experience and commonly solve urban problems.

2.1 The designation of the World Cities Day is a necessity for human development in the urban age

Today, more than 50% of the world population is tiring in cities, and by 2030, about 60% of the world population (approximately 5 billion) is expected to inhabit urban areas. As the hub of commerce, culture, technology, production capacity, and social development, cities have generated unparalleled challenges while bringing people with unprecedentedly rich material and spiritual wealth. Cities around the world cove roughly 2% of the land area of the earth, but consume as much as 60%-80% of the energy around the globe arid generate 75% of the total carbon dioxide emissions. Moreover, the quick urbanization also leads to problems like population expansion, traffic jam, housing shortage, environmental pollution, resource shortage, income inequality, cultural conflicts, etc. The sustainable development of cities has therefore become the most urgent challenge facing the world in the 21st century. The World Cities Day will focus on urban development problems, concentrate on efficiency improvement and technology innovation in the urbanization process, promote the implementation of effective management in densely-populated cities, reduce the consumption of resources and energy, and realize the healthy and orderly growth of cities.

Under the general trend of economic globalization, all countries rely on each other, impact each other, and jointly respond to global problems like climate change, energy security, food security, public health security, etc.. With the coming of the age of cities the coordination and settlement of many important affairs in economic, social, and cultural fields have deepened from national and regional levels to the urban level. Meanwhile, the identities of urban residents are increasingly diversified and the interests patterns a re becoming complicated with each passing day, which results in the situation where the traditional urban solutions are difficult to handle. The World Cities Day will explore and set up new combined coordination and consultation mechanisms which take cities as the subject.

2.2 The designation of the World Cities Day will effectively promote sustainable development of world cities especially cities in developing counties

Today, seven out of ten urban residents in the world live in developing countries. In the next several decades, about 95% of urban expansion will occur in the developing world. Main developing counties in Asia, Africa, and Latin America are turning from agricultural countries with the agriculture civilization and history of thousands of years to industrialized countries which focus on the urban society. It is inevitable that the rapid acceleration and expansion of cities will bring some negative impacts. Except universal problems that the urban development process results in, developing countries are facing specific problems in terms of urban-rural integration, economic transition, resource constraint, etc. The solution of these problems shall depend on the political wisdom of governments of all countries, the joint participation of the people of all countries, as well as the experience and lessons of various countries (especially developed countries) in city construction and management.

In the information age, market factors such as capital and talents are breaking the original regional constraints and freely flew around the globe, seeing cities as the nodes. Meanwhile, challenges like financial crisis, climate change, and cultural conflicts co-evolve at home and abroad and constitute challenges to developed countries' traditional urban management mechanisms. Practices have proven that the solving of problems on sustainable development of modern cities needs global solutions and no city can develop independently in the age of globalization. Therefore, the World Cities Day comes at a right time.

2.3 The designation of the World Cities Day conforms to the sustainable Development goal that the UN pursues

Since founded, the UN has always been advocating the goal- "to create a more beautiful world for the mankind". The World Cities Day focuses on issues regarding the sustainable development of cities, which is consistent with the development goals and working goals of the world on the one hand, and embodies specific needs in the development of the mankind and cities on the other hand.

The United Nations Conference on Environment and Development which was held in Rio in 1992 accepted the principle of "common but differentiated responsibilities" and reached a series of conventions related to climate change, biodiversity, and environmental protection. Over the past 20 years, although the world has achieved certain progress in terms of sustainable development, the progress was slow, and these conventions were not put into effective implementation due to the lack of funds, technologies, and talents in the globalized world, crises faced by the mankind are interconnected, and these crises can be solved only by strengthening the global cooperation.

The economic growth, social progress, and environmental protection, three pillars for sustainable development advocated by UN closely rely on each other, being important sectors that the sustainable development of cities covers and being associated with the future well-beings of the mankind. The success in the sustainable development of the world has never been associated with the urban development as closely as today and that is the reason why the rapid urbanization is included as the priority of the agenda of the Rio+20. In addition, it has been confirmed that the 3rd United Nations Conference on Housing and Sustainable Urban Development which will be convened in 2016 will be themed on the discussion over the sustainable urbanization and the future of cities.

So far, 106 international days have been recognized by the United Nations, among which international days that involve urban development issues include the World Telecommunications Day, the World Day for Cultural Diversity for Dialogue and Development, the World Environment Day, the World Habitat Day, the International Day for the Eradication of Poverty, the World Science Day for Peace and Development, etc. These international days focus on difficulties and challenges facing the city from different points of view, but international days directly taking the city as the overall concentration object remains to be designated Therefore, the World Cities Day is expected to be an important supplement to the family of UN international days. Via designating the World Cities Day, the UN may establish advanced consultation mechanisms as to issues on sustainable development of cities around the globe, strengthen the attention of governments of all countries to major problems and challenges in the urbanization process, further encourage individuals, civil society and non-governmental organizations play more important roles in solving urban problems and synthesize, integrate all resources in different sectors involving urban problems solutions.

The sustainable development of cities is a topic under the common attention of developed counties developing countries and under-developed countries in the world.

The World Cities Day will attract a majority of countries in the world to jointly discuss various problems the urban development process facing, and therefore significantly elevate the influence of the UN.

2.4 The establishment of World Cities Day will forcefully drive China's new urbanization

Since the past 3 decades, the urban development in China has achieved remarkable results, and the development mode and expedience & lessons thereof have provided precious references and reference value for developing countries. At present, the "new urbanization" that China is promoting sticks to the new urbanization path of people-oriented, synchronization of modernizations of industry, agriculture, and informatization, optimized layout, ecological civilization, and cultural inheritance which bears the Chinese characteristics and accelerates the coordinated development of all kinds of cities as well as towns and counties which is just the interpretation to the connotation of "sustainable urbanization".

The promotion in designating the World Cities Day shows the attention of Chinese Government to sustainable urbanization problems of China and the world is helpful for China to learn successful experience of various countries in urbanization and sustainable development, and learn the successful experiences of urbanization and sustainable development. The Chinese Government will provide experience and vigorous assistance in terms of fund, manpower and material resources, construct the platform where developing countries can discuss challenges and learn experience in the rapid urban development process from developed countries, and make contributions to sustainable development of cities.

The establishment of the organizing platform of World Cities Day and its in-depth cooperation with UN and other international organizations will effectively promote the local foreign diplomacy, the city's public diplomacy, enhance the globalization degree and international influence of Shanghai, and facilitate the building of "Four Centers" and socialistic modern international metropolis. All these will be conducive to Shanghai's role of the reform and opening-up pacesetter and pioneer of scientific development.

3. Permanent and Annual Theme of "World Cities Day"

Parties have agreed that the World Cities Day shall have a permanent theme, and each year will have different theme under this permanent aim which could manifest the objective, vision, and realization way of "World Cities Day", and would, through repeated appearance with the Logo, strengthen the in-depth understanding of the audience towards the brand of "World Cities Day". The annual theme may combine the hotspot urban issues and focus of the international community of the year, and change constantly on the premise of conforming to the general aim, with a view to demonstrate the timeliness and internationality. Through discussion, "Better city, Better Life" of the World Expo Shanghai is set as the aim, which not only indicates the close association between World Cities Day and Shanghai Expo, but also accords with the UN-Habitat's focus on the sustainable development of cities over the past years, and more the ultimate target and vision of holding the "World Cities Day". After discussion the theme of the first World Cities Days determined as "Leading Urban Transformation". The practices of countries' development indicate that only by carrying out economic and social transformation and ridding of the traditional urban development model featuring high energy consumption, heavy pollution, and extensive development can cities achieve the sustainable development. At present and in the near future, cities around the world are all facing the hot but difficult issue on how to deal with the relationship between transformation and development, which is worthy of worldwide research and discussion.

4. Setting of Chinese coordination body of World Cities Day and its main responsibilities

With the approval of The UN-Habitat Shanghai becomes the home court city of the first "World Cities Day".

In order to better drive the preparation and organizing work, on Sept. 2,

2014, Shanghai Coordination Center of World Cities Day was established in Shanghai. As the major execution and coordination body of China in "World Cities Day", Shanghai Coordination Center of World Cities Days has undertaken the publicity, organization, and preparation for the first "World Cities Day". Upon the completion of the ceremony, the Coordination Center will closely cooperate with the UN-Habitat and think tanks both at home and abroad through such activities as organizing forums, exhibitions and fairs, case study, promotion and communication, and knowledge sharing and training, etc, to assist government of different levels and social organizations, enterprises, and individuals in dealing with challenges confronted in the process of urbanization, and to jointly solve the problems of different cities both at home and abroad in their sustainable development.

5. Core Activities of First World Cities Day

5.1 Shanghai 2040 Summit Forum

Sponsor: Shanghai Urban Master Planning Compiling Work Leading Group
       Office

Organizer: Shanghai Urban Planning and Design Research Institute
       Shanghai Urban Planning Exhibition Center

The new round of urban master planning compiling work has been fully carried out according to the work arrangements of municipal Party committee and municipal government in order to further embody "planning with an open attitude" as one of the 1st "World Cities Day" series forum activities Shanghai Urban Master Planning Compiling Work Leading Group Office (the sponsor) held Shanghai 2040 Summit Forum on October 31, 2014. This forum specially invited officials of United Nations Human Settlements Program, mayor representatives of Seoul, Chicago. Milan and more and experts from the US Belgium and other countries co-attended and made keynote speeches. The attending guests discussed Shanghai's spatial development strategy in the future 30 years and provided experience references for the new round of urban master planning preparation of Shanghai.

5.2 Global City Forum

Sponsor: The Development Research Center of Shanghai's Municipal
People's Government

World Bank

Organizer: Shanghai Normal University

Support units: World Council on City Data

Science and Technology Committee of Shanghai Urban and
Rural Construction & Management Committee

Shanghai Urban Construction (Group) Company

In 2014, Shanghai initiated a research subject on development strategy for future 30 years which extensively mobilized domestic and overseas experts and social forces' active participation. By now, more than 70 research teams including the World Bank and Development Research Center of the State Council have been invited to carry out systematical and monographic research on the target tasks of 2050 of Shanghai from different perspectives such as the global vision, national strategy, professional field and more. After negotiated with the World Bank the subject of the Global City Forum was determined as "Shanghai, 2050-Rising Global Cities". The forum invited officials of United Nations Department of Economic and Social Affairs, experts from the World Bank, city mayors and famous experts and scholars at home and abroad to gather at the beautiful river bank of Huangpu River, discussing the global city development tendency, studying and judging the development strategy of 2050 of Shanghai, forecasting the significant issues of city development and planning the beautiful blueprint in future Shanghai.

5.3. 2014 international Health City Forum

Sponsor: China Association of Mayors

Shanghai Health Industry Development & Promotion Association

Organizer: Shanghai Rui Yin Health Industry Co., Ltd

Support units: China Executive Leadership Academy Pudong

With history developing and society progressing the design, Planning, construction and development of healthy cities will also enter a brand new historical period to keep pace with the times The promotion of new concepts. Demonstration of new mechanisms formulation of new standards and operation of new models will lead to a new discourse system that impact on cities' transformation and sustainable development continuously. Holding the tenet of "organizing forums with open attitude, establishing platforms constantly and building up a brand elaborately", 2014 International Health City Forum constructed an open frame of high tolerance, deep degree of participation and strong experience with the help of high technology and extensive social force to reach a joint development. 2014 International Health City Forum was held on October 31, 2014. The aim of the forum was to discuss and carry forward the healthy city construction concept of wider vision and bigger pattern.

5.4. China New Urbanization Forum

Sponsor: Architectural Society of China

Support units: Shanghai Municipal and Rural Construction and Management
     Committee
     Shanghai Municipal Transportation Committee
     Bao'shan People's Government, Shanghai
     Shanghai Planning and Territorial Resources Administration
     Bureau

Co-organizers: Architectural Society of Shanghai
     Shanghai Xian Dai Architectural Design (Group)Co., Ltd
     Tongji Architectural Design Group Co., Ltd

To review and summarize the urban and rural construction experience of our country, and explore an intensive, efficient and eco-friendly new urbanization development road by prospering architectural creation and promoting technological innovation, it is decided to hold China New Urbanization Forum & 60th Anniversary of Architectural Journal in Shanghai at the 60th anniversary day of Architectural Journal and the first World Cities Day globally. This forum will invite many academicians leaders from Architectural Society of China leaders from relevant departments in the Yangtze River Delta Area, famous domestic architect representatives, famous experts and scholars entrepreneur representatives, representative from institutions of higher learning and more to attend, and is a high-end industry meeting of architecture industry in 2014.

5.5. The 3rd International Forum on Public Diplomacy: Practice and exploration of city diplomacy—dialogue between China and Europe

Sponsor: The Charhar Institute, China

Clingendael Institute, Netherlands

Institute for Foreign Cultural Relations, Germany

Support units: China Public Diplomacy Association

Co-organization: Shanghai Public Diplomacy Association

China's city diplomacy practice always walks ahead of theoretical research City diplomacy either promotes the focal economic, social and cultural development, or makes important contributions to China's general diplomacy Since the reform and opening-up, with China's urbanization and urban internationalization accelerating day by day, the function of city becomes more and more outstanding in national development strategies and foreign contacts. How to push internationalization strategies and realize urban development strategic objectives through city diplomacy has also become an important issue concerned by many cities. The 3rd Public Diplomacy International Forum combines practical cases and academic discussion and establishes an exchange and interactive platform for domestic and overseas experts, scholars and government officials, which surely promoted China's city diplomacy work comprehensively and solidly.

5.6. Underground Pipelines and City Security Academic Forum

Sponsor: Shanghai Highway and Transportation Society

Organizer: Banshen Civil Engineering Consulting (Shanghai) Co., Ltd.

City underground pipelines are an important constituent part of urban infrastructure and the "life" of city. The leakage, fire, explosion collapse water logging, interruption of gas, water and electricity of underground pipelines will threaten the operation of tile whole city and seriously influence citizens' living quality and life security. By the end of 2013, the total distance of all kinds of highways in Shanghai has reached over 12 300km and the total distance of urban roads is over 4 860km. At present, the total length of all kinds of underground pipelines (including water, electricity, gas, telecommunication and more)has reached more than 100 000km. These pipelines are buried underground to supply materials, energy and information for the city. The Underground Pipelines and City Safety Academic Forum carried out discussions and communications concerning the planning, design, construction, current situation and technical measures of operation management and other aspects of underground pipelines at home and abroad, aiming to provide a platform for scientific and technological cooperation exchange for Shanghai's urban sustainable development and four-center construction, relatively complete underground pipeline system construction and substantial improvement on disaster prevention capability.

POSTSCRIPT

后 记

2010 年，中国上海世博会以"城市，让生活更美好"为主题演绎了人类、城市与地球三者之间的关系。2014 年，首届世界城市日纪念活动系列论坛之一——全球城市论坛又以"上海 2050：崛起中的全球城市"为主题，深入探讨了如何建设更美好的城市，促进城市可持续发展，让人们过上更幸福的生活，更好地迎接全球化、信息化和城市化深入演进带来的历史性变革。

本次全球城市论坛得到了联合国、世界银行、上海师范大学、世界城市数据联盟、上海市城乡建设和管理委员会科学技术委员会、上海城建（集团）公司以及国内外和上海市各界专家学者的大力支持，特别是汇聚了国际全球城市研究领域的著名学者和上海高层次专家，为未来 30 年上海城市发展战略和核心竞争力的提升出谋划策。本届论坛在上海国际会议中心设立了主会场，举行了开幕式、闭幕式、主旨演讲和两个平行论坛的专题演讲，并在上海师范大学设立了平行论坛分会场。论坛围绕未来 30 年上海城市发展和建设，形成了一系列富有启示性和前瞻性的观点和研究成果。为不使这些宝贵的观点和研究成果湮没，我们将其原汁原味地汇编成书，以飨读者。

本书的出版得到了世界银行、上海师范大学和上海世纪出版集团格致出版社的大力支持，上海市人民政府发展研究中心改革处、综合处、信息处和科研处的同仁为本书的编辑付出了辛勤的劳动，在此一并表示感谢！

In 2010, with the theme of "Better City, Better Life", Shanghai Expo vividly demonstrated the relationship among human, city and the earth. In 2014, themed on "Shanghai 2050: A Rising Global City", Global City Forum, one of the serial forums celebrating the first "World Cities Day", carried out in-depth discussion on how to build a better city to promote sustainable development of cities, let people enjoy better life and better embrace historic changes brought about by the progress of globalization, informatization and urbanization.

The forum received strong support from the United Nations, the World Bank, Shanghai Normal University, World Council on City Data, Science and Technology Committee of Shanghai Urban and Rural Construction & Management Committee, Shanghai Urban Construction (Group) Company and experts and scholars at home and abroad and those in Shanghai. The forum gathered prestigious scholars in the research field of global international cities and high-level experts in Shanghai, who offered their suggestions on the development strategy for Shanghai in the next 30 years and on the improvement of Shanghai's core competitiveness. The main venue of the forum was Shanghai International Convention Center, where the opening ceremony, the closing ceremony, keynote speeches and speeches at two parallel forums were carried out. Shanghai Normal University was the venue for the parallel forum. Centering on the development and construction of Shanghai in the next 30 years, the forum has achieved a series of enlightening and forward-looking viewpoints and research achievements. To make these valuable opinions and research achievements be known by all, we compile them into a book for readers.

The publishing of the book has received great support from the World Bank, Shanghai Normal University and Truth & Wisdom Press of Shanghai Century Publishing House. The book is mainly edited by staff from Reform Division, Comprehensive Reform Division, Information Division and Scientific Research Division of the Development Research Center of Shanghai Municipal People's Government. We express our thanks to them all!

图书在版编目(CIP)数据

　　上海2050:崛起中的全球城市:联合国首届世界城
市日全球城市论坛实录/肖林主编.—上海:格致出
版社:上海人民出版社,2015
　　(上海市人民政府发展研究中心系列报告)
　　ISBN 978 - 7 - 5432 - 2566 - 4

　　Ⅰ.①上…　Ⅱ.①肖…　Ⅲ.①区域经济发展-研究报
告-上海市　Ⅳ.①F127.51
　　中国版本图书馆CIP数据核字(2015)第229852号

责任编辑　忻雁翔
装帧设计　人马艺术设计·储平

上海2050:崛起中的全球城市——联合国首届世界城市日全球城市论坛实录

肖　林　主编

出　版	世纪出版股份有限公司　格致出版社 世纪出版集团　上海人民出版社 (200001　上海福建中路193号　www.ewen.co)	印　刷	上海中华商务联合印刷有限公司	
		开　本	787×1092　1/16	
		印　张	21.25	
	编辑部热线　021-63914988 市场部热线　021-63914081 www.hibooks.cn	字　数	448,000	
		版　次	2015年10月第1版	
		印　次	2015年10月第1次印刷	
发　行	上海世纪出版股份有限公司发行中心			

ISBN 978 - 7 - 5432 - 2566 - 4/F · 880　　　　　　　　　　　　　定价:128.00元